STARTING SOMETHING

An ENTREPRENEUR'S Tale
of CONTROL, CONFRONTATION
& CORPORATE CULTURE

Wayne McVicker

Ravel Media ■ California

Starting Something: An Entrepreneur's Tale of Control,
Confrontation & Corporate Culture

Published by Ravel Media
Ravel Media, LLC
www.ravel.tv

Printed in USA

Book design/typography by Sara Patton
Cover writing by Susan Kendrick Writing

ISBN: 1-932881-01-8 (Hardcover)
LCCN: 2004093746

Publisher's Cataloging-in-Publication
(Provided by Quality Books, Inc.)

McVicker, Wayne.
 Starting something : an entrepreneur's tale of
control, confrontation & corporate culture / Wayne
McVicker. p. cm.
 Includes index.
 ISBN 1-932881-01-8

 1. McVicker, Wayne. 2. Corporate culture—United
States. 3. Entrepreneurship—United States—Case
studies. 4. Neoforma (Firm) 5. Businessmen—United
States—Biography. I. Title.

HB615.M38 2004   658.4'21
          QBI33-2040

For Anni

Contents

Introduction

I made a few hundred million. I lost a few hundred million. But that does not in itself make this story particularly unique—considering the place and time: Silicon Valley, at the end of the twentieth century.

Back in 1996, my partner, Jeff Kleck, and I started a company called Neoforma. We started with a product. A good and needed product. But this product served a very large and complex audience — the healthcare industry. So we could only provide for its initial needs. Other people would be needed to facilitate its growth and ensure its survival. Our company had to grow into something beyond its product. As it happened, it turned into quite a large production.

This book is about control.

When we started Neoforma, Jeff and I were firmly in control. As we hired people and invited investors, we had to yield some of that control. Sometimes we gave too little. Sometimes we gave too much. Sometimes it didn't matter. Sometimes I wanted to scream.

This book is about confrontation.

Jeff and I knew that our ideas and product might stir things up a bit. In fact, we believed that the healthcare equipment industry could use quite a bit of stirring. So there was certainly some level of spunk and rebellion in us when we started Neoforma, but we really didn't mean to start a fight. We were young, but not that young. However, fights are what we got. One after another.

And this book is about corporate culture.

We had become frustrated with one company's culture. We left that company in a fit of rebellion and opportunity. When we had the chance to start from scratch, we were committed to building something creative and empowering—something more like us. But a culture's formation is complex and subtle. Everyone who touches a company affects it. The earlier they touch it, the more they affect it. In the beginning, Jeff and I *were* the culture. In the end, the culture had little need for us.

In 1995, as I began to realize that I might soon be heading down the entrepreneurial path, I was fortunate to come across Jerry Kaplan's book, *Start-up*. I read with great interest his story of the formation of a pen-computing company that would entrance, befriend and then be crushed by industry giants.

I was both entertained and educated by Kaplan's book. Now that I have been on a similar journey, I believe there is more to say.

This book is not a guide on how to start a company, though it should certainly be helpful for anyone planning to start something. This is not a history book, though its context is quite historic. Instead, it's a look at some of the peculiar ways that things get started. Some of this book is about business. Most of it is about how people—individuals and groups of people—interact with each other in new and unusual situations.

No complex series of events can be fully understood without some consideration of its context. The time and place in which this story took place distorted and magnified what might otherwise have been relatively mundane behavior. In the final years of the twentieth century, Silicon Valley was quite an unusual place. Everyone involved with a plethora of new businesses felt more important than they had ever expected to feel. That alone led to some interesting situations.

Any assumption that this story accurately reflects historical truth should be weighed against the fact that I have a perverse tendency to feel certain in the absence of uncertainty and to feel skeptical in the presence of facts.

While the name of the company on which this story is based is factual, and can be verified, the events described in the following chapters should be assumed to be at least partially fictional—being based primarily on the notes and memory of one person. In the interest of privacy and self-preservation, the names of most of the characters and some of the companies have been changed. For the most part, it's not who did what that matters. Instead, it's what they did — and maybe why they did it — that provokes thoughtful retrospection.

I must also mention that, regardless of my take on things, you should tacitly assume that the characters and events in this book all have equal and opposite sides. I, of course, only see what I saw.

October 1999

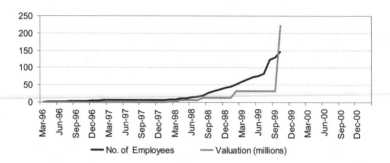

No. of Employees — Valuation (millions)

Medical supplies supply the next B2B wave

Take the temperature of the medical equipment supply industry and you'll sense the next hot batch of business-to-business IPOs . . . Neoforma.com filed Friday for an IPO . . . In its filing with the U.S. Securities and Exchange Commission for a $75 million IPO, Neoforma.com disclosed that it received a final $70 million round of private funding this month . . .

Red Herring
October 16, 1999

The Printer

Somehow, I ended up on the outside, looking in.

An initial public stock offering (IPO) represents a company's official launch into the delightful realm of public scrutiny. It is the time when a company steps into the public limelight, drops its drawers, and says—*Look at me. Here's what I intend to offer you.* To competitors, it is the first real glimpse at the company's pricing and positioning strategy. To investors, it is the first chance to evaluate whether this new offering represents a chance to make a killing.

As Neoforma's IPO documents were being sketched out, I kept hearing talk about the "Printer." I assumed that it was jargon for something I should already know about, so I just went along, nodding and smiling, without asking what it meant.

The Printer was actually a specially designed place where public companies' massive reporting documents are assembled by large teams of people, then electronically submitted to the SEC. Several companies are usually involved in various filings at the Printer at any given time. Each is assigned conference rooms and given access to an assortment of food and beverages.

Almost twenty-four hours a day for weeks, an amazingly large group of young lawyers, accountants and investment bankers—almost none of whom I knew—had been enthusiastically gathering and assembling mounds of obscure Neoforma information into crowded conference rooms.

A private company can have many secrets. There is very little requirement for the public disclosure of information. But once you go public, all of that changes. A public company can have very few secrets. And even those secrets are controlled by all kinds of legal restrictions.

The team of mostly young professionals assembling those mounds of information hardly acknowledged my presence when I visited. I don't know whether it was that they didn't know who I was, whether they were simply being polite, or whether this was such a common situation for them that I was barely worth their notice. Personally, I would've been incredibly interested in what might be going through the head of someone about to make a ton of money. And, in no way had I connected that *someone* with me.

They seemed so engaged in the process that it made me feel proud —if somewhat surreal—to be a part of it. I was impressed by how they could put so much into a process that they wouldn't directly benefit from. They seemed to be driven simply by the knowledge that they were at the heart of a unique and very exciting time.

Jeff and I were only bit players in the filing process, but we did visit the Printer several times to go over minute events in the early history of the company. Our biographies and the financial history of our investments in Neoforma were also being included. This would be the first time that anyone outside Neoforma would have complete visibility into my ownership of Neoforma.

I am a private kind of guy. I didn't like the idea of my personal information being published to the world in so raw a form.

Typically, only founders, investors and their lawyers and accountants know the ownership make-up of a private company. This would be the first time for almost everyone inside Neoforma to see the ownership position of any of the corporate officers, including me.

My own position was pretty staggering: four million shares of company stock. That is what I owned. I hadn't thought much about it before. But we were rumored to be filing a starting price at up to $10 per share. It didn't take much for me—and everybody else—to figure out that I might soon be filthy rich.

Because the bits of information requiring disclosure were changing constantly, it was impossible to pinpoint the day that the filing would take place. If we changed *anything*—made any strategic decisions, considered any new acquisitions, were party to any new legal actions, or even changed our snack policy—the filing date would be pushed back so adjustments could be made.

Our strategic funding round, which we were announcing in parallel with the filing statement, was a complex mess. All of the funding details, including any operational adjustments made to accommodate it, had to be included in the final filing document.

As we neared the second week of October, we knew that everything was almost lined up. Each day was going to be *The Day*. Then something new would rear its ugly head. Each day the tension would increase, even as each issue was resolved.

On the evening of October 14, just after finishing dinner with my wife, Anni, and my sons, Weston and Reece, I received a call from Jeff. He told me, "We're filing tonight! You might want to come down here."

I really hadn't thought that the actual submission of documents to the SEC was such a big deal. Anni and I talked it over. Of course I wanted to go, but there had been so many nights where Neoforma had intruded into our lives that I had lost perspective on what made this night any different than the rest. We agreed that I should go to the filing.

When I arrived at the Printer, there was a crowd of thirty or so people standing around, mingling. Only a small number of them were Neoforma employees. The atmosphere was electric, celebratory. Everyone was drinking expensive champagne. One of our PR employees recognized me and energetically handed me a glass. She told me that they had just completed the document and were ready to submit it.

Leading me through the crowd to a small cubicle. Jeff was there already. She pointed to the keyboard of a simple computer terminal. She told us that all we had to do was: "Push *that* button!"

The aisles were filled with unfamiliar, excited faces. Someone had a camera aimed at us. I felt silly, but proud. It was heartening that this group of intelligent people were giving up their evening to be here to watch us push a button. I was glad I had come and shocked that I had considered not being here.

We pushed the button—to cheers and toasts. In a month or so, we might be a public company.

I found out then that, despite the late hour, a group of thirty or so Neoforma employees—mostly long-time employees—had gathered at the company offices to celebrate. I drove there feeling quite disoriented.

At the door, someone handed me a Nerf gun. Slightly inebriated people were racing through the maze of cubicles, laughing freely, firing soft darts and balls at each other. The stress created by hyper-growth had been building for a long time. A lot of stress was vented that evening. I was a favorite target. I fired at a few satisfying targets too.

This is the email message Bob, our CEO, sent to Neoforma employees that evening:

> Today at 6:45 p.m. we closed on our Series E Preferred Stock financing in the amount of $70 million. At 6:50 p.m. we pushed the button (literally) and transmitted our S-1 registration statement to the Securities and Exchange Commission. At 7:03 p.m. we received confirmation from the SEC that they had accepted our filing with a filing date of October 15. Any of these events is a big event in the life of a company—having them all occur on the same day, within minutes of each other, is a pretty rare thing.

It wasn't until I read that message the following morning that I realized the filing date hadn't been the 14th. Instead, the filing was registered on the next business day, the 15th, my fortieth birthday. Forty was a big deal to me. Not because I was getting old, that didn't happen until at least 41, but because, ever since I was ten years old, I had always considered forty to be the age at which wisdom was achieved. I had told myself as a child that I would be ready to write my first book when I was forty. I believed that life experience would take that long to ferment. I am still waiting for the wisdom, but I have quite a bit of experience.

It was on that day that I made a formal resolution to write a book about my experiences at Neoforma. I believed that the richness and peculiarity of my experiences during these times was worth trying to communicate. It certainly felt strange enough to me to be worth exploring.

March 1996

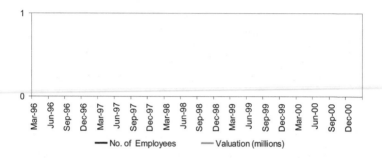

Neoforma incorporated.

March 6, 1996

Inking It

It was an inauspicious start.

Neoforma's official beginning can be traced to a day more than three years earlier than our IPO filing. At the time, I would never have predicted the scale and intensity of the course we were about to take.

I do remember that the building it all started in was far from flashy. A quiet, somber place, the bank's small attempts at welcoming us—a carpet here, some wood-grain there—were subservient to the formal processes involving the exchange of money. Sixties modernist design without the modernist attention to detail. Cold flooring, high ceilings. This was not a glamorous place.

We had selected this bank not for its prestigious name or its dedication to customer service—it was known for neither—but because it was located a couple of blocks away from the offices we were about to open.

But I did feel a sense of glamour as Jeff and I were directed, along with our wives, to the business desk.

Though there wasn't much to it, this was our official opening ceremony. We would each sign some forms and checks. These were just about the only physical requirements of this ritual. However, its completion would formalize our willingness to embrace real risk—not physical risk, but lifestyle risk. All risks share the same emotional basis — that one might return with less than one started with or nothing at all. When this risk is voluntary, it comes with the thrill of potential reward.

Our wives were there because the ten thousand dollars that we were each depositing to purchase the first shares in our new company was being transferred from jointly held accounts. When I think back, I am impressed how much support my wife provided at this big step. It took me a long time to appreciate the emotional investment Anni made that day. We had discussed the details and potential consequences of this investment at length, but in the end, she was making this decision primarily on the basis of faith in me. We were taking most of our savings and putting it into a place from which it might never return. And there was little doubt in any of our minds that this was only the first small step into an uncertain future.

While there was not enough money in the new business to allow me to leave my nice safe job yet, I was certain I was going in that direction. There was no turning back.

It represented a big turning point in my life: a turn away from one of the paths I had envisioned for myself in youth—the creative artist/architect and toward another—the developer of an idea into a business.

The first significant enterprise I had founded was a business I started at fifteen, some twenty-two years earlier, breeding tropical catfish. I convinced three fellow misfits at school that if we each put in $100 (a lot of money for fifteen-year-olds back then), we could create a fun and profitable business. I wish I still had those sheets of the calculations I had created to convince them. They were full of youthfully optimistic assumptions.

After two years of hard work, silly mistakes, small successes, little arguments over division of labor and relatively clean fun, we became bored, closed the doors and sold everything. In the end, we broke even financially, excluding labor. However, we made a huge profit developmentally. That felt pretty good at the time. I liked building a team. I liked the thrill of being emotionally and intellectually challenged.

I can't say how thoroughly I had evaluated the risks of this new venture prior to writing that first check. I had children to raise and educate. Mortgage to pay, marriage to nurture. I do know that I dismissed the risks quickly as I embraced this new challenge.

Jeff and I had some good ideas and a vision of better things. My new, less youthful, but equally optimistic financial projections indicated that Jeff and I might, between us, be able to make enough money over time to pay off our mortgages if we did things right. We believed that could make up for a lot of family neglect. And we felt that, after this formal ceremony of incorporation, we would go on to be good corporate citizens. Ready to follow the path tread by many before us. To contribute, with a little luck, more than we consumed.

April 1996

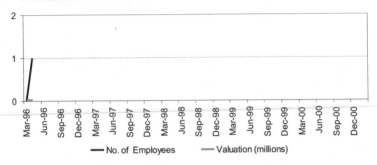

Chart axis: 2, 1, 0

Mar-96, Jun-96, Sep-96, Dec-96, Mar-97, Jun-97, Sep-97, Dec-97, Mar-98, Jun-98, Sep-98, Dec-98, Mar-99, Jun-99, Sep-99, Dec-99, Mar-00, Jun-00, Sep-00, Dec-00

—— No. of Employees   —— Valuation (millions)

Neoforma opens corporate offices in Mountain View, California.

April 1, 1996

Yahoo IPO closes at $33 after $43 peak

Yahoo's much-anticipated entry to Wall Street began with a bang this morning at $24.50 per share and hit a high of $43 before closing at $33. Yahoo opened at about 8:45 a.m. PDT and shot up to $43 an hour later, which equals $1 billion for the company . . .

Yahoo has been the talk on Wall Street and Silicon Valley since it filed for the offering last month, the most closely watched high-tech IPO since Netscape Communications made market history in December . . .

CNET News.com
April 12, 1996

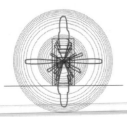

Front view of a typical radiation distribution from a medical radiotherapy machine. Early Neoforma software was loaded with exciting diagrams like this.

The Prequel

There was no master plan. A series of chance encounters planted the seed that was to become Neoforma.

Neoforma's first offices were located just a few blocks from my house in Mountain View, California, a suburban town near Stanford University and just south of the halfway point between San Francisco and San Jose. While expensive on a square-footage basis, our office suite had all of the overhead services we might need: administrative support, phone service, copy services, conference rooms, kitchen, etc. This was important because we had very little money for such investments. Our office doors officially opened April 1—the annual day of surprises and punchlines. We considered it an omen of sorts. The total capital assets of the company consisted of a computer, a secondhand desk and a chair.

At the time, I really didn't have a specific idea of where the Silicon Valley was. I knew it was somewhere close to where I lived, but I thought it ended geographically south of me. Since I was a local, I had never given any thought to being a citizen of that legendary place. It turned out that our office was right in the heart of the Valley.

As an architect, I had helped design buildings for some of the companies that gave the Valley its reputation for innovation. But living in Silicon Valley was not the same as participating in the culture of technology. That was less about geographic boundaries than social and educational ones. I crossed these boundaries quite late, quite gradually, and quite by chance.

For me, the seed of Neoforma was planted in 1987, when I received a call from Dwight, an architect I'd worked with many years before. He ran the Planning Department at Varian, a radiotherapy medical equipment company. Varian made big machines that fought—and sometimes cured—cancer.

Dwight was what you'd call "a character." Brilliant, and brilliantly flawed. Big mind. Big ideas. Big heart. A vulnerable, hippie/intellectual, struggling in the corporate world, he was absolutely unable to consistently distinguish between the good of an Idea, the good of The Company and the good of Mankind. He had little sense of prioritization, or supervision. But, what a mind! What a rebel!

Suffice it to say that, when he called to offer me a job, I was flattered. He offered me the challenge of bringing technology—specifically, computer design and drafting—into his department.

I was working in a large architectural firm at the time. I had worked there off and on since 1978. From the start, my fascination with technology, and its potential, had drawn me to the very cutting edge of the architectural profession. While most of the architectural interns were focused on the path toward licensure, I was playing with the new toys the company had acquired. In my spare time, I had taken over a pair of Apple computers and started programming some useful new tools for the firm. Later, I built more programs for the firm to help pay my college expenses.

When faced with inefficient traditions, I tend to obsess about changing them. Anything that repeatedly slows me down is an unacceptable distraction to me. I can't rest until I fix it.

Over time, I became increasingly frustrated with my peers' lack of enthusiasm for technology. And I didn't quite fit comfortably into any niche in the firm. My tendency to dress casually, if not carelessly, and the fact that I didn't wear shoes very often weighed heavily in the minds of my bosses against the fact that I was very good at my job. I decided that it was time for me to move on, but I didn't know where to go. And that's when Dwight called me. Dwight had worked with me at the same firm a few years back. I admired him very much.

I am sure that, in spite of my disgruntlement with the profession, I would not have considered this substantial diversion from the business of architecture had I not been reading *Nueromancer*, the futuristic science fiction novel by William Gibson. The business world Gibson portrayed was lit by the projection of images moving on interlaced monitors — frenzied, gritty, smart, complex, individualistic, unrestrained. I convinced myself that this was the proper domain for the contemporary architect. The corporate world would embrace my quest for reconstruction and progression. The visually creative stuff could come later. This would bring bright light to my dark corner.

I accepted the job at Varian. Barefoot in the land of cubicles. At the time Varian had only two computers in the marketing department. One, the "fast" one, was in the office of the head of marketing. The other was in my cubicle, with boxes of uninstalled software next to it. My job was to convert paper to pixels. Dwight had hired me because we had, working together in the past, shared an interest in the potential of computers to revolutionize architectural design.

Dwight talked on and on about how I should write programs to completely automate the three-dimensional design of hospitals. Of course, first I had to figure out what the heck a "medical linear accelerator" was and how the heck to use yet another computer drafting program—my sixth—to very quickly create drawings that architects could use to build departments to accommodate this big, complex equipment.

I was completely lost in this alien environment. At first, as I browsed mounds of ugly engineering drawings I was supposed to convert, I panicked. *What was I thinking? This ugly stuff didn't have anything to do with design. This is the most mundane job I could have gotten myself involved in.* But by the second day, I caught glimpses of the potential. The current processes were so archaic that everything in the place was going to have to change, fast and inevitably. And I could be a big part of designing that change—learning with it—and that idea felt pretty good.

Once I had solved many of the big problems, I began to tackle smaller ones. For example, we required the services of a nuclear physicist to help customers design facilities that would safely attenuate the radiation generated by the linear accelerators. Gene, our internal resource, was a very well-respected authority on radiation safety, but his recommendations were often untimely and generally incomprehensible to the likes of me. And he was going to retire soon. So I wrote some programs to automate the process of determining how much concrete or lead or whatever was required to shield the rooms.

I distinctly remember one day in my office a couple of weeks before Gene was set to retire. My boss, Evelyn, a short, fiery woman, whom I respected very much, but from whom I would seldom feel respect, introduced me to Jeff. Because of his closely cropped hair, conservative suit and confident manner, I instantly assumed that he was the new physicist. And I disliked him immediately.

In spite of the fact that the guys in my department all considered me to be "the college boy," I was, in fact, quite wary of formal education. I hadn't graduated from college. I had just played at it for awhile. It left me with a certain, unshakable scorn for the professional student. (Of course, this scorn was really based on a fear that those of a certain class could instantly identify my ignorance of protocol. And, for the most part, they could.)

There was some initial friction between Jeff and me over the computer program I had written. I had created it to essentially eliminate my dependence on the services Jeff had been hired to provide to my department. He pointed out some significant flaws in the program's calculations. This pissed me off. He did not act in the least bit impressed by what I had built. I argued that most of his points were irrelevant under most conditions. He argued that they could indeed be not only relevant, but critical.

Somewhere along the way, we stopped arguing as much and began collaborating on the next generation of this tool. We realized that we both shared a focus on making things better. His initial rejection of my work had not been a rejection at all. He simply had been more concerned with how it could be better.

More than once before, I had become good friends with someone I had initially disliked. It looked like that was going to happen again.

Since I had already built a tool that worked quite well for Varian, the new project had to be created almost entirely on our own time. And since it *was* our own time, we wanted to build the best, coolest, most feature-rich stuff we could build. What started as a relatively modest effort to build a completely accurate, linear-accelerator calculation tool would evolve into something much more.

We thought it would be great to add some graphics to illustrate the concepts and variables. And it would be great if we added sample drawings of common ways to solve various problems. Then there were all of the global regulations that could be included, so that everything would recalculate when different regions were selected. Between the two of us, there was no end to the possibilities. Jeff and I built easily on each other's ideas and, somewhere along the way, we inadvertently amplified each other's yearning to be free of boundaries.

Our brains started working overtime. What if we added other types of machines that Varian made — like after-loaders and simulators? And if we did have multiple types of machines, then, of course, we should include layout drawings for all types of equipment. And of course if we were including information on different types of *big* equipment, why not gather information on all of the hundreds of *smaller* items that went into each room?

After all, my department spent an inordinate amount of time supporting the decision process for third-party products. *Why not distribute this information to customers in software that they could use themselves?*

In fact, the more we thought about it, the more we realized that this tool we were building was so unique and yet essential to the radiotherapy installation process, that if we made it self-supporting it might even be — profitable!

We knew that customers would be willing to buy this program. While it was used entirely as an in-house tool, customers would often see it in action when members of my department were doing on-site calculations. Or they would simply see the pretty, detailed reports we produced. They were nothing like the scribbled reports they were used to seeing. Customers from all over the world began asking us about the software. They'd ask how much the program cost and if it worked with competitors' machines.

That gave us pause. Certainly every manufacturer had a similar need to compile this kind of information. *Didn't it make sense to consolidate these efforts?* Varian had just created a partnership with another, much larger manufacturer of medical equipment. Since I had to coordinate our planning tasks with this other company's, I had an opportunity to become friends with their head of planning. He verified that they did indeed have the same problems gathering information from within the company, aggregating it with information on hundreds of third-party products and distributing this information to customers in a useful, cost-effective way. Not only were the processes almost identical, but much of the information overlapped.

This simply didn't make sense. Maybe if we included all competitive and compatible products in our tools, Varian would benefit by reinforcing, in the customer's eyes, the fact that we were the clear market leader in medical equipment. After all, our equipment was better. Everyone in the company seemed to sincerely believe that to be the case. What would be the harm in showing it next to competitive products? Now *that* made sense to us.

Convincing management of this was an entirely different matter. Being the clear market leader, Varian's sales and service teams had long been in the habit of conveying only the minimum necessary information to customers. If the customers agreed that Varian equipment was the highest quality in the industry, why take the chance of messing something up by giving them some unnecessary piece of information that might confuse them?

When I had implemented an automated fax document distribution system, I received huge resistance from the sales organization. How would they know who was getting their precious information? Even the competitors would be able to get these documents. Of course, I, and everyone else in the field, knew that the competitors could and did get this information through customers already. That's how we got our information on their products. This double standard really irritated me. *Didn't we make good products? Shouldn't we support—to the fullest extent possible—the customers who put their faith in our products?*

The answer from sales was that I was "naïve." Control of information was the key to success in sales, they informed me. *Why would we even need salespeople at all, if information were conveniently and freely available on all products available in every category?*

A dangerous question indeed, since the power in a market-leading company lives in the sales department.

Even if we provided more information only on complementary— rather than competitive—products, I knew that there were better and far less expensive products available than what we were recommending. Tens of thousands of dollars could be saved on every room, if we were to provide a bit more information to our customers. *Wasn't that my job?* I was told by sales management to "Butt out."

But Jeff and I agreed that this was too important an issue to drop. Despite internal resistance, our program was now being distributed on CD-ROM to all of the service and planning offices, as well as to a few of the more progressive salespeople. Soon, at the request of the international salespeople (who weren't as far ahead in the market and thus were generally delightful, creative people), our program ended up in the hands of some customers for the first time.

Before long, it was clear that we had insidiously made our program into a key component in some equipment sales. Important customers were assertively requesting that we provide support for their non-Varian equipment as well.

We were now spending every spare moment expanding the program — every evening, every lunch hour, every weekend where possible and every spare moment on our business trips. And, slowly but surely, we began to spend some of our work hours on this too. Our bosses reluctantly put up with this distraction, since there were some salespeople who swore by our program—not the majority, but a few key ones.

Our program was particularly popular among the international sales and service groups. They had been frustrated by the lack of support they received from the U.S. and welcomed any tools that put more control into their own hands. To better understand how our program supported the international audience, Jeff and I went to the main European support office in Switzerland for a week or so. I know there were reasons other than our project for us being there, but I can't remember them. We knew the trip would increase our support within the company and, more importantly, give us several long plane flights and many uninterrupted evenings to work on the program.

We stayed at a small, modern hotel in the center of old Zurich I had discovered on a previous trip. By day, we would go to offices in Zurich and Zug to discuss assorted business issues, as well as to validate and garner support for our software. By night, as the locals lined the narrow cobblestone streets with tables for dining and socializing, we would grab a meal in whatever interesting restaurant we could find, and then return to the hotel to begin our real work. We had rooms across from each other at the end of a hallway. Since the rooms were too small for both of us to work in, we'd prop open our doors and yell questions across the hall to each other as we worked frenetically on our laptop computers well into the morning hours.

While sitting over our meals in this neutral land, far away from our jobs and families, Jeff and I spoke to each other with a candor that went beyond our project for the first time. We asked each other the hard questions: *What were our goals in life? Where was this whole thing going? Was this just a distraction, or could there be more to it? There was something here that was developing a life of its own. Was its life tied to ours? If so, how?*

We were working our asses off to build this thing, and people were benefiting from it. Yet there was no financial reward in sight. We were taking time away from our wives and children with no reward, other than the praise of some of the customers. *If we could sell this thing— and we knew we could—shouldn't we get a piece of the action?*

We each had hundreds of hours into this. *Could we convince management that this should be turned into a Varian product and sold? Could we convince them that, since we had developed this on our own, we should get a piece of it?*

I had tried in the past to get management to provide bonuses to my team for generating substantial profits on construction management projects, to no avail. If our guys were to get a piece of their action, then everyone in engineering would argue that they should get a piece of each new product *they* rolled out. *Where would it stop?*

Yet, we felt that this was something different, something fundamentally new — an opportunity to embrace the information age aggressively. There was this great new power in the storage capabilities of CD-ROMs, not to mention the distant possibilities of the Internet. Jeff and I agreed, then and there, to ride this thing to its conclusion, wherever that might be.

In the past, we had tried to go through Evelyn, my boss, to request fundamental changes, but we realized that she was probably not the person who would make this kind of decision. So we navigated down the slippery slope of personal empowerment by developing a proposal to present directly to Ed, the president of our business unit.

We knew that Ed, who had come from the service end of the business rather than sales, was far more open-minded and inquisitive about the power of information technology than most of the managers in the company. His was often the first computer to have the latest software installed. And he had made the effort to greet me in the corridors by first name long before we were ever formally introduced. That meant a lot to me. He was a man of contradictions—playful and serious, nerdy and shrewd, doubtful and confident. Most of all, he was a man we trusted.

I knew that Evelyn would be upset with this apparent disregard of her authority. She was very powerful within the company, and very well regarded and rewarded. But most people believed that she had gone as high as she would go. Anyway, I knew she would be very upset. That bothered me, but what could I do?

The members of my department would be upset too. They had already noticed that my previously frenzied attention to their needs had slowed substantially, as I had become more distracted. I justified it to myself this way: I had provided them with the tools and status to perform their jobs better, so they could afford for me to be less attentive. They expected me to keep pitching. And I expected them to step up to the plate.

I regretted that I no longer met their expectations, but I had contributed a great deal more than was required of me throughout my first eight years at the company, so a little selfishness was overdue. And I wasn't being entirely selfish. *What I was doing was helping the customers. That was important, right?* (Okay, the truth is, I had significant pangs of guilt about abandoning my department, but I did it anyway.)

I felt a bit alone with my moral dilemmas in dealing with my boss and my employees. Jeff had no employees and a more supportive boss. I discussed my concerns with him. Jeff was good at addressing such issues. He was able to articulately point to the selfish acts of others as justification of one's own self-interest. In fact, he would point out that if we didn't protect our own interests, we would get trampled, pure and simple.

His finely educated, self-righteous attitude conveyed confidence. And the projection of confidence can be very powerful indeed. Although I was very confident about a lot of things, I did not project unqualified confidence. Quite the opposite. I often embraced doubt as an opportunity for improvement, which could make me appear to be uncertain. But I was grateful for Jeff's ability to project certainty. I had learned in the past that partnerships with opposite personalities created opportunities for great balance. And, sometimes, great volatility.

Our proposal to Ed would be this: *Let us turn our software into a product. Let us sell it. Give us a small commission on sales.* Simple. We sketched out a basic business plan, complete with a financial analysis.

As we developed the plan, we began to see its faults. The marketing of the software by Varian would dilute our objectivity and would restrict our ability to work with Varian competitors. The profits we could produce would be large by the standards of two guys running a business, but miniscule by the standards of a business selling more than half a billion dollars worth of stuff each year. But we argued that it would have great strategic value and who knows where it might go in the long run?

Just to cover our bases, we added the option that Jeff and I could simply spin this project out as a separate business. A separate business could continue to support Varian's equipment without the risks associated with developing an in-house product.

We didn't really think much of this option until *after* we'd pushed SEND on the proposal and emailed it to Ed. But seconds afterward, Jeff and I looked at each other, eyes wide and bright. Somehow, we sensed that the latter option was going to be the likely one. We had each started companies before. We had a pretty good sense of the consequences of this option.

We cut our safety net that day near the end of 1995. If management said no, our loyalty and our commitment would be forever in question. My boss and my staff would never forget that my dedication had been elsewhere.

And we knew that we couldn't accept no for an answer. We were too far along for that now. We both spent a great deal of time discussing the implication of our actions with our wives over the next few weeks.

Each hour after pressing that SEND button felt like a day. We had sent a message-read request with our email, so we knew exactly when he had read it that afternoon. He did not respond that day or the next.

Jeff and I were as excited as kids and completely distracted from our other activities.

Jeff began to propose theories to explain the delayed response. "He just skipped and ignored our email . . . He is threatened by us . . . He is working with the legal department right now, trying to figure out a way to take all of our hard work away from us."

I didn't think so. "Nobody's trying to take anything away from us," I told him. "We're proposing something that really rocks the boat and we need to realize that it's hard for anyone to stay balanced on a rocking boat."

That dialog was the first indication of the nature of our partnership from then forward, suspicion and calm. Whenever Jeff's radar detected any hint of possible threat, he would jump to "what if . . . ?" and "they must be . . . !" He had an innate skepticism of people's motivations. I had an innate conviction that resistance was not necessarily the same as rejection. Of course, the middle is the right place to be. Intense back-and-forth would usually lead us to the middle.

In this case, Ed *had* paid attention to our memo. We knew he was paying attention because, a week later, he asked for more details. He wanted a more detailed business plan and answers to a bunch of questions.

We didn't know whether to be thrilled or frustrated. On one hand, we weren't being ignored. On the other hand, now we had to go through all this formality of justifications and projections. This was just slowing things down. We thought, *Either this is a good idea or it isn't. Why not just make a decision about which direction to go and, if it doesn't work out, we'll figure something else out when we get there?* We felt that we had put so much into thinking this thing through that we wouldn't be proposing ideas that didn't make sense. They should just assume we knew what we were talking about and accept our ideas out-of-hand. *Didn't they realize that our self-interest was integral to the company's interest?*

We wanted to just get going at full speed. But we dutifully answered the questions and expanded the business plan.

There was much back-and-forth with Ed, and then with Ben, a matter-of-fact but hard to read guy, who had been Ed's right-hand man as Ed had risen through the ranks. Nobody was quite sure what the boundaries of Ben's job really were. He didn't have specific authority, but was Ed's choice for a variety of special projects.

Ed gave us a preliminary thumbs-up, indicating his support for our efforts and preference for us to take on this project as a separate company. Ed didn't want our proposal to cause confusion among the rank and file, so he asked us to be discreet in our activities. He quietly assigned Ben to be our primary contact going forward.

Ben was a cordial, frank and frequently offbeat guy. While we weren't working with the top guy anymore, we liked Ben and felt that, even though he often seemed distracted, he would treat us fairly. He did.

While we tried to present everything to Varian in a balanced way, we *were* slanting the conclusions toward the formation of a new company. We began to explore all of the steps to starting a company—office location, name, legal structure, etc.

We needed to find our own lawyer to help us with the incorporation and negotiation with Varian, assuming that things went in that direction. I asked a lawyer I had worked with a few times at Varian for a recommendation. I really liked this guy and knew I could trust his opinion and his discretion. He was intrigued with, and supportive of, what we were proposing. It was the first time I had shared our plans with anyone outside Varian management or my family. His encouragement gave me much needed support.

He recommended an individual at a large law firm with offices nearby. The firm had expertise in company spin-offs. I made an appointment for the following week.

At the law firm, we were directed into a large, luxurious conference room. The lawyer we met was polite and formal. He treated us like businessmen, like men who made important decisions. This was a very new and invigorating feeling to me. Jeff and I acted very calm, but we certainly weren't feeling calm.

After an hour or so of listening to us and then presenting the strengths of his firm, he told us that he had to check one detail before we went any further. He had to see if his firm had any conflict of interest with Varian. He called someone in his firm and asked to have this checked into. We continued to chat for a few minutes until the phone rang. The lawyer had a quick conversation, nodded his head several times and hung up.

It turned out that there *was* a conflict. The firm had done recent and relevant work for Varian. They couldn't work with us. In fact, he told us that it would be difficult to find a large firm in the area that hadn't worked with Varian. So, he suggested that we work with a smaller firm. He had one in mind. It was formed by a lawyer who had previously worked at his firm. We thanked him and moved on, feeling a bit let down.

Later that day, when I was abruptly asked by Evelyn to come to her office, I had an immediate sinking feeling. By venturing outside the company, I knew that I was on shaky ground. Jeff's paranoia caught up with me at times.

As soon as I entered her office, I knew that she was upset. She was pissed. It turned out that, in order to verify the conflict of interest, the lawyer had called Varian's legal department. Evelyn was in charge of most sales contracts, so she worked regularly with the legal group. One of the people in that group had casually asked her why a guy who worked for her was scouting out legal firms that did not have a conflict with Varian.

She was *seething*. She was *very* upset that I had worked around her on this. She hadn't been supportive of the work I had done on this project and for me to have gone around her ... well, that was inappropriate. I explained to her that I had worked at Varian relatively selflessly for nearly a decade. I believed I deserved this opportunity. She disagreed. She felt that I had broken her trust. She was even more upset at Ed, who hadn't kept her in the loop on his decision process.

In any case, the news was out. Everyone was treating me differently now. Most, knowing how upset Evelyn was, distanced themselves from me. Those that were friends interacted with me in whispers.

As the news spread, I noticed changes in the pattern of my daily phone calls. A few individuals — mostly the maverick sales guys — were more respectful and familiar. With the rest, conversations were more formal and curt. I was slowly but surely being isolated from the body of the company.

To avoid further human resources confusion, Jeff and I wrote a letter to Ed requesting official authorization to explore the creation of a new company. Once this was signed, we made an appointment with the new lawyer. The lawyer met with us within a few days. We liked him and initiated the formal process of negotiating the spin-off. Jeff, wearing his NewCo (as we had come to call it) hat, positioned every deal point to slant completely in our direction. I feared that starting off with a deal that leaned heavily in our favor would create an atmosphere of resentment and it did. But many deal points that I thought would never end up in our favor, *did* end up in our favor. So Jeff's aggressive approach had its benefits.

The contract process went painfully slowly, but eventually a deal was made. We would be allotted a certain amount of money to get things going, but only enough to get started. In exchange, we would support Varian's customers and their use of the software for a period of time. And, they would get all of the intellectual property back if we discontinued support for the software within a certain amount of time. There wasn't much else to it. Things ended up so simply for two reasons.

First, while there was little business reason for Varian to support this new enterprise, there *was* good reason to get distance from it. If Jeff and I stopped supporting the software, some important customers might be upset. There needed to be some way to phase out Varian's role in the process without losing face.

Second, we *were* doing something interesting, even if it was a bit unclear what impact we would have.

I believe that Ed's unpopular decision to support us was based primarily on his support for our pursuit of an idea and subsequently justified by the legitimate business motives.

Jeff and I agreed to name the company Neoforma. More on that later. When it came to assigning corporate titles, we really didn't see much difference between CEO and President. Both titles seemed to sound equally important and inflated. We flipped a coin. Jeff got CEO. I got President. In many ways, this is the only way the coin could have landed. I was more naturally an inside guy. Jeff was more naturally an outside guy.

So, in March of 1996, in a tension-filled atmosphere, a formal agreement was signed between two corporations, Varian and Neoforma. Jeff and I agreed to stay with Varian for at least a year, but that day, our minds moved on.

During the later days of the spin-off negotiations, I had been getting administrative support for our project primarily from Patty, a young and complex woman who had worked as a temporary administrator in my department. When she was due to be released from her stint at Varian, I arranged for her to work entirely on Neoforma activities. I knew her to be resourceful, self-motivated and discreet. These were key characteristics I needed to help get the doors at Neoforma open.

That first day in April, on the first of hundreds of long lunchtimes at Neoforma, I stepped into our small office feeling like a new man. Patty was on the phone with a customer, a Neoforma customer. There was much to do.

May 1996

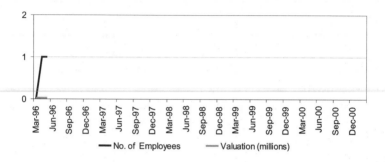

- No. of Employees
- Valuation (millions)

Microsoft Internet Explorer 3.0 Beta Now Available

Microsoft Corp. today announced the immediate, worldwide availability of Microsoft® Internet Explorer version 3.0 beta software, the next generation of its popular World Wide Web browser . . . For users, Microsoft Internet Explorer 3.0 provides a dynamic browsing experience for viewing content created in Java, JavaScript, Netscape™ Plug-ins . . .

Microsoft Press Release
May 29, 1996

The Frontier

I'd like to say that we had it all figured out from the beginning. That we knew the Internet would be the hot place to be. But it wasn't like that at all.

Our survival would depend on how efficiently we could get our message out to a diverse and potentially hostile audience. While we had great advocates using our software, we weren't certain how openly we would be welcomed by healthcare equipment suppliers.

One of our first tasks at Neoforma was to create an image for this new entity. Even though we only had one person, Patty, on salary, the company had too little money to survive for long. By this time, we had run the numbers enough times to see that the most lucrative path to profits would be to leverage our captured-customer base and get the bulk of our money from healthcare equipment suppliers. In our view, they had the most to gain.

Usually when a group of customers gets together in the form of a professional society, they adamantly shield their members from suppliers. They support themselves by doling out bits of customer information in exchange for the sponsorship of society events.

We planned to take this time-honored concept and project it into the digital world. We would gather together a group of architects and healthcare providers who shared a similar need for information to improve their ability to expand and build hospitals. We'd provide them with software tools, such as shielding calculations, room templates and product information, which met their needs.

We would get suppliers that shared the same customers to help us build those tools. They would sponsor the tools by paying us to include detailed product listings and images among a sea of unenhanced listings. Since we put this information in front of their targeted customers very early in the product decision process, this product placement was very valuable indeed. We had offerings varying from a couple of thousand dollars to tens of thousands. We justified these rates by comparing our service to the high cost and low return of traditional media.

We would give these tools away, charging only for the more advanced versions. It was kind of like shareware. We'd get a little money from the buyers and more from the sellers. Everyone would benefit. This process was far less expensive and more predictable than traditional customer aggregation. So, we had to get the message out to suppliers quickly. We had some initial success cold-calling suppliers, but we needed scale and speed to keep the doors open. We decided to send a brochure to a large number of carefully targeted suppliers.

This seemed like an old-fashioned way to start a grand wave of technology, but we knew that this was a very conservative industry. The business of healthcare was very serious indeed. Our official intro-duction as a company would need to be familiar and professional. It would also be very expensive for us. We would only have enough money for one shot.

Seeing the first brochure at the printer was a breathtaking experience. Its two folds opened outward, exposing a rich view of the world we were trying to create. It was conservative in layout with striking colors, expensive-looking, professional, exuberant, and beautifully eye-catching. At least it was as exciting as a brochure primarily about radiation shielding and medical room layouts could be.

To top it off, our new logo—a diagonal spiral—looked great on the cover. This was the first visual representation of our company. Our business was getting more real every day.

Our families got together that weekend to stuff thousands of envelopes with the brochures. We addressed them to thousands of manufacturers. The stacks of mail went out the doors on Monday. And, we waited.

We knew it would probably be several days before anyone actually received the brochures, but that did not make the fact that we received no calls from new customers on Tuesday any less disappointing.

Wednesday was a different story. Several manufacturer representa-tives who knew us called us to say some variation of, "Wow! You guys are really serious about this thing!" We also received some calls from companies that we had not spoken with before. Some part of me relaxed, just a bit.

We also needed to establish a presence on this new thing called the Internet. For the most part, I had only used the Internet for email and technical support for assorted computer devices, but I had seen enough to know that our products would rely heavily on it someday. If we wanted to project a vision of the future, we had to be on the Web from the start.

So, as we were producing the brochure, I called around, asking for a referral to someone who built websites. I knew a great deal about computers, but I knew very little about the Internet. I didn't understand how it worked or what software was used to make things work or even what the computers that ran things looked like. I didn't know why there was a "www" prefix in front of so many Web addresses.

What I did know was that this medium had the potential to solve many of the problems and reduce the costs associated with traditional media distribution. I asked people I knew who seemed to know more about this stuff than I did where to go for website construction. Nobody could give me recommendations.

It seemed that everyone was a novice at this. I was left with no resource other than the phone book. There were only a few listings under "Internet". Galatia was the first number I called where someone actually answered the phone. They only had six employees, but were poised to grow. They could do anything we needed. Now and in the future. Sounded good to me.

At first, our website was mostly a distraction for me. It was something I had to keep updated, but that was about it. My focus was on the CD product. However, the quick expansion of our products required us to change our information very often. So, with increasing frequency, we directed our supplier and buyer customers to the website for new information.

The problem was, the Internet was so new that we spent an incredible amount of time painstakingly explaining to manufacturers how to use a browser.

The good news was that, once they understood what we were doing, they embraced our ideas with vigor and started asking us if we could add this feature or that. One of their most frequent questions was: *Is there any way to keep our own product information up-to-date using the Internet?* Well, I assumed that this was possible, but I had to verify that it was practical.

We had been receiving more and more product literature from suppliers to scan and convert for use on our CDs. It was becoming a bottleneck for us. We had to input everything into the computers, then send it out to be reviewed by the suppliers. Additional changes were made by us, and then reviewed with the customer again. It certainly would make sense for us to put the editing control into the hands of the suppliers themselves.

I asked Linda at Galatia how much it would cost to create a secure interface on the website that would allow the suppliers to maintain their own information. The price was high, but easily justified. Since the master database I had written was resident on our own computer server, Galatia would have to track all changes made to their copy of the database. I would need to write the interface to capture this data and merge it with ours on a regular basis.

Within a couple of months, we were up and running. We now had a real, interactive application running on the Internet.

The customers loved the idea of this. A few even used it. What we found, however, was that *we* ended up using the Web interface quite often. It was simple to use and a very convenient way for us to change supplier product information while at trade shows, which had just now begun to have Internet terminals. The suppliers were very impressed when they saw their products *immediately* appear on our website.

My interaction with Galatia became a daily, then hourly occurrence. Our list of features to add to the Web interface grew rapidly. Since we had all of this supplier information on the Web, we thought that we might as well make it visible to those few Internet-savvy people who might prefer to get this information via the Web rather than a dated CD.

It turned out that there were quite a few people who liked the idea of getting this information via the Web. Our traffic started at a trickle and would slowly, steadily, become a torrent. Although our business model didn't change much, the medium of delivery sure did. We started to realize that, at the rate we were going, the CD might soon disappear. The Web projects quickly became more complex. The Web development bills grew larger. Much larger. As I paid each bill, my demands increased too. I needed more, faster.

I still worked my day job at Varian. I had to establish a routine that allowed me to be at home in the morning to help get my two young sons ready for and off to school. Also, it was important to me to be home and attentive during dinner, until the kids' bedtime. From what was left, I had to carve out enough time to allow me to keep up with an increasing workload at Neoforma.

I ended up with a routine that worked. I would get up at between four-thirty and five each morning, take a quick shower and get in an hour or so of work before the kids awoke. Each evening, I would begin work immediately after the kids were in bed, at around eight, until my mind slowed down — usually between eleven and two, sometimes later. For the first time, coffee became a critical part of my mornings.

With my hour-and-a-half lunch, this schedule allowed me to put almost eight hours a day into Neoforma on weekdays, plus Saturdays. Because of this schedule, I would often send messages to Galatia at one or two in the morning and then again at five.

Once I had maintained this pattern long enough, I tended to forget that not everyone kept the same schedule. As my pressure on Galatia increased, Linda remarked that it was unreasonable to be expected to keep up with the demands of someone who never seemed to sleep.

The pressure had increased not only because of our increasing demand for new features, but because the nature of what we were doing with the Web was so unique that it stretched Galatia's software and hardware beyond their boundaries.

We were doing things that hadn't been done before. Or, more accurately, we were hitting these new website features with a volume of traffic that hadn't tested before.

Under the weight of increasing interactivity, data and traffic, the site began to crash. Often. I grew terribly frustrated. In the middle of the night, perpetually short on sleep, these unpleasant discoveries would occasionally drive me to rage. And my messages would fly: *Why can't you just keep this thing running!!?? Why do I have to find these problems myself!!?? I have a business to run. This is supposed to be your expertise!*

Over time, I became a demanding and impatient client. We had clearly outgrown Galatia, but I still held onto the idea that they should be growing in pace with us. And they *were* growing, but not at our pace. I couldn't understand why.

The fact was that they had decided, long before I'd interrupted their peaceful existence, to pursue a more restrained and more human pace. The very characteristic I had selected them for was the one that forced us to leave them behind.

Eventually, we couldn't avoid reality any longer. We decided that we had to bring our Web development inside the company. By late 1998, controlling our website would become much too critical to our future to leave to an outside party.

By that time we had a rapidly growing equity value. We considered buying Galatia. This would be a great way to quickly acquire a trained staff. But almost as quickly as we thought of this course we dismissed it, knowing that the cultural gap between Neoforma and Galatia would be too great, even if they became part of our company. So, we had to hire our own programmers. Galatia graciously helped us transition our website services to inside Neoforma. And that was that.

We were a rapidly growing company that had simply left behind what didn't fit. They had watched us grow from a company with one employee and no Internet experience to a company with nearly forty employees that was becoming a major player in the hastening Internet race. While I did not slow down enough to adequately thank them, I hope they felt, as they watched us disappear into the distance, some pride over their contribution to our success. They were pioneers too. They had simply chosen not to run quite as wildly as we had.

June 1996

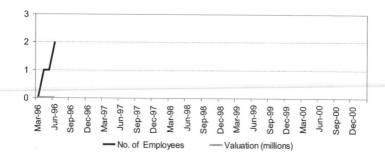

3
2
1
0

Mar-96 Jun-96 Sep-96 Dec-96 Mar-97 Jun-97 Sep-97 Dec-97 Mar-98 Jun-98 Sep-98 Dec-98 Mar-99 Jun-99 Sep-99 Dec-99 Mar-00 Jun-00 Sep-00 Dec-00

—— No. of Employees   —— Valuation (millions)

CompuServe, Microsoft Forge Major Strategic Alliance

CompuServe Inc. (NASDAQ: CSRV) and Microsoft Corp. today announced a far-reaching strategic alliance that includes a comprehensive technological partnership as well as marketing, distribution and commercial opportunities . . .

Microsoft Press Release
June 4, 1996

Borderline

There is nothing more frustrating than watching someone wear their fabric of memories and behaviors in such a way as to enshroud rather than enhance the beauty that is their unique potential.

She was charming.

I first met Cassandra when a very good friend and former business partner invited me to meet his new, attractive, very stylish girlfriend. The warning signs should have been obvious from the start, but expertise is tough to see around. Her subtle, flirtatious glances focused only on me. Her well-timed smiles, hints of inner wisdom, tidbits of an extraordinary life—as a professional ballet dancer, a pilot, a designer, a salesperson, a marketer—her fluency in many languages made her charming, mysterious, someone you would like to get to know.

After a particularly nasty breakup with my friend, Cassandra married someone else, moved to San Francisco and became a good friend to both Anni and me. I have always been exceptionally resistant to the wiles of charming people, but she caught me off-guard. We enjoyed being around her. Her presence was often very uplifting. Yet, as we got to know her better, we caught glimpses of a darker side—an inner turmoil—sides and corners disturbingly incongruous.

When we needed an extroverted, aggressive salesperson at Neoforma, Cassandra came to mind. The thought that hiring friends was a bad idea crossed my mind many times. Concern that she clearly had troubling gaps between her inner reality and outer projection crossed my mind. But her last job had been selling architectural services to hospitals. Her experience was ideal for Neoforma.

She agreed to spend some time helping us with sales—just part-time, just for a while. And she did very well! She would get on the phone and charm away. An expert, she knew that she would be calling people about fairly mundane products. She would be speaking with salespeople like herself. People she could connect with, listen to and spice up. She knew almost nothing about our product, but could project it to be whatever the person she was speaking with wanted it to be. I was still working for Varian, so I was only be able to come into the office for a long lunch every day to monitor her progress. Oh, and what progress! She was closing orders right and left. Big manufacturers too—the type of people I knew to be stubborn and immobile.

Sometimes I'd overhear her on the phone. Her accent and vocabulary would change completely, depending on who she was speaking to. She could always find something she had in common with the person on the other end of the phone. Sometimes, I knew that the common interest was not shared at all, but it sure made people feel special. I was a bit troubled by her use of deception in the workplace, but she *sounded* so sincere and she made people feel good. I admired her versatility and her control. Almost overnight, she became our shining star. We'd be rolling in money when everyone paid us.

Then one day, my good friend, Cassandra's ex-boyfriend, called me "just to say hi." He had heard that she was working for me and wanted to ask about her. He had heard that she had broken up with her husband, which was true. When he asked for her phone number, I hesitated, remembering how obsessive she had made him and I didn't give him the number.

He ended the call abruptly, with a warning: "You don't know who you are really dealing with when you're around Cassandra. Be careful."

It started with little things. I had to speak with an unhappy customer who clearly misunderstood what he bought from Cassandra. Then it became clear that many of the supposedly closed sales were actually simple expressions of interest, often more in her than the product. And, the more work that was required to get these deals closed, the less often she appeared at work.

When Jeff and I had a discussion with Cassandra, she painted a dizzily convincing picture of her vision of herself as a member of the executive team. She persuaded us that she would bring new commitment to her role in the company. We knew that when she was good, she was very good. So we gave her the position.

At the office though, things seemed to get worse and worse. Once Cassandra was a VP, Patty wanted to be vice president of operations. Cassandra pretended to support her completely. Yet, she would belittle Patty whenever alone with me. In fact, we were really being a bit indulgent having a full-time office manager when we really needed marketing and sales people. Since several customers weren't paying their bills, we were a bit tight on cash. So, we laid off Patty.

This was a very tough thing to do. After all, Patty had been our first employee. There was a lot of crying, on her part. Jeff and I tried to emphasize that she had outgrown us and could do better in a larger company.

I left the office that day in a dark mood. In spite of the heavy emotional drain involved in laying off or firing someone, I usually experienced a sense of relief afterward. In this case, I only felt that something wrong had happened, but couldn't explain why.

But there was no time for introspection. We had an international conference in Austria to attend. We had sales to make. We even had scheduled a side trip to Germany at the invitation of one of the biggest manufacturers in Europe. Yes, Cassandra was high-maintenance, but we could deal with that. After all, Jeff and I were both used to being thorns in the side of management at Varian. Anyone creative and driven would do that.

And, wow, could she work a show!! After the first day, as I walked the floor with her, she would pass people right and left that she knew by name. Many received hugs and expressions of familiarity exceeding what one would expect based on a one-day friendship. Whenever possible, she would slip into one of her many foreign languages to further that special bond she had created, and separate me from the conversation—evidence, I thought, of how much we needed her.

She would set me up to meet people in their booths. But I would get there and they would have no idea why they were talking to me, and I would have no idea why I was talking to them. We would dance around our mutual confusion, each unwilling to embrace our frustration at being seduced so easily into this meeting without a subject. I'd eventually be able to rebound and get the conversation under control, but I got quite tired of the embarrassment of not being prepared.

We also made a quick visit to Zurich, where we met with a friend I had become close to on previous visits for Varian. He was an architect, passionate about design and theory. He had the equivalent of my job in Europe. We shared a common passion for detail and the knowledge that we were far from the world of art and design we had dreamed we would be in by our late thirties. He had agreed to represent Neoforma in Europe and I wanted him to meet our team and discuss the possibilities.

As it happened, he had just separated from his girlfriend and was a bit down. Cassandra perked him right back up. They were instant soulmates, speaking alternately in French, German and Russian. Seldom English. He barely acknowledged me during the visit. Our new friendship and business partnership evaporated in his pursuit of her.

At the next trade show a month later, I noticed that nearly every meeting Cassandra set up for me was awkward, struggling to be more than it was. Some suppliers began to feel duped, but were not quite sure why.

When we hired two more smart, strong and creative persons to join our team, things really became surreal. Although we'd tried to confront Cassandra, she would expertly acknowledge certain things, deny others, and dilute the remainder.

As the deals Cassandra worked on became grander and the sparks around her grew brighter, the strain began to wear on her. She would be animated one hour, resigned the next.

What had seemed like a clever tactic—her ability to switch roles to suit the person she was talking to—began to seem like a problem. We slowly began to realize that, inside her world, she wasn't just putting on a show, she was really changing. At one angle she would be one person, at another she would be someone else entirely. Her expressions, accent, mannerisms, everything changed. And, I began to notice that one personality seemed to have no memory of comments made by another.

I cared about Cassandra very much. But, when I saw that look of a trapped animal, part of my heart froze. I knew what I would have to do. I knew what it was going to cost me, my family and Neoforma. But her friendship with our family would have to end. I would no longer hear from my friend in Zurich and some of our most significant customers were now socially close to her. I knew that she had pushed

Patty from the nest and manufactured walls between our other employees. She had to go.

When confronted with someone as intelligent and skilled at self-preservation, at deception, I couldn't help but question my own judgment right up to the end. I interviewed each employee in confidence: *Did she really say this? Did she really do that?* Some employees really seemed to think that I would be angry if they told me negative things about Cassandra. She had convinced them that my friendship with her was paramount. But in the end, they confirmed the tales that had led to my decision. I wasn't angry, only very sad.

After many unsuccessful confrontations and warnings, Jeff and I fired her. She went through so many extreme emotions and personalities during her severance that we couldn't keep up. Panic . . . denial . . . anger . . . pleading . . . righteousness. No charm though. The glue that had cemented her charm was dissolved in a torrent of tears.

I never saw her again. Anni tried to contact her, but Cassandra did not want to talk about it. The customers seemed to get over her, though some still asked about her years later.

I felt relief, exhaustion, inadequacy, and helplessness. *Why couldn't I tame such talent? Nurture such spirit? Make her feel good enough about herself to let down the charades?* I knew she felt bad about the damage she had done. That's why she became so desperate to sever all ties in the end.

To this day, I don't know if she became less expert in response to my awareness of her fragments or if I simply chose to ignore them from the beginning. I don't know if her many compartments were truly isolated or if she consciously used a new personality each time the current one was threatened. A little of each, I assume.

July 1996

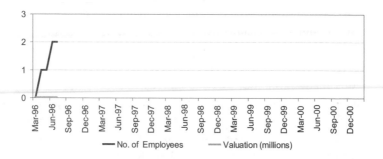

Product information screen capture from Neoforma CD-ROM

Two Worlds

By day, I was a disempowered middle manager. By night and on lunch hours, I was a respected business leader, speaking as an equal with the CEOs of major companies in the industry.

In our early days, we were still focused on the radiotherapy portion of healthcare. This was the area we knew best. In that in-between time, while I still worked at Varian but ran Neoforma, I existed in an odd, ethereal state. The guys in my department had given up any pretense of affinity to me. Since I was going to be leaving, I was clearly not in the power structure of Varian anymore. They were busy plotting to fill the void I had yet to create.

And, frankly, the day-to-day issues I faced there seemed incredibly petty to me now. Challenges that had previously excited me seemed suddenly to be quite mundane. Some of the people I had resolved to get along with were much more difficult to tolerate.

Needless to say, this split brought me quite a bit of tension. Each day I was teased by the pull of a new world, only to be pulled back to the old one again and again.

These feelings were brought to the forefront during my first trade show after officially founding Neoforma. This was one of the major trade shows in radiotherapy. I had represented Varian at this conference for many years. That year I would still be in the Varian booth, but representing both Varian and this new partner of Varian, Neoforma.

Jeff and I took turns in the booth demonstrating our software to an enthusiastic audience of healthcare professionals. Meanwhile, whoever wasn't in the booth was walking the floor, speaking with most of the vendors, including some Varian competitors. This was very exciting for us.

We were cautiously, but warmly, greeted by most of the vendors. There was a certain amount of confusion though. They ask us if since

Varian was the market leader in radiotherapy and Neoforma was sponsored by Varian, didn't that mean that working with Neoforma would bring them closer to Varian? We stressed that, "No, there is no such connection. Varian is simply one of our many customers." It was true.

We felt that, instead of being treated by the general populace of Varian as the loving offspring we thought we were, we were being treated as a tick that had finally been plucked out by tweezers. For some suppliers, those trying to buddy up with Varian, this news cooled their interest in us. For others, those that had long been pushed down by Varian's dominant market position, this news vaulted our status to that of long-lost friends.

Jeff and I struggled to make sense of our multiple identies. We were trapped between two worlds: one characterized by obligation, tradition and resentment and the other by optimism, uncertainty and jubilation.

August 1996

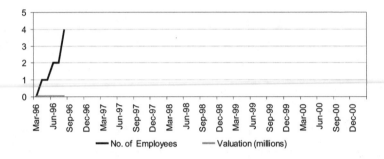

Casting

Our first steps and missteps in hiring taught us that the best ideas can be enhanced or destroyed almost overnight with the addition of each new teammate.

We weren't rolling in dough, but for a time we were making more money than we were spending. And the work was piling up.

To help catch up, we brought in a temporary administrator. Mona was a very quiet, seemingly simple, no-frills woman. Every task we threw at her, she handled with courage and ease. She quickly moved beyond administrative work to customer coordination, then content-production work, then software quality assurance, and more. When we had to pull overnighters to get a release of software out, Mona was right there beside us—temporary job or not. We eventually hired her, of course.

She moved through dozens of roles at Neoforma and ended up staying there longer than I. While my interactions with her became infrequent over the years, I did notice something amazing about her. She gradually evolved from a shy, somewhat plain woman into a very confident, attractive woman. While I am sure that motherhood and family life had a good deal to do with that, I'd like to think that the unbiased culture and abundant opportunities at Neoforma had something to do with it as well. She was one of the best employees we ever had at Neoforma.

From the beginning, I had been doing all of the computer programming, much of it based on code sketched out by Jeff. As my responsibilities and our customer base expanded, I realized that I needed to hire someone to augment and support our software. After all, I wasn't even a *real* programmer. I was just an amateur.

I provided a few search firms with a detailed description of the type of person I was looking for. Unfortunately, it turned out that people with the specific experience I needed were the hottest commodities on the market at that time. It was going to be tough to find anyone willing to work for a start-up without a track record, especially one offering the ridiculously low salary we could afford.

The applicants would ask, "What does your options plan look like?" And I'd say, "Options? Um . . . well . . . we don't offer options at this time . . ."

This would elicit an audible sigh on the other end of the phone. I could almost hear them shaking their heads above shrugging shoulders and glancing over to someone at another desk with a look that said, "See what I hafta put up with?"

Naturally, I had heard of stock options before. I had even received a small quantity from Varian. But I really didn't understand how they worked. I asked our lawyer about them. He explained what they were in terms that I almost understood and said, "Well, of course, you'll want an option plan set up to create incentive to your key hires. Costs a bit to set up though . . . so you might want to wait awhile."

I had always worked for a fair wage and a challenging variety of tasks. The options program didn't seem very important to me. I figured we'd get around to setting one up when the time was right. If I understood it correctly, options didn't mean much in a private company anyway and we certainly had no plans to be anything but a private company!

In came a trickle of résumés. I picked a few promising candidates to interview and set up meetings at Neoforma.

The early indications seemed good. While the people I interviewed generally had less knowledge about our specific programming environment and software support than I did, most had other skills that would complement mine well.

However, when we got to the salary discussion, things quickly turned south. These men and women were five to ten years my junior, had little or no college education, had very little experience, and were already making more money than I was! We couldn't offer them anything close to what they were expecting.

This went on for months, with no success. The headhunters became impatient with me, as I kept lowering my expectations rather than raising my salary target. Finally, one of the headhunters called me and said, "There is this guy who fits your needs perfectly. He has the experience you need and is willing to talk about some kind of profit-sharing model rather than taking a high salary." Well, this sounded promising.

I made an appointment with the guy—Isaac. He fit one stereotype of the opportunistic programmer—intelligent, sloppy, soft, arrogant, cocky and childlike. I disliked him, but he did seem to have the experience we needed.

He had worked primarily in large and established companies, so I made a point of clarifying that we were a start-up company without the infrastructure and support he was used to. He'd have to install his own software, set up his own systems. He'd have to learn our existing program mostly on his own and he'd have to be self-motivated about improving it. We were expanding to a second, adjacent office to accommodate him but our furniture was sparse and unsightly.

He assured me that these issues were trivial and that he had far more experience than we would ever need. Our negotiation was very aggressive and abrasive. He finally agreed to grace us with his presence, though it would be two more months before he could join us.

When the day finally came for him to join us, everything was creaking under the weight of the incomplete tasks that were waiting for Isaac. I called the office in the morning to make sure that he had arrived and was relieved to hear he had.

But by the time I got to the office at noon, Isaac was nowhere in sight. He had quit.

After waiting two months for the arrival of a guy I didn't even like, I was beside myself. My anger was the most intense I had ever experienced. I must've looked like a caricature of rage—face flushed, ears burning, knotted muscles. I was near overload, but managed to calm myself down somewhat before I called Isaac's cell phone. "So . . . what seems to be the problem?"

I could tell that the level of my calm confused him. There was some hesitation on his end. "Well . . . I looked at your software in some detail this morning. And I am not the right guy for you. There is too much to do. I'm going back to the firm I was working for. I've already called them. They're fine with it."

I could hear a fuse in my head pop. My anger rose beyond acceptable levels. The circuits overloaded. "NOT THE RIGHT GUY FOR US!?! WE STOPPED HIRING! WE WAITED TWO MONTHS FOR YOU TO JOIN US! AND THEN YOU CHANGE YOUR MIND AFTER A COUPLE HOURS? WHO THE HELL DO YOU THINK YOU ARE TO PLAY WITH US THIS WAY?!"

My rage, of course, had little effect on Isaac. But it did make me realize a thing or two about the importance of our culture. This guy hadn't *felt* right from the beginning—even though he had *sounded* right. I had focused on his computer skills—which can be learned—instead of more important and innate qualities—like an arrogance, born of insecurity—that would have made him difficult to work with, even if he'd stayed.

Staring at two months' backlog of work, I certainly couldn't appreciate it at the time, but he had done us a favor by leaving. He had not only kept our culture intact, but he'd reminded me how important it was to preserve it.

After venting the last of my outrage on the headhunter who had sent Isaac to us, I began looking at résumés again. There were a few promising candidates. But the next interview did not go well.

When I shook hands with the attractive woman in the lobby, I could tell at once that she was doing everything she could to present an image of calm and confidence. It must've been very hard for her because she was clearly trying her best, but she was not succeeding.

To make it worse, I noticed, as we went into the conference room, that she was dragging an eight-foot length of toilet paper behind her. Apparently, in her nervousness, she had caught it on an edge in her pants and dragged it along with her.

Nobody else had seemed to notice, but I was nonplussed. I'd already realized how nervous she was. *How was I supposed to put her at ease while pointing out that she was trailing more than a little toilet paper behind her?* There was a risk that she would be horrified to the point of immobility. I couldn't tell her. And yet, how could I ignore it—especially if the end of it still stuck out under the closed door? The situation was macabre. I sat there visualizing what would happen if someone absent-mindedly pulled the thing from the other side of the door or she got tangled up in it as she stood to go. I struggled to focus on her words—and heard enough to realize that she had overstated her capabilities, so she wouldn't be a good fit for the job.

As I waited the appropriately respectful time before ending the interview, I began to experience a sense of dread over what might happen as she left the building. Yet I simply sat there, feeling incredibly guilty that I hadn't found a more courageous way to handle the situation.

She may have had bad luck coming in, with a trail of toilet paper behind her, but she had amazingly good luck going out. Her tail did not get snagged on the door. And no one seemed to notice. The normally busy corridor was unusually empty. The receptionist did not have visibility below visitors' waists, so she couldn't see anything out of the ordinary.

I watched as this earnest woman, trying so hard to please, walked out of our offices in shoes that were clearly too tall for her to walk in comfortably, with her black pantsuit trailing that embarrassing white banner. I could only hope her luck would hold and it come off on its own before she noticed it.

Then we found Dante.

Finally, a candidate who felt right! Dante gave the impression of being a young, slightly large guy. Actually, it wasn't so much that he was large as that his suit was small. It was obvious that he didn't have much occasion to wear a suit and had somewhat outgrown this one. I did appreciate the fact that he made the effort to dress up for the interview though.

When I got to know him better, I found that Dante never wore constraining clothing voluntarily. It was T-shirts and shorts every day of the year, except for weddings, funerals, trade shows and interviews.

Dante was willing to take a salary cut in exchange for the opportunity to expand his experience. He was willing to work at whatever would help the company. He didn't ask about our options plan. He was a bit less experienced than I was looking for, but something felt right about him—and I was learning to go with my instincts about who would fit our culture.

I liked and hired him on the spot. He was eager, curious, persistent —the opposite of Isaac. He was willing to ask questions when he didn't understand something and to offer advice when he did understand something.

If he had a concern, he expressed it, but he never complained. He took responsibility, aware that each situation was a direct result of his decisions. He took his decisions seriously. I had the pleasure of watching him grow, in a very short time, from a talented young man into a mature leader. He was with us when we had to work all night, as Mona was. And, like Mona, he outlasted me at Neoforma.

I hired a few more people over that next year, but it wasn't until the beginning of 1998, when we would first receive some investment money, that I began hiring more people in earnest. I did so at an increasing pace that would eventually overwhelm me.

While Jeff spent most of his time seeking additional investment and selling our services to some of the largest suppliers in the industry, I used my time trying to spend that investment well.

The most substantial and important investment we had to make was in building a team to carry an enlarging vision forward quickly. We had entered the Internet race. This was something we had not anticipated, but we were up for a challenge.

Of the first hundred employees of Neoforma, I hired—directly or indirectly—about seventy-five of them. Jeff interviewed many of them and shaped the decisions too. While this was a very diverse group of people, they shared a core set of values. They sowed the seeds of a new culture.

A year or so after we had left the company, Neoforma asked Jeff and me to present the history of Neoforma to a group of new employees. Looking into the eager eyes of those new recruits, I had a strong sense that that same culture survives today. I hope so. We had been rejected by the culture at Varian. And we went on to form a culture that was more like us. This is the nature of evolution. We are compelled to reproduce ourselves in the world in any way we can. And we are deeply enriched when some of our traits live on in what we have created.

November 1996

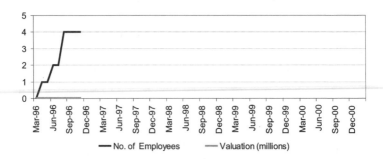

— No. of Employees ———— Valuation (millions)

Department Toolkit Now Available

Neoforma Inc., in collaboration with Varian Oncology Systems (VOS), has developed a software-based planning tool and product catalog for radiotherapy departments . . . Eventually, there will be a Department Toolkit for the entire hospital . . .

Centerline
Fall '96

Confidence

We *were* going to change the world. All we had to do was let the world know.

The largest U.S. trade show for medical equipment is held every November in Chicago. I had attended, and dreaded, this show for many years.

Booth duty consisted of standing in uncomfortable clothes for long hours, mostly hoping that a customer would walk in and ask a question I would know the answer to.

In 1996, I went there with a new mission: to convince a good portion of the six hundred vendors attending that there was a better way to get in front of their customers.

While there were fifty thousand attendees at this conference, most were not in the middle of a critical decision process. And of those that were, a very small portion would stumble into any particular booth among the hundreds of vendors. And of those, very few would actually remember the products they had seen when it came time for them to make their decision. Also, they were only one of many people usually tasked with making each decision.

Our products could change that.

Since our software on the Web and CD was used as an integral part of the planning processes, everyone visiting our website or using our CD was at the decision sweet spot. *Didn't it make sense to put your products in front of these professionals the Neoforma way?* Of course it did.

That was the spiel. So far, so good.

The thing is, I am an introvert. My casual social interactions tend to be awkward, stilted events. Niceties escape me. Witticisms slip into my brain moments too late for effective delivery. Proper nouns—such as names and sports teams—are stored in a largely inaccessible place in my brain. Add to this the fact that I am neither tall nor imposing and look many years younger than my age. More often than not, I even mispronounce my own last name when introducing myself.

Yet I found myself, once again, in a huge, crowded hall, filled with unfamiliar people. And it was my task to walk into as many booths as possible, identify the decision-makers, and convince them that I was going to change everything.

Sometimes I was met with open hostility and asked to leave. Most of the time, of course, I was met with courtesy. After all, most people were mildly interested in what the Internet would mean for their business in the long run and I seemed to know something about it. And it helped that everyone was bored with doing booth duty.

When I met with the junior sales guys, they seldom had heard of Neoforma. But a surprising number of the execs *had* heard of us. Some were truly interested in exploring our business proposition. Most were simply interested in listening to what I had to say, rather than doing anything about it.

For the most part, I took rejection well at this conference. In fact, I fed on my frustration, walking the aisles with a devout certainty that we would forever change this industry for the better. I was confident that Neoforma would someday become a name recognized by most of these companies. As I've said, I didn't necessarily convey my confidence well, but my ability to talk about this new company that I believed in so strongly was growing.

At the end of each day, Jeff and I would tell our stories of the day— the successes and failures, the eagerness and stubbornness, the challenges and opportunities. We felt exhausted, but above all, we felt privileged.

With a little time, and a little luck, we would make a fundamental improvement to this old, entrenched industry of healthcare. We knew it.

January 1997

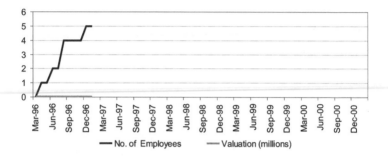

Mar-96	Jun-96	Sep-96	Dec-96	Mar-97	Jun-97	Sep-97	Dec-97	Mar-98	Jun-98	Sep-98	Dec-98	Mar-99	Jun-99	Sep-99	Dec-99	Mar-00	Jun-00	Sep-00	Dec-00

—— No. of Employees   —— Valuation (millions)

Zona Research Indicates Microsoft Internet Explorer Share Now 28 Percent

. . . A Zona Research study released today reports that use of Microsoft Internet Explorer in corporations has more than tripled to 28 percent of total use in the past three months . . . Independent studies confirm corporations moving to Microsoft Internet Explorer from Netscape Navigator . . .

Microsoft Press Release
Jan. 28, 1997

The Majors — Part One

We meant well. We were focused on making things better in our little corner of the world. How could we have imagined that we were causing such a fuss?

When we started Neoforma, Jeff and I considered ourselves, in part, to be champions of the small company. Varian, the big behemoth, had dominated its market with an iron hand for decades. Good companies were being squeezed out in such a monolithic environment.

Most of the companies we worked with were small. They had the most to gain by our alternative to a direct sales force. But as we grew, we did work with some big companies too. At first this was with small divisions of large companies. Eventually, our connections with one division in a company would lead us into other divisions.

We discovered quickly that, in the eyes of these companies, Varian was just a stubborn little company that had captured a lucrative market by luck. These other companies were willing to lose a significant amount of money fighting for a foothold in Varian's market. It was a matter of pride.

It took us awhile to adjust to the idea that there were bigger fish out there than Varian — in the form of some huge, multinational equipment manufacturers. Then we had to adjust to even bigger fish. Some of the healthcare distributors were absolutely monstrous in size, with tens of thousands of employees.

We were only familiar with the equipment market, but began to bump into the supplies companies quite early. They often had a small selection of items that we considered to be equipment. We assumed that the distributors would not be threatened by us. Equipment was a very small part of their business. We would just be providing one more channel for them to sell within. And it was about that same time that we became familiar with the group purchasing organizations, or GPOs.

In the early 1980s, healthcare providers had banded together into groups of up to thousands of hospitals, in an effort to control the soaring prices they were paying for supplies. They had grown into powerful forces in the healthcare industry, with several managing tens of billions of dollars in annual purchases.

GPOs negotiated good prices with manufacturers in exchange for a commitment to a certain volume of purchasing. Since the GPOs were often owned by the hospitals they served, there was great pressure within hospitals to support these agreements.

While the GPOs primarily saved money in the supplies market, they also had a large influence over the equipment manufacturers. I knew very little about GPOs from my days at Varian—other than the fact that they were disdained, feared and treated with reluctant respect. The loss of a single contract with one of the large GPOs could doom a company's financial results for years.

Because most equipment was purchased in irregular cycles, as part of large projects, most capital equipment items had not been successfully aggregated by the GPOs. Since capital equipment was our area of focus, we were quite comfortable that we would not be seen as a threat by the GPOs.

What we didn't know—what we didn't have the egos to imagine—was that Neoforma had started showing up on GPO and supplier strategy whiteboards in early 1997—quite literally under the category of *Threats*.

As part of our Web strategy, we had created a messaging system on top of our catalog. We knew that we would eventually be able to capture revenue from buyers of equipment when they had become accustomed to using our website to source their products. So we began channeling carefully framed leads from our site visitors to thousands of suppliers. The leads went via email to those few companies that had email addresses, the rest went via an automated fax system. We did not charge for this service.

At first, most companies were very irritated with us. *How dare you get in between our customers and us?* But as the leads increased in quantity and quality, manufacturers and distributors were more cautious in their response to us. They had seen what the GPOs could do to a company that resisted them. They didn't know what to think of us.

Two years later, when interviewing executives from these companies to fill positions at Neoforma, I was astonished to hear how much we had been dreaded and feared.

In those days, we had assumed that nobody was paying much attention to us, but many were already working on ways to keep us out of their game. When I discovered later how much attention we had been getting, I thought, *If only they had just come to speak with us then, we could have all worked together to solve some of the big problems facing the healthcare system!*

Of course, the businessman in me knows that it doesn't work that way, but I have never been able to shake the piece of naïveté that embraces the idea of mutual benefit.

February 1997

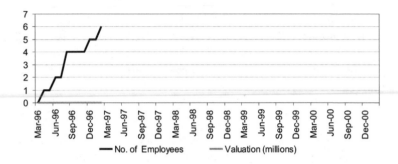

No. of Employees   Valuation (millions)

The Contract

Sometimes a shove from the nest leads to flight. Sometimes it doesn't. Time would tell.

As my confidence in Neoforma increased, my situation at Varian continued to decay.

One day, I was congratulated by a workmate at Varian for my move to Neoforma. I said, "Thank you," But this was news I was not pleased to hear—considering that I had not yet given my notice.

I had indeed been coordinating an eventual departure date with my boss, Evelyn. I couldn't bear the daily ritual of watching the clock slowly spin each morning, waiting for the time I could go to Neoforma for lunch.

Now that we had put in our promised year at Varian, both Jeff and I agreed that one of us needed to be at Neoforma full-time. There was so much to do.

Since I was engaged in most of the operational issues, it made sense that I should be the first to move. Neoforma did not have enough money to sustain me for long, but the sales were increasing. With our current growth we should easily be able to pay me a salary— that is, if Jeff and I both agreed to invest some of our own money. We estimated that about fifty grand each would do the job.

Neither of us had much money saved. We were both just beginning to invest in college funds for our kids. But we figured we could each just pull together about fifty thousand dollars for a short-term loan to the company. With our current revenue projections, we estimated that we would be able to pay ourselves back within six months. We would survive by holding off paying the balances on our personal credit cards. We had each run our cards up quite high, paying for company expenses.

Anni and I were able to come up with the money by leveraging the equity in our house. But we owned the house along with my father-in-law. He had helped us get into our house several years earlier by investing in it with us. Even though our first mortgage balance was very high and we only owned part of the house, there was just enough equity in our share to borrow eighty thousand. That would be enough money that we could invest the fifty thousand and use the balance to make the loan payments.

Since Neoforma was doing so well, this seemed to be a reasonable risk. We had to rush the loan through since I would never qualify after moving to Neoforma.

I had calculated a salary reduction that would put me at the absolute minimum salary I could take to allow Anni and me to pay our monthly bills. That way the impact on Neoforma would be minimized. Jeff agreed that when he soon joined Neoforma his salary would be the same. I felt safer, knowing someone else was willing to take the same risk.

So, while I was prepared to make the move to Neoforma I didn't expect to be the last to know *when*.

It turns out that my boss had simply let a departure date slip out during a meeting. Clearly, she felt that I needed a boost to get over my hesitancy. This would not have been my preference, but it worked. I agreed to consult with Varian for a period of time to help transition my exit. Then I counted the minutes until my departure.

There was a small going-away gathering held for me in one of the conference rooms. The atmosphere was awkward. Nobody was quite sure if I was leaving on good terms or bad. When Ed, the president of the company, showed up, it made me feel good. I had been there for nearly ten years, working energetically to solve every challenge I faced, yet I felt that I was leaving hardly any impression behind. People come and people go.

I knew that wouldn't be the case with Neoforma.

March 1997

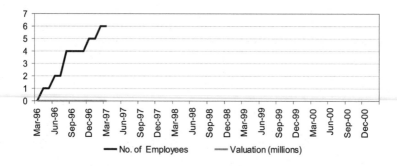

Word of Mouth

We hadn't really expected to be in the business of helping to ease the discomfort of rats, but once things got going, there was really no way of knowing where they might lead.

In 1996, at the request of the local Varian salesmen, I had traveled to Australia to show off the software Jeff and I had written. One of the venues I had gone to was a prestigious teaching hospital. Around a conference room table, I had presented our software to a group of thoughtful medical physicists who spent their lives exploring things I couldn't understand. Sitting there, viewing my demonstration of what would become the foundation of the Neoforma software, they had conveyed a surprisingly energetic curiosity.

An eager man in a lab coat interrupted my demonstration to tell a colleague enthusiastically that he had been able to get the specifications for a certain piece of radiotherapy equipment made in the U.S. He was thrilled that he had been able to get this information from across the world while the manufacturers slept. And he was most thrilled that he had been able to get it *in a couple of hours.*

He had searched many different websites to locate the correct manufacturer. Then he had searched for some time within that manufacturer's site. But he eventually found what he was looking for much faster than the current method of spending hours calling colleagues to locate a fax number, sending a fax and then waiting until those lazy Americans got out of bed.

I asked him what the product was. By a lucky coincidence, I had that particular product catalogued in our software. In seconds I was able to pull up the same information he had in his hands. They liked that idea and would soon join the thousands of visitors to our website.

After being with us for only a few months, our very talented website designer/marketing guy was helping to expand the catalog from our CD onto the Neoforma website. He developed techniques for directing thousands of new, curious visitors from all over the world to our website every week. An intelligent artist/entrepreneur with a mischievous sense of humor, Todd reveled in the challenge of bringing people to our domain. His road signs were cleverly crafted to convey uniqueness and stimulate curiosity.

Under his influence, our site became the perfect destination for the increasing number of brave souls poking around the Web, seeking information they couldn't find any other way. Todd's perseverance and creativity changed everything.

In March of 1997 our online catalog was still relatively small, containing information on only a few thousand products. However, the email inquiries sent by visitors using our website to suppliers were of great and intriguing variety . . .

I provide technical advice to a number of TV series and movies. It is my job to ensure that medical scenes are "technically" accurate within their "artistic impression." If you are a fan of ＊＊＊＊ and have watched their high-tech medical scenes, you've seen some of my work. I'm presently working on a feature movie . . . I wish to obtain info on specialized equipment and availability for its use in this movie . . .

And . . .

＊＊＊＊ is a medical device manufacturer currently looking for a new vendor for ＊＊＊＊. We purchase roughly 12,000 per year. Please send any information and pricing to . . .

And . . .

We need to buy 2 million 1 cc disposable syringes with 24 gauge push on needles. C&F price [Middle Eastern country]. Target price US$ 4.40 each.

And . . .

We are in need of blanket warmers to be used on rats during surgery . . .

People from all over the world were looking for all kinds of stuff. Expensive stuff. And they seemed to be very grateful to have found a way to connect to those who could meet their needs.

The variety of stuff they were looking for went far beyond our initial scope. What an interesting challenge, connecting this community together in some way that made sense to everyone involved!

If everyone benefited from what we created, then it should be easy to come up with a model where the costs were balanced with the gains—especially when single transactions were often worth millions of dollars.

We were definitely onto *something* good here.

April 1997

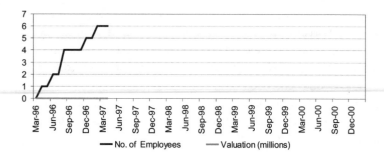

Legend: No. of Employees — Valuation (millions)

The Mentor

When we entered this new society — the world of the technology start-up — we felt quite lost in some ways. It was difficult to know how to navigate the many established, yet unfamiliar channels of communication without a guide. Jeff and I were lucky.

We were referred to Jack by the large law firm he had left to start his own practice. We didn't think that a relationship with an attorney was a big deal. We just wanted someone who could help us set up a new corporation and negotiate a good agreement with Varian, that was all.

Jack didn't work that way. He was a big, warm man with eyes that expressed enthusiasm for any challenge — a man full of charming eccentricities, eternally late for meetings, always sliding into the room with apologies, offering drinks and food left over from his previous meetings.

At our first meeting with him, Jack's eagerness and respect for innovation quickly put us at ease. He asked good questions, about us and about our business. He paid attention to what we said, but I felt him probing us with his eyes more than with his ears. I could see that he was making a quick decision about Jeff and me — not about the company we were forming. He was someone who relied on his intuition. We liked him very much.

After a half-hour of questions, he began to brainstorm ideas on how we could expand our business. Some suggestions were laser sharp, others wildly off course, but all were welcome. He suggested that we should get some investment money to grow our ideas. We hadn't thought about that possibility. We figured we would have enough money to get us through to profitability. So Jeff said, "No, we don't think we'll need any money."

But it *was* reassuring to know someone familiar with raising money, if for some reason we were to need extra money someday.

Jack actually seemed to think we might be able to make this idea of ours work. Prior to this, other than from our families, we had received support from a few people, but not much encouragement, and definitely not expressions of confidence. He opened a view to a world where risk and sacrifice were encouraged, even appreciated.

We had to remind him at the end of the first meeting that we had legal details to attend to. He offered a very low fee for the work he would do, saying that he would make it up when we grew. He rattled off what we needed to do. We agreed, and then he called in an assistant to take care of all the pesky details.

Over the next year, Jack inundated us with ideas. Every week he sent me envelopes stuffed with articles, clipped from a multitude of obscure periodicals, scrawled with cryptic notes and suggestions. Links to articles and websites flooded our email inboxes. This guy never stopped connecting ideas together. He could validate our ideas with technologies that were ten years away.

Jack always had smiles and encouragement for us. He effused sincere belief in us every step of the way. I could tell that this was how he conducted all of his business. His emotions were always on.

However, I sensed ferocity beneath his gregarious exterior. A client of his told me that Jack was an absolute tiger in the courtroom and I believed it. He could be very convincing, due to the intensity of his conviction.

I was sure that his passionate emotions must take a toll on him. He could not win every battle, yet I knew he could not accept losing a battle he cared about without suffering. I must admit that I worried sometimes about whether he paid too much for this unbridled passion. But he was always there for us.

We finally realized in early 1997 that our own financial resources weren't enough to manage our rapidly expanding business plan. Our personal debts were growing. We remembered Jack's belief that we could get money from outside investors. That seemed worth exploring.

We met with him and, as casually as possible, asked how we might get investment money, if we were to need some. Picking up on our hint and ignoring our caution, he said, "Well, if I were to invest some money in Neoforma, then I could introduce you to some people I know who might be willing to follow."

And it was that simple. We had our first outside investor. Jack wrote us a check for twenty-five thousand dollars on the spot. This was an extraordinary amount of money to us. I felt very proud of his confidence and took his investment very seriously.

Within another year, Jack would tell us that his firm was too small to handle the body of work our growing company needed. He helped us transition to a large firm and bid us, "Good luck!"

Thanks to him, we had already had more than our share of luck.

May 1997

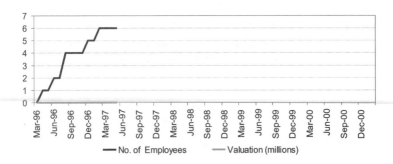

7
6
5
4
3
2
1
0

Mar-96 Jun-96 Sep-96 Dec-96 Mar-97 Jun-97 Sep-97 Dec-97 Mar-98 Jun-98 Sep-98 Dec-98 Mar-99 Jun-99 Sep-99 Dec-99 Mar-00 Jun-00 Sep-00 Dec-00

—— No. of Employees　　—— Valuation (millions)

Amazon.com IPO skyrockets

Silencing any doubts about its chances on the public market, Amazon.com (AMZN) ended the day $54 million richer as its long-awaited initial public offering soared 30 percent above its opening price . . . The IPO raised $54 million for Amazon, giving the company a market value of $438 million . . .

CNET News.com
May 15, 1997

Businesses Find the Web a Friendly Mall

For all the hype over online commerce, cyberspace has yet to prove the retailing miracle many hoped it would be . . . What's missing? The answers seem to be everything . . . value, a great experience and added convenience . . . But business-to-business is another story . . . Forrester Research Inc. predicts business-to-business trade online will swell to more than $65 billion by 2000 from about $600 million in 1996 . . .

Investor's Business Daily
May 19, 1997

Angels

Our first taste of outside investment created an almost instantaneous craving for more.

When Jack made good on his promise to connect us with potential investors, we scrambled to produce a short business plan and slide presentation. The business plan would be sent to several angels.

Angel investors are private individuals who invest small amounts of money—say twenty-five to two hundred fifty thousand dollars—in the early stage of companies. Most angels have made their money as entrepreneurs. They know a great deal about the situation these new businesses are in. They have been there.

Within a month, our first meeting was set up. Jack gave Jeff and me directions to a house in the upscale community of Los Altos Hills. This meeting was going to be a bit unconventional. Most first presentations and discussions were held in conference rooms. Meeting on neutral ground kept meetings from getting too personal. This kept the potential investor shielded from personal feelings that might get him or her suckered into an otherwise irrational investment.

Jeff picked me up on a cloudy morning. We followed the directions into the hills, up winding roads, and parked next to a locked gateway. We stepped out of the car and caught a glimpse of a large house over the gate. Shrouded by trees, the estate had been designed to evoke among visitors, in equal measure, feelings of insecurity and importance. It worked.

Jeff and I looked at each other with trepidation and pleasure, then pressed the intercom button adjacent to the gate. Although the place looked empty, we were quickly buzzed in. As we walked toward the house along a path across a large expanse of lawn, a glance to our right revealed a small collection of pristine luxury and collectors' cars in the driveway.

The house was formal, but not quite classical, not quite opulent. A casually dressed man who looked to be in his fifties greeted us at the door. Our first glance inside the house revealed a marbled entry containing a full-size suit of armor and an elegant spiraling staircase. The man introduced himself as Shawn.

His carefree manner, long hair and casual attire provided him with an intriguing aura of conscious success and well-tailored rebelliousness. Jack had told us that Shawn had made more than a hundred million from the sale of his software company some years back. He was retired, but active in helping companies get off the ground. When I later asked him why he continued to invest in small companies he told me, "You can only play so much golf, you know."

Here was a man who had taken on IBM in his day—and won. He deferred to no one. With practiced skill, this all came across within minutes of greeting us.

He guided us through an elaborate, art nouveau archway into a formal living room. Seated within the darkened room, in somewhat more formal attire, was Wally. A successful heart surgeon, Wally, in addition to being an angel investor, was a director and vice president at a medical device company. In contrast to Shawn's more assertive manner, Wally was calm, studied and modest.

Seated across from them around a dark wooden coffee table, Jeff and I nervously, but confidently, introduced ourselves. When I proudly indicated that I was an architect, their eyes widened eagerly. Wally said, "You're a software architect?"

Software architects are the men and women who design how everything in a program is going to work together, a very important role.

When I answered proudly, "No, I'm a real architect . . . as in buildings," Wally was visibly disappointed. I didn't know until then that architecture was not a desirable background for an entrepreneur to have. Those with artistic temperaments tend to be far more wedded to their ideals than their pocketbooks. Investors wanted their investments protected by founders driven by the fame of fortune.

In future discussions, when my background was being presented by one set of investors to another, my management experience was emphasized and my architecture license was minimized or not mentioned at all.

Jeff and I demonstrated our software and discussed our plans. Wally and Shawn both seemed impressed. Wally asked many good questions. We became increasingly comfortable as we realized that we were able to answer them competently.

Shawn asked many questions too. Many, many questions. He dug in every nook and cranny, questioning everything he heard. He was on a mission to find our biggest flaw. It didn't take long for him to find it. "You guys are clearly not salesmen. How could you sell this on a big scale?" After all, investors would only put money into a company that had *big* potential.

We could tell that our responses were too vague for Shawn. He didn't understand how, in spite of its substantial market size, we would get a large amount of money out of the healthcare industry.

Wally was more optimistic. With his background in the hospital business, he knew that once we had a solid grip on this conservative industry the growth potential was huge. He was more comfortable with our loose ends than Shawn was.

The meeting went on for several hours. Before we left, Shawn gave us a tour of the house. He pointed out the rooms that he and his wife had recently remodeled. He wasn't sure how they would take advantage of the upgrades, since this was the least used of their houses. But he was sure that they'd figure out something to do with it.

Wally and Shawn indicated that they would discuss Neoforma with each other and a few friends in the industry.

Two weeks later, Jack let us know that Wally and Shawn were interested in investing in Neoforma. We were thrilled. Because of their expression of interest, we began thinking about ways to accelerate our growth by putting more money into our website development. We thought that, since the first investors we spoke with were so interested, it would not be long before these or other investors put some money in us. We felt comfortable spending money a bit less conservatively.

Wally and Shawn were especially concerned about what customers really thought of what we were doing. Wally set us up to present our business ideas to a group of purchasing managers at a local hospital— so they could directly gauge customer interest. The presentation went very well. But it was only a single group at a small hospital.

Wally also wanted to know how we would be received by larger buyers, so he picked up the phone and called the persons responsible for acquiring equipment for the largest hospital system in the country. (He *was* a well-known doctor after all.)

Wally set up an appointment for the following month. I flew across the country to their headquarters with Jeff and Shawn. We presented our current and future software to the two key people responsible for selecting equipment for the entire hospital system. That meeting went quite well too.

Jeff and I had discussed it and agreed that if this meeting went well, it would probably only take a few weeks to finalize the funding. But to our surprise, instead of proceeding to financial term sheets, Shawn continued to ask us for more details — longer-term financial projections, a more detailed business plan, more sources for market size evaluation. And his language was becoming increasingly cautious.

Then his inquiries suddenly stopped. He had told Jack that he thought we needed far more money to pull this thing off than we were asking for. He said that he wasn't sure if he was ready to invest in us. He had to think about it.

After weeks of waiting for a firmer answer, we found out that he was traveling. In fact, he wouldn't be around much for a few months. He said that he'd keep thinking about us and maybe we could connect when he returned to the area.

When Shawn disappeared without a firm yes or no, Wally became more hesitant. Investors seldom want to invest alone. Knowing that others are willing to take the same astronomical risks is the best indication that the risk is worthwhile.

But Wally did continue to meet with us, sometimes alone, sometimes with someone else from the healthcare industry. At the beginning of each meeting he would be cautious and skeptical, but by the end he would be enthusiastic again.

Jack had trouble getting other investors to meet with us. For various reasons, he just couldn't get us in front of many investors. The couple of meetings we did have were unproductive.

Having made the decision to pursue funding, we *were* getting a bit nervous, but we were so charged-up by the great stuff we were doing that we knew the funding issue would work itself out. In the mean-time, we'd figure out a way to bridge the money gap with our own money, and maybe some family money. Just for a little while.

June 1997

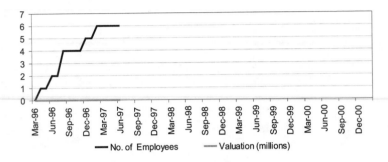

The Audience

The unsatisfied customer is the most important customer.

One day, I was at home showing off the Neoforma website to my father-in-law. At the time, he was a dentist, computer-illiterate, impatient and prone to doing things the old, familiar way, unless the new way was unequivocally proven to be vastly more efficient.

Although our database had few dental products, he *was* able to find some products he used. He checked out the feature that allowed visitors to send email inquiries to vendors, but he was skeptical of its value.

"Why would I use this, if I could just pick up the phone and call a vendor, negotiate a good deal and be done with it?" he said. Then he paused for a bit, smiled and added, "Now, if I could send a message to several vendors at once—that might be a real timesaver. Can I do that?"

When I told him that we didn't have that capability yet, he was disappointed. The ability to broadcast requests to a multitude of vendors simultaneously was a great idea. Yet I had seen nothing like it on the Web. So I sent a specification to our developer that weekend.

By the end of the next week, we had implemented the new feature. A visitor to our website could search through thousands of products, pick a category of interest, write up a message, and send it to some or all of the manufacturers of that type of product. A process that took hours previously could now be done in seconds. And we didn't even charge for it.

We did not announce the feature when we posted it on our site. However, within ten minutes of being live, a visitor sent the first broadcast message to multiple suppliers.

By the next day, the system was being used for hundreds of messages—in ways we had never envisioned. At its peak, twenty thousand messages a week were being sent from buyers to sellers. We knew we had significantly improved the lives of many people.

I felt very good about that, even though it hadn't been my idea.

July 1997

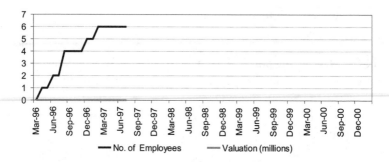

A Square Peg

Being unique is great. Except when you're not like everyone else.

Even when it was looking likely that angels like Shawn and Wally would fund us, Jack insisted that we keep exploring other paths. He said he knew consultants who specialized in helping small companies get big funding. And then there were also the venture capitalists (VCs).

We had revenue, increasing website traffic, a patent application filed for our planning and email systems, and respectable angel investors about to put money in us. It was time to figure out what we wanted to be when we grew up.

To get others to see us as grown-up, Jack said we had to show what we were going to look like years from now. We thought this was ridiculous. We knew we would grow up big and strong, but held no illusion that we could imagine exactly what that would look like.

Jack had a tough time comparing us to any other type of company out there. We were *kind of like* an Amazon.com or a Yahoo for the healthcare business. We were *kind of like* a couple of private companies that were being funded (Ariba and Commerce One). But we were *not really* very much like any of them.

We certainly didn't serve the consumer market, where growing sites with huge traffic were quite the buzz. And we weren't providing infrastructure, the software tools integrated into the way large companies run their day-to-day business, where enterprise software companies had made huge sums.

We were a company focused on improving a particular process in a particular industry. Since we couldn't be classified, most large investors weren't interested in speaking with us. They were seeing plenty of consumer Internet and business infrastructure companies to keep them busy.

We vigorously resisted classifying ourselves. We thought that it

was a good thing that we were so different from other companies—
that showed how unique, creative and special we were, didn't it?

We discovered that, when it came to funding, uniqueness was not
a good thing.

What we couldn't know at the time was that, two years later, more
than a hundred companies would get funded by describing how they
were like Neoforma. Too bad that couldn't help us in 1997.

August 1997

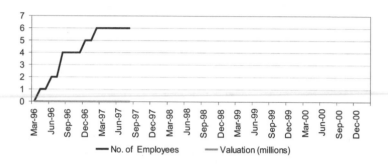

	7																		
6																		
5																		
4																		
3																		
2																		
1																		
0																		

Mar-96 Jun-96 Sep-96 Dec-96 Mar-97 Jun-97 Sep-97 Dec-97 Mar-98 Jun-98 Sep-98 Dec-98 Mar-99 Jun-99 Sep-99 Dec-99 Mar-00 Jun-00 Sep-00 Dec-00

—— No. of Employees ——— Valuation (millions)

Microsoft Completes Acquisition of WebTV Networks

Microsoft Corp. and WebTV Networks Inc. today announced
the completion of Microsoft's acquisition of WebTV for
approximately $425 million in cash and stock.

Microsoft Press Release
August 1, 1997

We at The Herring are convinced that highly focused and
quietly successful niche companies that fit into the
convergence applications model will redefine corporate
computing, changing companies' transaction approaches
from task orientation to process orientation . . .

The Red Herring
August 1997

The Producers

Every big industry has them. They supply the nutrients required for abundant growth.

Alexander and JP were *players*. Builders of buzz. They had been involved in rapidly building the valuations of several local companies—companies vibrating with potential to make it big—companies to be pursued.

Jack told them about us. Afterward he sent us an email:

> *Alexander and JP want to meet you. They are well-wired in the venture community and could help us position for additional alternatives to Wally and Shawn . . . though, as you will hear . . . their views will be more tuned towards how you can RAMP very, very quickly . . . with much much more mone . . . presumably from the venture community . . . though, of course, they are also connected to private money including from their own group.*

We met Alexander first. He was a fiery Greek, all knotted energy and quick emotions—a man with strong convictions. He always held his convictions very firmly, at least until someone knocked them free by the sheer force of intelligent argument. Once dropped, these convictions were easily left behind and replaced by new, stronger ones.

He greeted us respectfully, though impersonally. He talked a bit about his partnership with JP. He told us that they only worked with two or, at most, three companies at a time. They were currently deeply embroiled with their latest company, Junglee, which they would sell to Amazon.com a year later for around $180 million, so they weren't seriously looking for a company to work with. But if the opportunity were good enough, they *might* consider taking on one more company . . .

"Besides," he said, "You guys are ten to fifteen years older than the other founders we deal with. Your extra experience means we wouldn't have to hold your hands as much."

I suppose I could have accepted this as a compliment, but, for the first time in my life, I felt old. I had usually been much younger than the people I worked around. To these guys, I was nearly over the hill.

He casually dropped the names of influential people, sowing seeds. He made it very clear that they were *not* angel investors, that they only played in much bigger leagues. He asked "What angels are you working with now?"

We told him about Wally and Shawn. He shrugged off their names, obviously not impressed. Those guys were clearly not players in his league. "We would definitely get you better valuations than they could."

Then he barraged us with questions.

"How many customers are there in your market? . . . How much money do they spend? . . . Where do they spend the most money? . . . Who are the decision-makers? . . . Does your software scale up easily? . . . How are you going to accelerate your sales?"

We had answers to these questions. We thought they were good, solid, mature answers. "We are going to use our incremental sales growth and a little outside money to improve the website, do some advertising, hire a couple salespeople."

He seemed to be agonizing in his chair as Jeff and I took turns presenting our careful growth strategy. I could see by his sighs, darting eyes and the shakes of his head that he was frustrated, but trying to be polite.

Jeff and I communicated our concern through well-practiced glances: *He doesn't understand us. Clearly, we are going over our information too quickly for him.*

We started to include more specific details of our plans.

That was it for Alexander. He couldn't take it anymore.

"COME ON, GUYS! THAT'S ALL BULLSHIT. I MEAN, HOW ARE YOU GOING TO MAKE NEOFORMA BIG? VERY BIG! Your plans sound fine, but if that is the road you're choosing . . . you don't need me and JP."

Oh, *now* we got it. He wasn't focused on our product at all. As soon as he had at least some superficial understanding of what we were doing, he didn't want to know more about our product—only about how big our market was and how we were going to dominate it.

Once we calmed him down, he asked us, "What is your exit strategy?"

Jeff and I looked at each other. I said "Um . . . what exactly do you mean . . . exit strategy?"

He was exasperated again, "I *mean* . . . how you are going to get a return on your investment?"

"Well, first we'll put Jeff on staff, then increase both our salaries . . ."

That was the last straw. Alexander stood up, emoting distaste for our small thinking. He thanked us for our time, shook hands and raced out the door. "You need to think about these things. I'll talk to my partner about you guys. Like I said, we are quite busy now."

Jeff and I were devastated. Here was a guy who could propel us from one world to another and he thought we were too timid to interest him.

We, who were risking everything, were too cautious to see the opportunities in front of us. What kind of world did these guys live in? Well, I guess we wouldn't find out.

A few days later we heard from Jack. "I talked to Alexander today; he was impressed with both of you and believes that Neoforma is *very fundable*. He should be able to get a very decent valuation from VCs. But he has some scheduling problems this week and next, so it looks like the next meeting with him and his partner will have to be in a few weeks. I asked him to make some time and give us some dates and he said he would do so."

What a disquieting feeling!

We thought we had failed completely, yet here he was coming back to us for more. He had teased us with what we could be, then shown us how little we were. It almost seemed like he had planned it that way . . .

Now he managed to make us feel excited that we were still under consideration, but made sure that we had to wait several weeks for the next step. So this is what it meant to be a player.

A few weeks later we did meet JP. Alexander arrived first. When JP arrived, Alexander bantered with him. JP had just been named one of the 20 Most Influential People in Technology by a major business periodical. An article with his picture would be on the cover of *The Wall Street Journal* the following week. Another article would focus on how he had made twenty million dollars by investing during a single phone call in a deal an acquaintance had put together.

JP was polite, contained, quiet, reserved, and a bit mysterious. Like Jeff and I, it seemed that these two partners had sought balance through their opposite.

"You know that Alexander and I are really tied up now, but he insisted that I should at least meet you two," JP said. "So. Tell me about your market."

We were more prepared this time. We had been gathering information about the spending characteristics of hospitals and the demographics of suppliers. We quoted a few numbers, freely tossing around the word *billions*. "Of course, we are only going for a small percentage of that market."

But they had heard what they needed to hear. Billions. "Are you sure of those numbers?"

I said, "Well, they are actually low, because they only factor in one segment of the industry. But they were all we could dig up for now." ·

JP said, "Do you know what kind of opportunity you have here?"

Jeff and I looked at each other. I said, "Well, yeah, of course we know how huge this market is. That's why we're doing this. We can save everyone in healthcare huge amounts of money. We figure we can do quite well by taking only a small share of that savings." We were thinking, *Well, duh . . . It's about time someone believed us!*

JP and Alexander glanced at each other. JP switched modes, became serious. "I'm not sure that we have time to help you now, but our share of the company for helping you would be 3% each. On top of that, we would invest some of our money, as well as getting money from some people who always invest with us. We'd quickly pull together a half million or so. Then we'd go after some real money. Don't give us an answer now. Just think about it."

Then there were more handshakes as they rushed out, promising to get back with us.

We were very relieved. We had all but given up on Wally and Shawn. It seemed like Alexander and JP were very interested in us.

And they claimed to be able to quickly get the money we now desperately needed—more than we needed, actually.

A week later a message came through Jack. Alexander and JP liked us, but had decided that they couldn't handle another company until sometime next year. They wanted him to make sure and pass on the message that they'd keep in touch.

September 1997

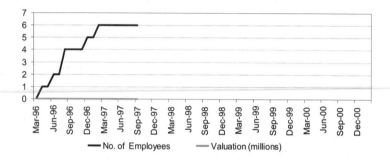

New Rules for the New Economy

Twelve dependable principles for thriving in a turbulent world
. . . 12: The Law of Inefficiencies . . . In the Network Economy,
don't solve problems, seek opportunities.

Wired
September 1997

Top Billing

It made sense at the time. We made practical decisions and underwent simple transitions. I'm not sure it could have gone any other way.

I was getting frustrated, and a little bit insecure. Thousands of people— the keepers of the world's health—were telling us that we were helping them. The demand for information from our website went well beyond our projections. *Certainly, our service to the world's hospitals should be valued by someone? Aren't successful businesses built on satisfying needs? Why—if I believed so much in Neoforma—couldn't I convince investors as well as I could effectively anticipate customer needs?*

In our early days, I had taken the lead over Jeff in talking to potential investors during our presentations. I knew more about the details of our services and I was good at convincing investors of the value of our services. But it had become clear that I was not as effective at promoting the financial potential of Neoforma.

Potential investors wanted us to show them that we were going to build a huge demand, very quickly, for something very expensive. Ultimately, that's what I wanted too, but in a much more organic way. I wanted to build the value for the customers, then prove the value to the company. Investors wanted us to prove the value to the company, then build it for the customers.

Jeff was much more adept at telling investors what they wanted to hear. With stunning aptitude, he became skilled at using the investor's language, painting pictures of what we would grow into and how we would leverage the huge size of the healthcare market. He was comfortable with the lack of connecting dots to a particular destination, such as an IPO. I was not.

We argued about whether it was right for us to project an image of ourselves as a very large corporation selling hundreds of millions of dollars of software and services each year. We didn't doubt that this was possible, but frankly, we would have been quite happy to sell a few million dollars' worth of software each year.

Investors did not want to hear that. They wanted large returns in exchange for taking the risk of investing early. Ten times their investment within a year or two was the absolute minimum acceptable return. A number of companies had recently proved that these kinds of returns were possible and they wanted to achieve the same thing.

So we painted a picture of how we might be. How we *would* be. A big picture. And once we started displaying that picture, we caught intriguing glimpses ourselves of what *could* happen to us with a company that matched that picture.

In one of our many discussions with our potential angel investor, Shawn, he asked us, "So, what do you see as your roles in Neoforma, when it grows large?"

We both had the same answer to this one. "We are certainly experienced enough to run the company, however it grows. But our real interest is in building the company and its services, not in running the company for the long run."

And this was completely true. But answering this question out loud made us truly examine what we might get *from* the company, beyond the obvious satisfaction of knowing we had created a livelihood for hundreds of families and improved a part of the world that affects everyone.

Some light was shed on this when Alexander and JP set up a meeting to check in with Jeff and me. Even though they had put us off for now, they didn't want to miss out on some positive change in our status. During the meeting Alexander asked us, "What do you want to get out of Neoforma . . . You know, how much money would you need to get if, say, someone offered to buy the company from you right now?"

Jeff and I looked at each other, then took turns trying to respond to this question. We knew that he wanted us to say some big number, as an indication of how driven we were to make money, but we had no idea what that number might be. And we had no idea how much we would really be willing to sell the company for. We hadn't thought about that possibility before. We had always seen ourselves as integral to the business, not separate from it.

Our responses were awkward and uncertain. "We know we're building a business that will be worth a lot some day . . . and . . . we wouldn't want to miss out on benefiting from that growth. However, we are realistic. You know, if someone offered us $10 million today, we would probably seriously consider it."

Now I must stress that neither of us had ever imagined getting more than a million dollars from Neoforma, let alone $10 million. But $10 million seemed like the right number to use that day.

Alexander grinned briefly, then turned very serious and said, "Well, that *is* a lot of money. Now just how do you think you would get a valuation that would get you that kind of money? You certainly can't do that without a huge shift in your business model. You need to capture, and get a cut of, every transaction going through the website. And you need to get big . . . fast. You are the First Mover in this space. To benefit from the huge returns that go to the First Mover, you have to be very aggressive!"

The way that he said this implied that, if we hadn't thought about what we wanted from Neoforma—besides goodwill and a salary—we were far too timid to pull off something *big*. Something really *significant*.

Then Alexander and JP abruptly ended the meeting and hustled out of the conference room. That was the last we would hear from them for some time.

Jeff tried to convey in a follow-up message that we *really were* greedy enough to promote and sell the business, if that sale would return value to the investors. But Alexander did not respond, relying on his silence to speak for him.

That's how our transition from founders to investors began. Even though we had yet to receive any outside investment, we began thinking very differently about the company. Suddenly, we realized that shareholder value might be as much of a factor in our decisions as customer value.

We needed to balance our desire to adopt this new vision with our desire to keep the doors open and our families solvent. But the more we talked about it, the more we agreed that we could do all of that and accommodate this new criteria. We could be founders *and* investors.

After all, if our other investors were going to make money, so would we.

It was a very odd feeling for me to think that making money might be an acceptable pursuit unto itself. It didn't feel all bad. If we were able to build everything we wanted to, faster and more grandly than we'd ever thought possible, maybe that was okay.

October 1997

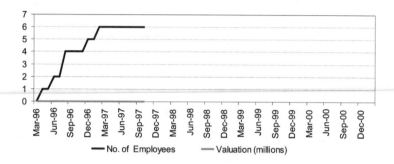

The Web

Who would have thought that the medium could become the message?

We were still basically giving away CDs loaded with catalog information and calculational tools to help hospitals and architects. I know that sounds kind of dry. But it was the size and scope of it that was exciting.

It wasn't the information or the tools; it was the way that this stuff was organized that made it so cool.

The disk had little playful animations, illustrating various actions. The abrasive collaboration between Todd and me had led our CDs through an aesthetic wonderland. We experimented with odd, but cool interfaces. We created fun and unique ways to get through this myriad of new information.

I am sure that we drove our customers nuts with the constant changes, but the newness and potential of it all made us innovate at a frenzy.

I loved the design aspect of this process. I didn't think of myself as a programmer. Computer code was simply my sculpting tool. I learned each new function with only perfunctory attention. To me, each function was like a new architectural material. I had to learn its properties in the context of the structure I was trying to build. The materials had no significant interest for me. The creation was my focus.

We only charged hospitals for the more powerful versions of the tools. We were increasingly convinced that the bulk of the money to support the whole thing should come from the suppliers.

So, the more suppliers, the more money. The more money, the more fun we could have building stuff that helped others. What more could we ask?

But we were battling with how to fit the huge amount of catalog information required by a typical hospital onto the CDs that we were successfully distributing. There just wasn't space for all of the information and pictures.

And no matter what we did, much of the product and supplier-contact information was obsolete almost as soon as we distributed the CDs.

The Internet was the perfect solution. Once we went online, the number of people using our online catalog doubled every month. Previously, we'd been committed to continuing our CD development. Looking ahead, we weren't sure we needed to anymore.

When we had started Neoforma, relatively few people were using the Internet for business and Internet connections were generally slow. Now things were changing. The rapidly increasing number of visitors using the catalog on our website proved it.

The Internet was still very young and unproven, but if we really wanted our efforts to make a difference, we knew that we would need to tie our fate to that of the Internet. Nothing else would fit our ambitions.

So in October, after much debate, Jeff and I decided to stop the CD development entirely. We printed up enough disks to support the professional society distributions we had committed to and sent them out. We even refunded money to hospitals that had paid for the professional version of our tool and to suppliers that had paid for product placement on the CDs we weren't going to distribute as widely as promised.

It was difficult, taking this step away from the known, finite, rewarding path to an unknown, risky, yet potentially infinite path.

In an Internet company, I would need to rely on others for our technology. I knew every line of code and field of data on the CD. But I had little idea of how to put information into a browser. I wasn't familiar with the properties or details of how things were managed behind the Web.

I wasn't comfortable navigating in this new world, but I trusted myself. I was usually a fast learner. If the Internet was to be the source of our bread and butter, then we couldn't continue to rely so much on an outside firm for our website development. I had to learn some Internet basics and then I had to hire someone to take us beyond the basics.

I figured it wouldn't be too difficult to find someone to help us develop Internet technology that was as cool as what we had produced on our CDs.

While Alexander and JP had made it clear that they couldn't devote much time to us, they did offer to help set us up with people they thought might be able to help us. Alexander knew that my familiarity with software programming did not extend far into the Internet world. He and other potential investors had been nervous about my lack of formal programming education. Graduates of MIT, or some such prestigious school, were always much more impressive as technology company founders.

So Alexander set up a meeting for Jeff and me to meet a properly educated technology guy. We met Scott at his small, starkly furnished house. Much younger and more polished than the two of us, and properly educated as a technologist, Scott was clearly living the life of an entrepreneur-to-be. His computers were the centerpieces in his living room.

After brief introductions and background summaries, he demonstrated the Internet technology that he and some buddies were developing into a business. In fact, the reason Alexander knew Scott was because he wanted Alexander to line up some funding for him.

Alexander told us that he had decided not to fund Scott because his business model was a little weak, but he hadn't told him yet. Alexander did recognize the value of Scott's clear understanding of Web technology, however. He felt that if Scott were to work with an experienced team like us, the best of two worlds would unite.

Scott *was* doing some neat stuff. Clearly, he understood how to design cool and complex Web pages. All I would have to do was figure out how to communicate my ideas to him and we could continue our wave of innovation and service.

But as I excitedly spoke with Scott about how what he was doing could help take our business to the next level, it became immediately clear that Scott was simply trying to sell us on his own business. I could tell that he assumed Alexander had brought us in to help evaluate his technology.

When we broached the subject of combining his technology

expertise with our business model, Scott cordially accepted our offer to consider the idea, but I could feel his lack of enthusiasm. He saw himself as a *founder*. Since we had been in business for a year-and-a-half, he could never claim that status if he joined us. There was too much eager money out there waiting to support a guy with his credentials. So, after some additional wasted conversations, we politely parted company.

Ultimately, Scott did found an Internet company. He raised impressive amounts of money from notable investors and created some very fun and popular stuff that was enjoyed by millions of consumers, until his company became one of the multitude of victims of the 2000 bust. He sold the business for pocket change, just months after closing a twenty million dollar funding round.

Our experience with Scott's need to be the inventor, rather than the collaborator, did not bode well for our search for a key collaborator in the Internet world. I started thinking that this bridge between the CD and the Internet might turn out to be a bit more substantial than I had imagined.

November 1997

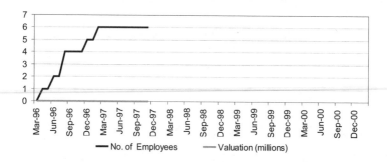

No. of Employees — Valuation (millions)

Seller, Beware: The Buyers Rule E-Commerce

The laws of E-commerce are being written by buyers, not sellers. The future won't be pretty for companies that don't start paying attention now . . . Some cutting-edge companies will find ways to leverage this new buyer-centric environment to their advantage . . .

Fortune
November 10, 1997

Tweening

The moments we felt strongest always seemed to coincide with the moments we were most vulnerable.

In addition to the difficulty of filling in our technology team, we had other new challenges to meet. Compared to the nearly infinite data available on the Internet, our previously deep and robust product catalog on CD flattened to a shallow, sparse database.

Jeff and I had started in a relatively secluded and manageable nook in healthcare, radiotherapy, which mostly involved using big scary machines to shoot carefully aimed, invisible beams of radiation at cancer tumors. Due to the fact that so many of our website visitors were also connected to the much larger radiology business, which included a broad spectrum of diagnostic equipment, we had begun collecting information on products and manufacturers too. Several of us spent most of our evenings entering new information in our databases.

But however energetic our efforts were, we could only gather information on a couple of thousand products from a few hundred manufacturers. This represented a small subset of the products available. And many of our radiology visitors also wanted information on products that were outside the boundary of the radiology department.

There were several companies that sold comprehensive, paper-based directories of healthcare products, but I couldn't think of a way that we could afford to pay them enough for them to allow us to republish that information freely to our visitors. In fact, I was certain that they would see us as their competitors.

Then I noticed that these directories used information from the Food and Drug Administration (FDA), the government agency that regulates all healthcare products, and wondered how they acquired their information. It turned out that the FDA website published into the public domain all the information they had regarding all healthcare products. This wealth of information was published in a form completely useless to someone seeking help on purchasing a product, but there was a wealth of information on fifty thousand products from ten thousand manufacturers. I just had to figure out how to get it out of the website in some usable form.

The current company that JP and Alexander were sponsoring, Junglee, made something called a wrapper. A wrappers was a computer code that could gather huge amounts of data from websites and then republish it with other data on a new website. I figured that, maybe, I could do something similar.

So nearly every day and evening for a month, I wrote clumsy computer programs to gather, clean and organize this large database of public information. My technical limitations made many of the steps manual, mind-numbing ones, but in the end, I was able to create a pretty good set of data to add to our site. I was nervous that the huge amount of data might slow down the site, but it didn't.

I sent the updated database to our developers and waited anxiously to see the results through our website. Suddenly, with a simple search on our site, anyone in the world could get information on nearly every healthcare product available.

Playing with the search engine, I was able to find just about any conceivable product. And I wasn't the only one. Due to Todd's ability to make our database visible to the generic search engines, our number of website visitors grew quickly and geometrically.

There was no denying it, Neoforma was suddenly a player in a much bigger world than we had anticipated. We had real muscles to flex.

Now that I had completed this consuming project, and seen its scope, I could no longer hide from the problem of how we were going to live up to our meatier profile. We had so much to do and so little money to support it.

Anni and I were now broke and deeply in debt to my father-in-law. Jeff and his wife were now broke and deeply in debt to Jeff's father-in-law. Both fathers-in-law had been very generous to have trusted a substantial amount of their money with their daughters' husbands. We would not have survived without them. Jeff and I had been careless in using these personal sources of money. Both fathers-in-law had made it clear to us that they expected to get the money back.

Our funding prospects had cozily sheltered for the holidays. And the stock market was jittery. That made investors jittery. It made my father-in-law jittery too. In fact, these jitters made my father-in-law inquire for the first time how far in debt I really was.

He panicked when he realized how close I really was to the edge of survival and became very concerned that he might not only lose his investment in me, but that the equity he shared in our house might be at risk too.

He had a simple solution to that problem. He demanded an immediate payment of forty thousand dollars to reduce my debt to him to acceptable levels.

My euphoria from our new website additions dissolved immediately and was replaced by an equally intense sense of dread.

How could Anni and I come up with that much money when we were completely broke? He was my wife's father. I did not have the luxury of avoidance.

But, of course, for those who have chosen to risk everything, there is almost always more money somewhere. *Isn't there?* At least, that's what I'd always believed.

The potential of this Neoforma project had simply grown and grown. I refused to allow a little thing like money slow us down. So, Anni and I cashed in our last safety net—the retirement money from my ten years at Varian. The nearly one hundred thousand dollar account would yield just over forty thousand dollars, after paying taxes and early withdrawal penalties.

Problem solved.

Now, we just had to figure out how to keep this monstrous database up-to-date.

December 1997

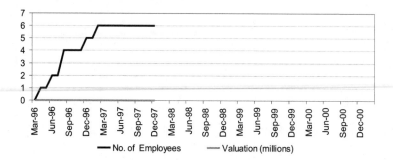

—— No. of Employees	—— Valuation (millions)	

East Meets West

As we were becoming increasingly immersed in the aura of the Valley's start-up culture, it became more difficult to imagine a company being any other way. The precarious edge seemed a natural place to perch. Occasionally, I was forced to face the fact that our way was not the only way.

As I watched the sun rise outside the airplane window, I silently rehearsed my upcoming presentation to ECRI, a non-profit company often described as the *Consumer Reports* for healthcare professionals. They produced one of the few comprehensive directories of medical products . . .

> Hi . . . I am the president of a rapidly growing, six-person, Silicon Valley, start-up company. We have just released a huge directory of healthcare products and companies on our website— about the same size as your healthcare product directory. A lot of people are using it.
>
> The main difference between our directory and yours is that finding information on our website is much faster than finding it in your book. Oh . . . and . . . our site doesn't cost anything to use.
>
> Now, I would guess that your directory represents a very small percentage of your company's revenue. So, you should let us help you take that old paper directory and bring it to the larger audience on our website. You have the means to maintain it. We have the means to publish it online. In exchange for your content, we'll direct leads to you. Doesn't that make sense?

Well, it made sense to me anyway. I figured that ECRI would easily recognize that the value of their paper directory was dissolving fast and that the Web was a far superior medium for the distribution of large, frequently changing directories. That was a given. The hard part would be convincing them that Neoforma was the right partner.

I was already convinced that ECRI was the right partner for us. We had published a huge directory of products and a large number of people were accessing our directory of medical products using a powerful search engine. But real doctors were using our information to make real decisions about important stuff. We were getting emails like this:

> *Our ICU recently received a patient from Texas. Our respiratory therapists are not familiar with the type of trach this patient has. Could you please send any information you have ASAP.*

Lives were on the line. We had to make sure that this information was kept accurate and up-to-date. I knew that we didn't have the staff to do it well. I also knew that there were several companies who did have the staff to do it. If we could partner with one of them, we could let them handle the content, while we continued to focus our energies on building the website.

I had researched and contacted the two for-profit companies that maintained paper directories with content similar to ours and had given them some variation of the speech above. They were cordial, but patronizing. They were cautiously supportive of the idea of working with a company like us, but let me know that it was very low on their priority list.

I was so passionate about the importance of getting information out to a broad audience that I had failed to adequately show my appreciation for the value of the information these companies had spent years gathering. To them, I was a robber, brazenly giving away information that was valuable to them. Who was I to suggest I had a new and better way for them to do business?

With passion driving me, I plowed through their resistance, not because I was oblivious to the value of their information, but because I knew that the world would be a better place if this information could reach more people.

But this was not necessarily a motive shared by them. They weren't insensitive to the social benefit of their information, but they were used to the balance between the prices they charged and the number of customers they had. They were not comfortable having some new upstart come along and stir things up.

They had to assume I was a flake, but they weren't certain enough of my irrelevance to be rude or dismissive. We agreed to keep in touch, but I did not feel any connection to these companies.

Then I called ECRI. I wasn't sure if an investment-driven, start-up company like Neoforma would be compatible with a non-profit, focused entirely on the Social Good. But they did have a good reputation.

ECRI was a bit more difficult to contact than the others. I was able to find very little information about them. They didn't even have a website.

I tried asking some of our customers for more information about ECRI. They told me that ECRI had the most reliable and unbiased information, but they didn't really know much about the company.

At the trade show where Neoforma officially announced its expanded directory, I approached some ECRI employees in their booth. From the start, I sensed a refreshing attitude from these guys. They seemed very interested in exploring other ways to distribute their information. Rather than being focused on guarding and *preventing* the distribution of their information, they were focused on how the quality and, most of all, the integrity of their information would be preserved. I could address those issues easily.

And, I liked these guys. They believed in the value of their contributions to the world's healthcare community. I had learned that I didn't need to like people to work with them, but it sure helped when it came to building trust.

They were very open with me, until I began to ask them about ECRI's plans for the Internet. Immediately they became evasive and vague. They told me I would need to speak with Tony, one of their vice presidents. So a couple of days later, I set up a meeting with Tony at ECRI headquarters.

The directions they gave me led me to what seemed to be an almost rural part of Pennsylvania. Driving my rental car through a primarily residential neighborhood I scanned the street for the address. My first time through I saw no indication of ECRI. After my second unsuccessful pass, I was concerned I was on the wrong road. It didn't look like a neighborhood where I expected to find a corporate office.

On my third pass, I spotted a simple black sign with white numbers, obscured by the shadows of the trees lining the street. There was no business name, but the numbers matched the ones on my directions. I pulled onto the driveway in front of the sign, stopped, and peered over the steering wheel at a picturesque, tree-shrouded landscape.

Some distance up the driveway was what looked like a manufacturing building. I checked my directions again, shrugged, and drove up the drive, passing several small signs clearly indicating that trespassers were not welcome. Since there were no other signs, it was difficult to determine whether I was a trespasser or not.

I am a stickler for promptness, so at five minutes before my scheduled arrival time, I stepped out of the car, put on my suit coat and looked for an entrance. The December air was much colder than my Silicon Valley blood was used to. My thin suit did little to cut the chill. I was anxious to get inside, but there was no clear indication of an entrance or lobby. I spotted an area of dark windows over a slight rise in the front lawns, at the far corner of the otherwise windowless masonry exterior.

At the end of the path I arrived at a darkened glass door with the letters ECRI painted above. *Whew . . . at least I was at the right building.* While I now knew that I was on the correct property, I was still not sure I was at the right entrance. I pulled on the door handle and stumbled backward due to its lightness and ease of movement. Some part of me had expected the door to be locked, or at least unyielding.

I stepped out of the light. As the door rattled closed behind me, I faced a glass wall with another door in it. I knew instinctively that this door was not unlocked. To my right was a wall with a window that reminded me of an all-night gas station security booth, except that I was in the enclosure looking out. I stooped to speak through a small opening in the glass.

A large woman gazed suspiciously at me through the glass. I tried to sound confident and friendly as I said, "I'm here to see Tony Montagnolo." His name was difficult enough to pronounce under normal circumstances. I was content that I managed to speak most of the syllables in order.

She frowned, as if I couldn't possibly be so important as to warrant a meeting with Mr. Montagnolo. I was thinking that I probably should not have worn my usual California business outfit, a nice but informal sportcoat and T-shirt combo. She asked, "Do you have an appointment?"

I told her I did, feeling pleased to convey that I was following the rules. She pointed at a log book on a pedestal on my side of the window and told me to sign in. She picked up the phone and quietly announced my presence.

I was startled to note that other visitors had arrived earlier that same day. I couldn't help but feel a bit disappointed that someone else had discovered this secret place before me. After a pause, the receptionist nodded into the phone and hung up. "Mr. McVicker . . . Mr. Montagnolo will be with you in a moment. Please have a seat in the lobby. Here is your badge. Please wear it at all times."

She buzzed open the vestibule door, handed me the pin-on identification badge, and pointed to some chairs in the dark, spare lobby ahead. Instead of sitting, I wandered in front of the assorted plaques and documents on the walls. Each plaque reinforced ECRI's position as a conscientious defender of All that is Good.

I also perused a wall display, posted with their assorted brochures. I could easily see how many of their products and services could fit seamlessly into our website. I decided that we would probably need to buy ECRI someday. The added value of the two companies' information would be spectacular. The irony of this arrogant fantasy was not lost on me, but it did not diminish my sincere belief that purchasing ECRI would simply be one more logical step toward providing efficient global access to needed information.

After waiting for the appropriate period of time—so as not to feel too important or unimportant—Tony greeted me. We shook hands as he asked if I had been able to find the place okay. I said, "Sure . . . no problem. I'm glad to be here. It would help to have a sign out front . . ."

Tony grinned at my comment, and then led me down a long, dark corridor with a solid wall on the left and interior windows on the right. The left wall was mostly empty, except for a display case that held what appeared to be some type of traditional Japanese clothing. The windows on the right exposed transparent meeting rooms and what looked like laboratories beyond. The décor would have made a subway designer proud. For the first time, I saw hints of people moving about in the distant rooms. Above a door at the end of the corridor was a sign that read: QUIET!

The door opened into a large windowless office area, filled with unusually tall acoustic partitions. The office felt completely still and silent. I assumed that most of the cubicles were empty, but, as Tony led me to a conference room, I saw that every cubicle was occupied by someone who looked busy doing something. Some were even speaking quietly into their phones.

I thought of the Neoforma offices, where six of us shared two small offices, along with our phones, servers, fax machines and printers. The idea that someone could promote silence, separation and isolation to such a degree was disorienting to me.

Once we were comfortably seated in a conference room with a wall-size world map filling one end, I asked Tony to tell me about ECRI. As he spoke, I tried to classify him. He wore the glasses and casual-conservative clothing that fit my image of information technologists. He was a bit younger than I was, which made me concerned that he might not have adequate authority to pursue a strategic partnership.

Tony did not begin by telling me about the products and the services of the company. Instead, he told me about how the company had been founded more than thirty years ago by a doctor, Joel Nobel, who had witnessed terrible patient injuries caused by the use of faulty medical devices. He founded ECRI to test and report on the safety of common devices. Everything they did sprang from that mission.

Tony went on to emphasize the not-for-profit nature of the company. He described how, as a trusted reporter on the medical device industry, ECRI went to extremes to avoid any appearance of conflict of interest. Each year, every employee was required to submit their tax returns to the company, so the company could confirm that no one was investing in, or otherwise benefiting from, any medical device companies.

I began to understand why visitors were not welcomed with open arms.

After Tony finished his summary, he asked me to describe Neoforma. I gave my practiced spiel with sincere enthusiasm. He asked me a few questions that conveyed that he *was* closely watching the evolution of the Internet and *was* aware that the impact on ECRI could be substantial. However, unlike my meetings with his competitors, he clearly understood that the Web was more of an opportunity than a threat.

Tony seemed to be genuinely enthusiastic about the possible benefits of working with companies like Neoforma, but he informed me pointedly that ECRI was in no hurry to embrace the Internet or any particular partner in that arena. They were just now converting a number of their publications from paper to CD-ROM. That was quite ambitious enough to keep them busy for awhile.

He said, "I don't want to discourage you from keeping in touch with me, but, frankly, I have no idea if Neoforma is going to be a winner or loser in the race to come. I don't know if you are a competitor or opportunity. And I don't think you will be received well by the GPOs.

"We are very slow and cautious here. By the time we are ready to seriously consider a proposal as aggressive as yours, you might not even be in business. And even if I supported and presented a plan to abandon control of the product directory to our executive committee, of which I am a member, they would not receive it well. We need more time to figure out what the Internet means to our business. But . . . I like some of your ideas and I will certainly think of Neoforma when the timing is right."

I was quite discouraged by his polite dismissal, but I was used to hurdling over obstacles, so I asked him, "Who else can I speak with in the company? Perhaps Dr. Nobel would be interested in a demonstration of our website?"

Tony made it clear that *he* was the right contact for me, that he was responsible for future technology initiatives, and that working around him was neither appropriate nor advisable.

As a consolation, he suggested that Neoforma might benefit from adopting the ECRI product categorization scheme, which was the closest thing to an international standard. That way, if we did work together in the future, it would be easier to connect our information to theirs. I was frustrated by this clear signal that our conversation was near its end. I am sure that my polite agreement to pursue common standards did not mask my displeasure or impatience.

We parted company, promising to keep in touch.

I did keep in contact with Tony. I called him every month or so to remind him that we should be working together. As the months passed, Tony became less responsive to my calls.

Meanwhile, as greater numbers of hospitals used our website, the importance of maintaining the quality as well as the breadth of our content became increasingly critical. By March 1998, we had discovered several instances of outdated information in our database. It wasn't bad for a database of tens of thousands of items, but it wasn't good enough for me. I knew that small inaccuracies, ignored now, would cascade into huge problems in the future. If we weren't going to be able to use ECRI data, then we needed to quickly build our own team to manage the website's expanding content.

We needed smart, literate people who were familiar with the products used in a hospital. I let the headhunters I was working with know that I was looking for nurses. I figured that there must be plenty of underpaid and underappreciated nurses who were tired of the day-to-day clinical grind.

When one of the headhunters told me she had found the perfect candidate, I was excited, until she told me that the candidate was a doctor, not a nurse. I said, "There's no way I can afford a doctor. I told you what I was willing to pay!"

She said, "No, wait 'till you meet with him. He is willing to work for less than he's used to making. And he wants to take some time away from the clinical environment and put his energy into something that contributes broadly to the improvement of healthcare. Talk to him. I have a feeling that you'll like each other."

So we interviewed the doctor. He introduced himself as Anil. And I quickly recognized him as a fellow iconoclast. He was so sure of himself, yet so innately unsettled, so intensely curious. He would also be tough to hire. He'd already had job offers that would pay substantially more than we could, and they would be far less risky.

But something in that risk, and our persistence, compelled Anil to join our small team. His first task was to bring quality to our quantity. He tackled this task with passion, vigor, and, at times, impatience. He was used to getting things done quickly. In the clinic, he was king. If someone didn't get something done right now, a patient would be at risk. He brought that immediacy with him into Neoforma.

Over the next several months, he hired a group of nurses and other clinical professionals. Without exception, all of them that survived the first couple of weeks of his demanding supervision were among the finest employees Neoforma would ever have.

But in spite of the amazing quality of this content management group, there was still the issue of quantity. As the number of products in our directory grew past fifty thousand and the number of manufacturers grew past ten thousand, I was still convinced that we could be far more efficient if we worked with ECRI.

In the past, Jeff had not been as concerned about the content quality issues as I was. There were other things to focus on—like making sure that we had enough investment capital to keep the doors open. However, by October 1998, he was becoming as concerned as I. Our slow but sure movement into the public limelight made it very difficult to ignore or accept outdated information on our website.

Once he decided that we needed to find out what was really up with ECRI, Jeff was determined to stir things up fast. He lectured me, as he was inclined to do whenever he saw me drift into the realm of self-imposed ethics: "Not everyone's driven by a sense of public good the way you are. You know from our Varian days how each person in an organization has his or her own motives, fears, and desire for power. Tony may have the responsibility for a partnership with us, but you can't get anything significant done with a company unless you are talking with whoever is in charge. Remember that we would never have been able to spin Neoforma out of Varian if we had not worked directly with Ed, the Boss."

So without hesitation, Jeff picked up the phone, dialed the front desk of ECRI and said, "This is Dr. Kleck, CEO of Neoforma. I am going to be on the East Coast next week. I was hoping that I could meet with Dr. Nobel for an hour when I get into town."

It was that simple. In minutes, he had set up the meeting I had been unable to get for nearly a year. I was pissed for a few minutes;

then, when I got over my damaged ego, I was thrilled to be reminded that Jeff and I made a pretty good team. I briefed Jeff on my latest ideas for a meaningful partnership.

Upon his return, Jeff grinned and said, "What a strange company! Anyway, you haven't met Joel, have you? He's not quite what I pictured. First of all, he wears surgical scrubs to work every day . . . which is a sight to see."

Jeff's meeting with Joel had been short, but it had gone well. They had spent much of the meeting discussing Joel's time as a doctor on a naval submarine and Jeff's theories about the future of assorted medical imaging technologies. I was frustrated to hear that Jeff hadn't discussed any of my proposals with Joel. But Jeff had staged a follow-up visit for me. And so, one year after my first visit to ECRI, I was going to meet the Boss.

Many things had changed in that year. Neoforma was a much more established company, with more than thirty employees. I was a bit more mature or, at least, experienced. I was much more realistic about what it would take to attract the interest of a conservative company like ECRI. What hadn't changed was that we needed a cost-effective source for our basic catalog content. We had better things to do than reinvent the wheel.

And I still believed that ECRI was our most real threat as a competitor and our best opportunity as a partner. I had designed a new model for supporting our architectural planning content on the website. I knew I could convince ECRI to work with us on it if I could convince their founder that I was sincere when I said that the primary motive behind Neoforma was the improvement of healthcare. I knew that I usually turned off investors by expressing our mission too enthusiastically, but I had decided that a little enthusiasm would be okay here.

When I finally arrived at ECRI for my second visit, I was ready to be open and sincere.

A woman greeted me cheerfully in the lobby and hastily guided me to the same conference room as the last time, explaining that Dr. Nobel was on the phone to an important person in some exotic country. She said Joel would be with me as soon as possible.

I waited for quite some time. I would have used this time to catch up on my backlog of phone calls, but this half-underground, window-less, concrete building was probably the only place in the state that did not receive a cell phone signal. I stood and studied the large world map on the wall instead.

In the midst of contemplating whether they should replace the map, since it still indicated the USSR, a man came into the room that could only be Dr. Nobel. Clothed in threadbare surgical scrubs, he appeared to be in his early sixties. The sparseness of silver hair on his head was more than amply made up for on the readily visible portions of his arms and chest.

His greeting was hurried, apologetic and cautious. He asked me to call him Joel. Nobody in the Valley called me Mister, so I didn't think to ask him to call me Wayne.

After we sat down at the table, he cheerfully bemoaned the complexities of working with so many international companies and governments. With a few simple statements, he was telling me that he was busy, casual, important and focused on big issues. His tone and manner reminded me of several of the angel investors we had spoken to — specifically Shawn and Denis, who had founded their own companies. They also had quickly established their credentials as successful entrepreneurs in a fashion that was direct and unassuming. While their comments could be seen as arrogant, they were simply expressing who they were in the quickest way possible. I realized that I was probably beginning to define myself in a similar way. I sensed this underlying bond between us almost immediately, in spite of the huge differences on the surface.

He abruptly asked me what brought me to ECRI. As I summarized first my previous communications with Tony and then my new thoughts and objectives, he listened intently, displaying what appeared to be mild amusement. I expressed some frustration at how little I had accomplished with ECRI over the last year. He smiled, sighed and said, "Yes, they are very protective of me. They don't want me shaking things up with too many new ideas."

I was startled that he would speak so openly with me. He went on to explain that ECRI was run by an executive committee that included him, but that he didn't have any greater vote than the rest. Decisions from the top to the bottom of the company were driven by consensus.

I had always been very skeptical about the value of decisions being made that way and I told him so. I asked him how any decisions were made at all. He laughed and said, "ECRI is very slow to make any decision. I am often frustrated by this, but because the decisions are made through an inclusive process, once a decision is made, things get done efficiently because the entire organization understands and is behind it."

I was beginning to run into substantial leadership issues as Neoforma crossed the thirty-employee mark. His words gave me some pause, but I couldn't figure how an organization moving at the speed that Neoforma was could apply his experience.

He talked a bit on how confusing the whole Internet thing was to him. He was all for easy-access information, as long as there was support for the institutions that had created the information. With a generous use of words like *youngsters, whippersnappers, troublemakers* and *hotshots*, he described how *free* information was a threat to *quality* information. I was prepared for this argument and used his cue to demonstrate my ideas on the computer I had brought. He seemed pleased by what he saw and asked me to create a formal proposal and set up an appointment to present it to the executive committee.

A few weeks later, I presented our proposal to their management team. They seemed enthusiastic. A few concerns were raised. I modified the proposal to address these concerns. I submitted it to the ECRI team. There seemed to be general agreement on both sides to move forward. Since they had a larger legal department than we did, we agreed that ECRI would draw up the formal contract. This is the stage where all of the small and previously glossed-over or missed details are addressed.

The end-of-the-year holidays were coming up. I knew that we couldn't expect to get anything back until after the start of the year, but I was thrilled that the deal was essentially complete. Just formalities from here. I could move my focus elsewhere for 1999.

When no contract arrived from ECRI in early January, I called Joel to check on its status. He said their legal department was simply backlogged. It might take a little time to get this to the top of the list. Frustrated that a month had already passed, I volunteered that Neoforma could draft the final contract instead of it sitting in their legal queue. He agreed.

In a week or so, I submitted a contract to Joel.

Four months later, in spite of almost daily communication, both sides were still bickering over a few sections of the large document. We just couldn't seem to work it out on the phone.

I believed that the only way to get this thing done would be to meet in person. Since I had full authority to approve the agreement for Neoforma and ECRI needed the approval of many, I made my fourth visit to ECRI. I tried to make it clear that I didn't want to travel to ECRI unless every decision-maker was available. Joel probably thought I was joking when I said, "I am not going to leave until the contract is signed."

I flew east on a Monday. I didn't think I would need the entire day Tuesday to complete the agreement, but I scheduled my return flight for late Wednesday just in case we needed Wednesday morning to finish up. I figured that we'd probably celebrate the completed agreement over drinks Tuesday evening.

I arrived in their offices at nine Tuesday morning. I would have preferred to start earlier, but I knew that most of the people at ECRI did not get in early. When the receptionist asked who I was going to meet, I went down the list of the execs I was supposed to meet with. I got quite far down the list before the receptionist was able to find someone in the office.

I had only spoken with Susan briefly on the phone. She was in charge of one of the business units I needed to negotiate with. She seemed a bit flustered when she greeted me in the lobby. She asked, "Who were you going to meet today?"

"Well, in addition to you I have a list of four others."

She said, "Me? Oh, well, I'm sorry, but I'm right in the middle of something. I can't get together with you today. Who else were you meeting with?"

As I read each name, she informed me that the person was either embroiled in a deadline or was out of town. She said, "I'm really sorry for the confusion, but I'm afraid you'll just be wasting your time if you stay here."

She saw the panic—and something more disturbing—in my eyes. I was pissed! I had traveled all the way out here thinking everyone was taking this deal as seriously as I. I felt the sudden, uninvited adrenaline rush I recognized as rage. This was a rare state for me, so it took me a few moments to regain control. I tried very hard to appear calm.

In my most restrained voice, I said. "Perhaps you could look more closely at the schedules of each person who is here. I won't need much of their time. I am available at any time, day or night. And if you let me know when the two guys who are out of town are due back, I can set up a time to meet them. As I told Joel, I am not leaving until this agreement is signed."

When she saw that my stubbornness would not be abated, she shook her head and said, "Well, if you don't mind waiting in the conference room, I'll check everyone's schedule again. I can't promise anything though." Her tone said she hoped that I would, indeed, mind waiting.

With a backlog of development work on my laptop computer to do, I actually welcomed the time away from phone and email. So I settled into the conference room and got to work.

Susan updated me an hour or so later: "I can't set up specific times, but Angela might be able to meet you sometime later this afternoon. It might be tomorrow though. And I definitely can't meet with you today. Perhaps we can cover the remaining issues over the phone next week. Stuart should be back in the office tomorrow, but I don't know what his schedule looks like. Tony is out of town all week. Joel is out until Thursday and probably won't have any time to meet with you this week. Since he needs to give us final approval, you'd have to wait until next week to get anything signed."

I politely said, "I'll be happy to meet with you, Stuart, Angela and Joel whenever you are available. I don't have any remaining issues with Tony, so it shouldn't matter that he's not around. I'll be right here until we get this done. I have plenty of other things to do."

She glanced at my computer and the piles of paperwork I had scattered around the table. I could tell she was upset, but what could I do? I was not going to let this product directory issue hang over my head for another week, or month.

And there was the issue of my pride. For six months, I had been telling the content team back at the office that an agreement with ECRI was imminent. So I ignored her frustration and got back to work. Passing employees glanced at me through the conference room's glass wall with noticeable curiosity.

I did not meet with anyone that day, but Susan stopped by my new office late that afternoon and told me that Angela could see me for a couple of hours the following morning. She'd let me know if she and Stuart could find any time to meet with me.

I called Anni at home and reluctantly told her that I didn't think I was going to get out of there until Thursday. She could tell that it was important to me and made the mistake of saying, "That's okay . . . take whatever time you need to get this done." Now they really weren't going to get rid of me.

The next morning, I did meet with Angela and settle the remaining issues that affected her. There was no news on getting time with Susan, Stuart or Joel.

Thursday morning, when Susan walked into my office in the conference room, I could tell that she was losing patience with me. "I thought you were flying out last night."

"I told you that I'm available until we get this worked out," I said, pleasantly. "No rush . . . I'm enjoying this time away from the office."

She said, "I don't see why you have to stay here. I'm sure we can work out the remaining issues over the phone."

I said, "It's okay . . . really. This is important to me."

She was clearly agitated as she left the room.

Around noon, Joel walked into the room, "So, Susan tells me that you've moved in here. You must be serious about not leaving."

There was no hostility in his voice. He appeared to be amused, but not necessarily pleased, by the situation.

I said, "That's true. I'm willing to take whatever time is necessary to make this happen."

He sat down and addressed me seriously. He told me that he liked the idea of working with Neoforma, but that he couldn't get comfortable with the financial model. He couldn't pursue a partnership that was as encompassing as the one I proposed without more confidence in its viability.

I couldn't believe what I was hearing. Their agreement that the nature of the deal was worth considering did not necessarily indicate an intent to move forward. It was suddenly clear that they had had no intention of actually closing a deal any time soon. Even as I processed this information I realized that I had known it all along. I had simply been unwilling to accept that outcome.

I summarized to Joel how we were going to fundamentally improve the quality of healthcare with the joining of their information with ours. I outlined how each point of the deal would accomplish this. I told him that the business issues were secondary. I said, "Do you want to do this or not? I am not asking if you like the business terms. I am asking if you think we have a shot at doing great things together."

He paused, and then acknowledged that he thought we could indeed make something important happen.

I said, "Good. Now, let's figure out what it will take for us to really get this done . . . this week . . . right now."

He outlined the monetary and contractual assurances he would need to make the deal. We haggled awhile, but made quick progress, now that we were dealing with the real issues.

He excused himself from the room for awhile. When he returned, he had set up times for me to meet the remaining members of his team.

The meeting times slipped. Old issues were slowly addressed. Words in the contract were analyzed, moved around, removed, added in. New issues rushed to fill the void. Finally, by Friday afternoon all of the issues had been tidied up.

At about four in the afternoon Susan told me, "Okay, all we need is for Joel to approve and sign the final agreement."

"Great. Let's get him in here."

She said, "Umm . . . he has left for the weekend. But, that is just a formality at this point. I'll catch him first thing next week and send you the signed contract right away."

I am sure she saw that now familiar disturbing look in my eyes. I said, "I didn't know he was leaving this early. I told you that I'm not leaving without this complete. You're an executive. Can't you sign the agreement?"

She acknowledged that she could, technically, but Joel would still have to approve it. I asked, "Isn't there some way to fax the contract to Joel for him to review, then you can sign it and I can go home?"

She looked at her watch, "Well, I don't know if he is available to review this now. He's left for the weekend. And I have plans for this evening."

I said, "That's okay. I can be here anytime this weekend."

I could tell by her frown that the only thing worse than being late for her evening engagement would be knowing that I was still in Pennsylvania over the weekend. She said that she would try to contact Joel.

Susan returned a while later to the conference room. Sure enough, she had been able to fax the latest draft of the contract to Joel and get his comments. He only had a couple of small semantic changes, which I agreed were acceptable. She left to print out the final document for us to sign. I was thrilled and exhausted. I was looking forward to getting home.

Then Susan returned. I could tell by her grim expression and empty hands that there was a new problem.

Joel's protection of ECRI's reputation for absolute integrity led him to measures we couldn't imagine in our part of the Valley. I had already been surprised to learn that all email going into and out of ECRI was channeled through one carefully monitored email address and Internet access was only available via supervised computers in their library.

Now I discovered another control he'd instituted. To reduce the possibility that information might be inappropriately accessed and removed after business hours, all computer printers in the building were automatically rendered inaccessible after 6:00 p.m. It was after 6:00 p.m. Not even senior executives could access the printers after hours or on weekends. Since it was after closing on a Friday, everyone had left for the weekend, including the network administrators.

Susan was ready to go home. So was I. We had slightly different views on what that meant. To her, it meant that the final contract revisions would be made next week. To me, it meant that we would hand-write the changes, initial them, and sign the darned thing. I made this suggestion. She looked at her watch, shrugged, and complied with my suggestion. I was ready to go.

She led me through the silent, darkened building to a back door. We shook hands and parted ways—me to my rental car, her to her life. As I drove back to my hotel, I wondered for the first time if the visit had been worth the effort. Now that my compulsion had been satisfied, I saw the partnership I had just created in objective terms for the first time since I first proposed the deal.

In my obsessive drive to completion, I had made compromises that I should not have made. And much was changing at Neoforma since those early discussions. I hoped that the value I had visualized could be delivered now that so many other factors were driving Neoforma in directions I had not anticipated.

As it turned out, we did add some truly great functionality on the Neoforma website by incorporating ECRI content, but the partnership did not meet either of our expectations. Neoforma headed in a direction that diluted the value of the partnership almost as soon as the contract was signed. And, as I might have known, the fast-paced Neoforma culture and the methodical ECRI culture were not a good mix. But the partnership did deliver in an unexpected way.

After signing the agreement, Joel gave me a great deal of advice on balancing the give-and-take of control in a growing organization. I will forever value the lessons he taught me.

As for those scrubs, he would say that he wore them because they were comfortable, efficient and cost-effective. But I never bought it. I think he wore those scrubs to remind himself, and those around him, every day, why he had started ECRI. He had been wearing that outfit when he first witnessed a problem that had to be fixed. He had started a company out of stubborn conviction and had been met with a hostile reception. And he had survived. The world is truly a better place because of that man and his scrubs.

January 1998

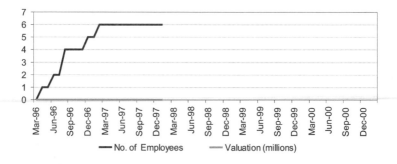

— No. of Employees	— Valuation (millions)

Board Meeting Minutes

New Investors and Board Members: Moved: Dr. Denis Coleman and Wally Buch, M.D., each invest $100,000 and join the Board of Directors of Neoforma according to the conditions in the stock purchase agreements and letter agreement prepared by Jack. Passed.

Officers: Moved: Denis Coleman be appointed vice-chairman and keep the minutes of meetings. Jack continues to be secretary. Jeff continues in his role as chairman and CEO. Wayne continues in his role as President. Passed.

Neoforma Board Meeting
January 20, 1998

The Screenplay

In the rare moments of calm between nearly unrelenting stretches of tumultuous rapids, we would sometimes, just for a moment, relax our control over things. Seldom did this respite prove to be beneficial.

Jeff and I had been putting increasing amounts of money into Neoforma—first, our own money; then borrowed money. By the end of 1997, we were running into dangerous territory. We had increased our spending—slightly, but significantly—based on our assumption that we would receive funding from someone long before the end of the year. And our need to do that was not going away. All indications were that Neoforma would run out of money by the end of December.

Well before December, we had both exhausted our personal resources. If we did have to close the doors to the offices, we were so far in debt that it would probably take us a decade or more to dig our way out. Anni and I had absolutely no buffer left. Anni's job couldn't even cover a week's worth of the bills that were stacking up.

Then in early December—eight months after beginning the process of fundraising—Jack brought another possible investor to the surface: Denis Coleman.

I was a bit intimidated by Denis. He had written one of the first wildly successful utilities for the personal computer. To sell his product he had formed a company that would become one of the largest software companies around. I had not heard of the programs Shawn had built, but I had several of Denis's company's programs on my computer.

It turned out that Denis was a very modest guy. He looked and acted like an engineer, one who simply faces each new challenge without preconception. With his modest manner, I would never have guessed that he had been a successful software executive. He was curious, cautious, enthusiastic, and very honest. I liked his directness. It allowed us to cover ground with him very quickly. He asked probing questions, but didn't seem to need the same resolution that others did. He accepted that there were things we could not know yet. He made decisions based on what was here now.

We felt that, if we could just get Denis and Wally together, we might be able to get our funding in place by the end of the month. By holding off on paying some bills, I could just barely manage Neoforma's finances until then. I'd be able to pay all of our employees—except me. But I told myself that that wouldn't matter. I'd simply pay myself in January, as soon as our funding round closed in December.

I'd also have to postpone hiring Stephen until then. We'd planned on hiring Stephen to start a real sales program for us. He seemed like the ideal guy to upgrade our sales efforts. But he was used to making real money. Even if he'd agreed to take half the money he was used to, we wouldn't have been able to pay his first paycheck.

Of course, we had to keep this pesky little fact that we were running out of money to ourselves. It simply wouldn't do to discuss our need for haste with investors-to-be. That would give them too great a leverage on us.

So when Denis suggested that we start by trying to find a time to meet with a group called the "Band of Angels," I tried not to panic. I knew this loose assemblage of wealthy investors met one evening each month to peruse new business opportunities. Each new business was sponsored by a member of the group. The assumption was that most companies presented would get several interested investors to join the sponsor in an investment round. It was obviously good for the new business, but it was potentially good for the presenter as well. There was great prestige in bringing a company to the group that provided strong returns.

Denis indicated that he would be willing to invest in us, but that it might be better to get a larger group together. Jeff and I met with the president of the Band of Angels at a well-known deal-making restaurant a few days before Christmas. The meeting went well. He indicated that he could *probably* get us on the schedule—maybe as soon as March! (*"That'd be just fine,"* I heard a little voice in my head saying. *"Only we won't have a company in March!"*) The words that actually came out of my mouth were something appropriate and casual, like, "Okay, sure. Just let us know when."

Denis and Wally had yet to meet each other and both were busy for the holidays. So Jeff and I agreed to meet with the two of them sometime in early January.

Our calm, professional demeanor at the meeting had almost no relationship to the actual frenzy building inside us. Jeff and I were on the phone with each other incessantly during the next two weeks. *We had to figure out how to make this work.* We couldn't watch it all disappear when we were this close!

I tried to disguise my despair when I was around my family. But sometimes, when I looked at this, all I could think was, *"What have I done, putting my family at this level of risk?"*

As my sons opened presents at Christmas, I found myself close to tears. I smiled and tried to be enthusiastic, while inwardly building some new walls to contain my feelings. Behind those walls, I found myself on an ocean of helplessness that made every minute seem like an hour.

Somehow, January finally arrived. We began making the calls and leaving messages. There was no response. With our precarious position increasing by the day, the uncertainty nearly choked us.

Finally, we got a call back from Denis. Hiding our desperation, we set up a meeting with Wally and Denis at Jack's office for the following week.

I spent nearly every moment of my time that week convincing our creditors to keep working with us. Things were about to turn around, I said. It sounded better than it felt, when I said it. I could only hope I was right.

As we drove to the meeting at Jack's office, Jeff and I were feeling despondent. By this time, we were so tense, we couldn't even pretend to cheer each other up. When Jack greeted us, however, he was enthusiastic, smiling from ear to ear. His pride was obvious. These were the moments that he lived for. He told us that he thought these guys were ready to sign the investment documents. We were skeptical. This had already gone on for nine months.

Wally and Denis had spoken to each other on the phone, but this was their first face-to-face meeting. Jeff and I nervously reviewed Neoforma's recent progress. We all reviewed the investment paperwork. The atmosphere was calm and serious. Wally and Denis discussed financial terms with Jack that I did not fully understand. His answers seemed to satisfy them. Once everything was reviewed, there was a pause in the room.

"Okay. Well . . . everything looks good to me!" Denis said, in an animated tone that was music to my ears. He turned to Wally and pulled his checkbook out. "Let's get this done."

Wally seemed momentarily startled. It seemed that he hadn't actually expected this to be done *right now*. Wally went through a series of motions I would later become quite familiar with—a serious pause, a slight frown, a subtle hunch of his shoulders, a deep breath and a shake of his head—and then the quick steadiness, the eye contact, and the smile—the stages of settling into a decision. When he was done, Wally pulled out his checkbook too.

Jeff and I tried to act casual, as the papers were ceremoniously signed. We discussed Board of Directors issues. Handshakes were exchanged. Then Jeff and I drifted out of the room. My emotions were bound so tightly at that point that I can't remember feeling anything. But I do remember that the sun's glare seemed to be particularly bright as we walked to the car. My eyes hurt. Perhaps they even watered a bit.

We had not only been bailed out in the final hour (or just beyond it), but we'd been funded by very prestigious investors.

Months before, Jack had encouraged us to begin a banking relationship with an institution that would be able to help us manage our growth. Now that we had a future to manage, we chose the Silicon Valley Bank, a firm of local legend. It had been the initial bank of choice for many of the most successful technology companies in the Valley.

When Jeff and I walked into the bank, we deposited two hundred thousand dollars into our new account. The teller did not raise an eyebrow at that amount. Either we didn't look like the young punks we imagined ourselves to be or the tellers in Silicon Valley had gotten used to six-figure deposits by young punks.

Two hundred thousand dollars—I had no idea how we could ever spend that much money.

There was no press release, no big celebration. We were much too exhausted for that. We had come to the brink of destruction, taken a few steps into the aftermath, been stricken with terror by what we saw —then the hands of Denis and Wally had reached out over the abyss and pulled us back.

After a quick shudder and a nervous, backward glance, it was on with the show.

With enough money in the bank, we could turn our attention back to the business with renewed energy. The business looked the same, but the infusion of cash had expanded our objectives. *Return on investment* was the only way to repay Wally, Denis and Jack. Jeff and I shared a deep sense of gratitude—but also obligation—about their investment in us.

So when our new investors emphasized that our priorities for the next month should include the production of an expanded business plan, we willingly agreed. Our only reluctance was due to the fact that we had produced business plans several times in the past and each time, potential investors had made it clear that we had fallen very short of producing a *real* business plan.

By nature, Jeff and I relied on observation and intuition for our business decisions. We tended to communicate our reasoning in qualitative rather than quantitative terms. For instance, we knew that the healthcare market was big enough. It didn't matter to us *how* big it was. We cared about the *product*, not the *business*. So naturally, our *plans* always focused on the *product*.

This made outside investors nervous. What was obvious to us was not obvious to them. Wally and Denis knew that we would need more money to build Neoforma and that our earlier business plans did not adequately display our huge potential. So they insisted that we have someone else write a *real* business plan for us.

The idea that someone else could possibly know any more about how to position our business than us was troubling. It even hurt our feelings, just a bit. Wally and Dennis gently nudged us. "You guys have too much to do to waste your time fussing with the details of a business plan."

They were pushing us toward the big picture—away from the details. That's what successful leaders do, they told us. And we had to be successful leaders, if we were going to get them a return on their investment!

It wasn't enough to be profitable. A profitable business does not return money to investors. A big business does.

The view our new investors saw was much larger and more panoramic than the one Jeff and I saw. They not only wanted a business plan that included that vision, they wanted to see that future in black-and-white. We agreed to let somebody else do it.

Denis recommended Sasa, a young and enthusiastic Stanford Ph.D., MBA, XYZ, etc. This guy had even been the President of the Harvard Club of Croatia. His great enthusiasm for whatever he was doing made me a bit uncomfortable. I was afraid my overt enthusiasm might look like that too.

Sasa tackled the creation of a new plan with precision and vigor. He solicited from us every quantifiable piece of information about Neoforma and the healthcare market. What he couldn't get from us, he ferreted out from an array of research sources.

When he collected our résumés, I sensed his disappointment with mine. It was nowhere near as impressive as his or Jeff's. From my own point of view, I was an Architect! I couldn't understand why that seemed so insignificant. But the reality was that I didn't have the kind of credentials that predicted a sure path to success—in the way that going to certain schools and racking up certain degrees could do.

So it appeared to be in the best interest of the company, if I were presented in Jeff's shadow. We had struggled enough with funding over the past year that I was quite willing to trust the judgment of outsiders in shaping our image for the outside world. I figured that I, and our employees, would certainly know that I was still running the company's operations, so, at the time, it didn't seem to matter much.

As Sasa compiled his research, he became increasingly excited about our opportunity. "The healthcare products market is huge. There isn't a lot of information about equipment like you have on your website, but the supplies market is very well documented. We can extrapolate from those numbers."

I told him that the supplies market was very different than the equipment market and was of little interest to us. He insisted that, since we had such good data about supplies, we should include supplies in our market segment. "Wouldn't it sound much better to say that we were targeting the $150 billion equipment and supplies market rather than the measly $50 billion equipment market?"

I couldn't argue with that—or, at least, I *didn't* argue with it. We did have some supplies listed on our site. Who knew how much we would focus on supplies in the future?

After two months of work, Sasa delivered a hefty document that defined our long-term business plan. I never even read the whole thing. I was much too busy, and I knew that the plan reflected where the company *could* go, not necessarily where I thought it would or should go. For the good of the investors—and I was one of them—maybe I didn't need to make every decision on the company's direction. With the completion of this document, Jeff's role as leader of the company became official and our investors started taking an outspoken role as well.

When Sasa delivered the business plan to me, he said, "You know, Wayne, I have no difficulty at all showing how Neoforma can be wildly successful in the enormous healthcare market. It's trying to imagine how you could possibly fail that baffles me!"

February 1998

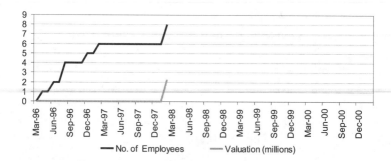

| | No. of Employees | Valuation (millions) |

Identity

In time, we would become known for what we had accomplished. For now, we were known only for what others imagined us to be.

We knew investor feedback had started in earnest when Wally sent Jeff and me this email regarding a meeting at a potential new law firm:

> *Denis and I met with Casey today for about an hour. He is perfect for us, as I am sure Denis will agree. I suggest that one of you call him as soon as possible to set up an appointment to meet him. You will be impressed. He is very excited about Neoforma, but hates the name.*

At just about the same time, Alexander and JP wanted Jeff and me to meet with Andrew, a well-respected man from a top management consulting firm. He was the kind of guy people were supposed to listen to. One of his partners had just written a book about the importance of communities to the successful websites. The book was all the rage. Everyone was using its jargon as the justification for the decisions they were making.

Jeff and I set up a meeting with Andrew. He was a very impressive guy. I really don't remember anything about his appearance or style, but I remember that he was able to see and express the relevance of things that escaped most of the investors we spoke with. He really seemed to get it! And he said so. He told us that he really liked what we had to say, but that, of course, we'd have to change the company name.

Many investors we met had expressed concerns about the name. It just didn't sound like a BIG company name. (*And the name you pick should have no more than two syllables—one is better.*)

The name had to *mean* something, but nothing negative. We emphasized that the name *did* mean something—to *us*.

When we had come up with the name originally, we had used a very scientific process to name our company. Jeff made lists of words, prefixes and suffixes he liked. So did I.

First, we sat down to see if we could agree on a simple name from one of the lists. When it was obvious that neither of us was adequately enthralled with any single name from the other's list as the name for our company, we started putting words and word segments together, combining a word on my list with a word on Jeff's list.

Jeff's list was made up primarily of sleek, zippy, modern prefixes and suffixes. Like *post-, neo-, e-, i-* and *manta*. He was enamored with *Squid Inc.*, until he discovered that hundreds of other people had already discovered that oh-so-clever name.

My words were mostly descriptive, laced with obscure meanings or derived from the Japanese spelling of Western modifiers like *plan, form, finestra, kyaro*—well, a lot of artsy entendres.

Putting the two lists together produced mostly unbearable stuff. We cringed at them. And it worried us. If this was what happened when the two of us collaborated, we were in trouble. (From that time on, we decided to split tasks rather than work together on them whenever we could.)

In spite of extreme stylistic differences, a few combinations kept our food down. Then, as we searched via legal trademark searches and Internet searches they were knocked out, one by one. There were clearly many people out there as desperate for company names as us. And they got them first.

However, one combination yielded fun results — *Neo-form*. We didn't quite like how it sounded, but the meaning was consistent with how we viewed what we were doing—creating an entirely *new model* for doing important things. And nobody seemed to have thought of this one before. Jeff called upon his four years of Latin and added an *a* to the end of *form* to make it flow better.

The only return on Web searches was *neoformans*, which is the name biologists assign to newly discovered, as yet identified organisms. Pretty cool. Well, at least two high tech, kinda ambitious, kinda nerdy guys thought so. We kept the *ns* off of the end to keep the name easy to pronounce.

However, it wasn't really about a specific name at all. In expressing their dissatisfaction with the company's name, these investors were actually expressing a desire to be associated with the *birth* of the company. They knew Jeff and I had started the company. We were its true parents. But to invest their hard-earned money, early investors wanted to believe that their support of the company would fundamentally affect the company, that they were feeding it the nutrients it needed to grow. The name had to mean something to *them*. What it meant to Jeff and me was no longer relevant.

So the chain of emails started. Dozens of messages containing lists of name ideas flooded my inbox — from current investors and their friends, from future investors and their friends. Everyone commented on everyone's ideas and lobbied for their favorites. The message strings went on for weeks. It drove me nuts.

I tried to act supportive and open-minded, but most of the ideas were repugnant to me. They had nothing to do with the company. I had lived with our company name long enough that the name itself had developed meaning to me. It meant — well, it meant, *our company!* Neoforma meant Neoforma. I just didn't get why this wasn't obvious to everyone.

Microsoft means something, now. Back a few decades, those two word fragments put together were meaningless — kind of small and nerdy sounding. The meaning came much later. That's how it is with most companies.

After weeks of tense and distracting wrangling over name choices, everyone verbally shrugged and agreed to keep the name the same, for now. Neoforma didn't sound so bad, compared to some of the new favorites.

"But," they added, "that logo . . . it's gotta go."

I had an associate tell me that he thought some people might, when glancing at it out of the corner of their eye, think that the diagonal maze looked kind of like a swastika. Somebody thought that someone, somewhere, tilting their head and looking at a certain angle, might one day make an association that would be unacceptable . . .

Now, maybe my architecture and graphic arts background keeps me from seeing the logo with an amateur's eye, but, as a professional,

I can say with authority that our asymmetrical, non-rectilinear maze did *not* look like a swastika.

It was a very cool logo and I was pissed that some obtuse association could restrict the use of an entire family of graphic symbols. A check mark looks pretty silly and mundane, until a few hundred million dollars worth of branding is put behind it.

I was annoyed by the sense that people were raising questions about the name and the logo, just for the sake of changing things and raising questions. The whole thing seemed like a pointless waste of valuable time. And, to make it worse, this was only the beginning.

Every time we brought in new investors, they complained about the name and the logo.

Every time, days were wasted on this issue of starting over.

And *every* time we brought in new management, the image had to be reborn.

Even the analysts and bankers complained about the name.

But the customers didn't. They simply saw what we were and associated our name and logo with it.

I did finally give in on the logo. They wore me out. Some glitzy ad firm created a new one. I couldn't bear to take part in the process. I tried to act supportive of the new logo. It was okay, but it was blandly conventional. With a quick search of the Web, I was able to find a number of nearly identical logos being used by dotcom companies. I guess that's why so many people seemed to like it. It was familiar.

The name didn't change. While the investors and marketing people continued to debate endlessly, the reality was that, by this time, the name Neoforma had been published in too many places to justify changing it.

Eventually people stopped complaining about the name. Eventually, when people would hear the name Neoforma, they would think of—well, Neoforma, just as Jeff and I did. In retrospect, I wish I had held out on our logo too.

March 1998

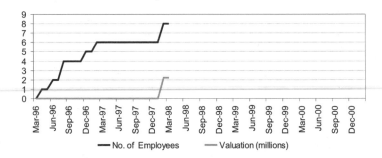

Legend: — No. of Employees   — Valuation (millions)

X-axis: Mar-96, Jun-96, Sep-96, Dec-96, Mar-97, Jun-97, Sep-97, Dec-97, Mar-98, Jun-98, Sep-98, Dec-98, Mar-99, Jun-99, Sep-99, Dec-99, Mar-00, Jun-00, Sep-00, Dec-00

Y-axis: 0–9

Scientist sues Baxter Healthcare over listing in Internet catalog

A scientist . . . is suing a biotechnology company he claims improperly allowed one of his inventions to be advertised on an Internet catalog of medical devices . . . A check of the Web site, the Neoforma Healthcare Product Directory (www.neoforma.com), on Wednesday found no reference to . . . his catheter.

Associated Press
March 25, 1998

A Hard Landing

One moment I was on a ladder reaching over my head, installing some electrical wiring. The next instant I was falling. One of the aluminum supports had suddenly buckled.

It takes very little time to fall twenty feet, but I remember having time to wonder how I could possibly have found myself rapidly descending upside down in the air without the slightest warning. And after landing, the pain did not come until I had plenty of time to contemplate the fortunate fact that carpeting had been laid over the restaurant's concrete floor only one day earlier. I suppose I could have sued the plumber who loaned me the ladder, but it didn't occur to me.

This episode from many years earlier came to mind when we heard about the lawsuit. That feeling of helpless dismay at some instantaneous change of state.

Of the forty thousand products listed on our website at the time, one of them was apparently outdated. It was bound to happen. It was just bad luck that we happened to step into a pool of unquenched anger.

What was this guy thinking?! He could have simply picked up the phone and called the number that we listed at the bottom of every page on our website and said, "Hey, I noticed the name of my product erroneously listed as being distributed by Baxter. What's that about?"

To which we would've said, "We're sorry for the misunderstanding. We simply listed your product as it had been listed by the FDA. Just a minute . . . Okay, check your screen now. The listing has been permanently removed. Nobody will ever see it again. Thanks for letting us know." It would really have been that simple. But he had a grudge to embrace.

I can't imagine any moral position in which filing that lawsuit was more productive than making a phone call. I suppose it was easier in many respects. He didn't even have to face us or Baxter to initiate the lawsuit. What power. What a great way to turn a simple problem into a fierce, costly battle. The process can be very profitable to astute opportunists. And it can be very unpleasant for unwary bystanders.

Years ago, I called Jake, a friend who happened to be a lawyer, to tell him about some simple comments I had heard regarding a business in which he was a partner. My only motivation was our friendship. I thought that the information might help him.

Jake became agitated. He asked where I had obtained my information. When I wouldn't reveal the source, he did not hesitate for a moment to tell me, "Well, you can't hold that information back. I'll subpoena you. You could go to jail, if you don't tell me."

I didn't share my source and he didn't subpoena me, but I learned just how deep our friendship went. I was sorry to see that he viewed the world from such an adversarial position that he couldn't even recognize a kind gesture from a friend.

Naturally, I didn't speak much with him after that. Then, years later, he called me out of the blue. He was very friendly and asked if I could recommend some investors for two healthcare device companies he represented. I could only think, *How can you be asking for a favor after threatening to throw me in jail for trying to help you?*

I did forward those companies' business plans to one venture firm. I knew that, in this boom time, they would not get special consideration unless I followed up on them, and I didn't follow up on them.

But the encounter with Jake still rankled. I had already been personally offended by a legal threat when the Baxter claim turned up. My sense of moral indignation would have been triggered by this trivial lawsuit regardless, but the timing of what was quickly becoming our official media debut could not have been worse.

Just before the AP article appeared, Jeff and I watched the sun set as we rode in a taxi on the way from the airport to our Chicago hotel room. We had been invited to visit Allegiance, the largest distributor of healthcare products to hospitals, and their sister company, Baxter, one of the most important manufacturers of healthcare products.

After years of dialog, we had finally convinced these companies that we *might* not be the enemy. In fact, we *might* harbor ideas and tools that could provide them an even greater reach to customers.

At the time, large suppliers were very concerned about how Internet companies might upset the balance in their relatively stable markets. We had come far enough to appreciate how tightly the big suppliers held onto the status quo. Their bonuses and earnings were completely driven by quarter-to-quarter results. We had discovered how powerful inertia can be.

After two years of polite but persistent badgering by us, one of the larger nuts had begun to crack. We had successfully worked with big suppliers before, but never with the potential of becoming an integral part of their business process. This time might be different. Allegiance was treating us as if we might be important. Our Internet catalog could improve the way they communicated with their customers.

We were eager to use our new investment money to open their shell a bit more. So Jeff and I flew to Illinois to meet with several executives at their corporate offices.

As we checked into the hotel, a polite woman at the front desk handed us a note: "Call office ASAP."

We had setbacks frequently enough to know that we were about to receive bad news. As we solemnly rode the elevator up to our floor, we each silently browsed our internal list of problems, trying to guess what awful thing it could be this time. This was a technique we had learned well. If we assumed the worst, we would usually be relieved by how trivial the actual problem was. It allowed us to convincingly convey confidence to our employees during the many times of crisis in our early days.

We reached Todd in the office. He asked us if we had already seen the press release in our email. We told him that, no, we hadn't.

He said, "Well, check it. You're not going to like what you see. We're named in a lawsuit against Baxter. Some guy from New Jersey is suing them over a listing on our website. Of course, we removed the listing immediately after Baxter called us this morning. The lawsuit doesn't target us, but it doesn't bode well for your meetings out there."

Fortunately, we had been able to remove the listing before the press investigated the issue.

Jeff called our contacts at Allegiance and Baxter. They told us,

"Yes, we know about the lawsuit. Yes, we know that it is a frivolous issue. We have a long history with this guy. But the corporate office has told us that we can't meet with you until the lawsuit is settled. I'm sorry. We were really excited about working with you."

We all knew that even a frivolous lawsuit might take years to settle. It was like effectively saying that we wouldn't be able to work with these very important companies. Ever.

After the call, as we stared out at the darkened city from the dimly lit hotel room, our view was dominated by randomly scattered rectangles of light against dark. Movement within some lit office building windows indicated unfinished work. Flickering light from behind blinds on some hotel windows indicated evening cityscape.

Our "worst case" technique had backfired. This was *worse* than any worst case we could imagine. At least nobody else was there to witness our despair and disgust.

We never did find out what happened in the lawsuit against Baxter. We assume that since we never had to do more than write a letter explaining the course of events, someone recognized the triviality of the whole thing and dismissed it.

But for us, the damage had been done.

April 1998

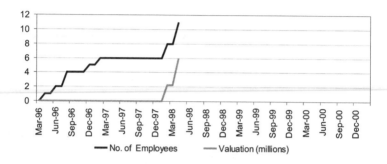

| | No. of Employees | Valuation (millions) |

Ariba Technologies, Inc., the leader in Operating Resource Management Systems (ORMS) for Global 2000 corporations, today announced that Intel Corporation has made an investment in Ariba. In addition, Ariba and Intel will initiate joint marketing activities to highlight the benefits . . .

Ariba Press Release
April 22, 1998

A Round Hole

Being unique is great. Especially when everyone else is like you.

Business-to-business. B2B. That's what they were beginning to call our *space*. That's how they were describing what companies like Neoforma did.

The number of Internet companies creating a huge buzz—and investor gains—was increasing dramatically. Most of those companies catered to consumers, not businesses. They were called business-to-consumer. B2C.

Driven by the desire to discover the next big thing, some investors were casting their eyes on Internet companies that served businesses rather than individuals. The argument they suddenly adopted: business between businesses was much larger, more repetitive and more predictable than businesses that dealt with fickle consumers.

Ariba, one Silicon Valley Internet software company that served businesses, was among the new darlings of the local investment community. They were creating quite the buzz. Following up on earlier investments by top venture capital firms, Ariba was receiving investments from large corporations. Strategic investments of this type were an early indicator of upcoming initial public offerings (IPOs).

The IPO is the Holy Grail for early investors. One early investment in a company that hosted a successful IPO could make up for a dozen bad investments.

A handful of other business-to-business Internet companies were getting attention too. The press was writing about some of them. Except for that one mention of us in an obscure (possibly defunct) lawsuit, the press didn't have any way of knowing about Neoforma yet.

Smelling blood and seeking an exclusive, Alexander and JP, our long-lost potential angel investors, reappeared with breathtaking speed and requested a meeting. We didn't expect much.

After Jeff and I provided a very brief update on our activities since we had last seen them a few months earlier, Alexander abruptly said, "Okay, here's what we are going to do. We'll get together between half a million and a million dollars to get this company going. Then we'll immediately go after the tier-one venture firms to get a follow-up investment. Once they know that we have invested in you, they'll want to invest too . . . at a much higher valuation."

Then Alexander and JP jumped into a private, but overtly audible, dialog. They discussed the people they would call (dropping recognizable names) and when they would call them. Then they moved on to the people they'd call next. They orchestrated the next two funding rounds in a matter of minutes. Their energetic, well-rehearsed brainstorming was contagious. Ordinarily independent to a fault, Jeff and I leapt into their stream of consciousness and let ourselves be swept forward.

And that's about all there was to it. A couple of weeks later, we had more than a million dollars in the bank. I would never meet most of the investors that participated in that funding round. And in fact, the investment round had been oversubscribed. We actually had to turn money down.

Wally and Denis were happy, for the most part. In two months we had increased the value of their investment by a factor of five.

But both Wally and Denis warned me, independently and sternly, "Those guys can take you far, but you must be aware, they're sharks . . . out for a large, quick meal. No more. No less."

So, almost overnight, Neoforma became a B2B Internet company serving one of the largest industries in the world, healthcare. At least, that's how it was branded.

It was nice to have our laborious arguments converted into a tagline. Saved a lot of time. A square hole had been created to hold our square peg. Or maybe we had been rounded off a bit.

May 1998

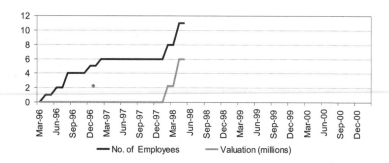

| | No. of Employees | Valuation (millions) |

Public Relations

A million bucks was just an entry fee.

Now it was time to play the real game—time to get some real money from a top-tier venture firm and the prestige that goes along with it.

You see, the value of a dollar is, pretty much, a dollar. Except when the dollar is really just the ante to a larger bet. Then it's somewhat more than a dollar. The greater the bet, the greater the prize.

We knew that we were holding good cards, but outsiders didn't know who we were yet. So we had to look sharp and confident to potential investors. We had to look comfortable in an unfamiliar world.

Everyone wants to bet on a proven winner. Since neither Jeff nor I were proven winners, Alexander and JP had selected the investors in the previous round carefully. They picked people who had made successful bets before.

Then they began to groom us for our new roles. They introduced Jeff and me to other entrepreneurs, teasing us with offhand stories about how these guys had just sold their companies for a fortune, or were about to. We were being trained to project the image that we knew without question we were Players.

Frankly, I was more interested in figuring out how best to spend the million bucks we had. I just wanted to run the business, to help and excite more people by making innovative and valuable software. The rest was just a distraction to me. That's why Jeff made a better front man. He enjoyed the challenge of playing his part convincingly. Little did we know that we would need him to leverage this talent almost continuously for years to come.

Jeff has an amazing ability to instantaneously integrate new information into his vocabulary. He was able to take the most technical or esoteric jargon from one meeting and correctly use it at the next. I knew him well enough to know that he was sometimes winging it, but he became very adept at communicating with even the most sophisticated investors and business partners.

Once we moved beyond angel investors, my role the investment process became largely limited to helping prepare presentations. I was okay with this role, because it gave me time to focus on operations.

Though I was trying to keep my attention on running the company, I must admit that it was pretty interesting watching Alexander and JP work the Scene.

They knew that the next funding round would need to come from a venture capital firm that other firms would blindly follow in future, much larger funding rounds. And so on. The venture firms that are followed blindly are called *top-tier*. There is no hard and fast rule for who is top-tier, who is second-tier and so on, but there are a handful of firms that are universally recognized as the top of the top-tier.

Alexander and JP made sure that at least one of the top-tier venture firms was represented on our list of investors, via Bret Emery, whom we had not met, but who had invested heavily in our previous round. Bret was a free-lance investor, but he was also connected to the prestigious venture firm, Venrock. As the venture arm of the Rockefeller family, Venrock was definitely near the top of the top tier, although their East Coast origin made them somewhat less sexy than the local Sand Hill Road venture firms.

Although Bret was a carefully selected investor, Venrock was not necessarily our venture firm of choice. Alexander and JP looked at it this way: either we would shop the top Sand Hill Road venture firms by dropping the old-money Venrock name, or we would shop these Sand Hill Road firms and then go back to Venrock, positioning these upstart venture firms against them. Or both. They always had multiple positive scenarios for each decision they made. The direction they pursued would be based on where the quickest valuation ramp-up could be achieved.

The fact that the top-tier venture firms funded only one in a thousand of the businesses they reviewed was irrelevant to Alexander and JP. The Internet was hot. Neoforma was an Internet company serving a huge market. And most of all, Neoforma had been vetted by Alexander and JP. Why wouldn't venture firms fight for the privilege to bet on us?

The firm they really wanted was Kleiner Perkins Caufield & Byers (KP), the current number-one VC darling of the Valley. In the intensifying stock market of mid-1998, it was generally believed that any company funded by KP was almost guaranteed to be successful, or at least famous. And when it came to raising money, that was pretty much the same thing.

Alexander and JP were staging everything to increase the chances of getting Neoforma funded by KP. If they succeeded, in addition to their increased chance of financial reward from Neoforma, their position as super angels would be greatly enhanced. They would get access to more and better deals. And they would be able to get bigger pieces of these future deals. That's how things worked.

So the idea was to create maximum buzz by visiting four or five top-tier venture firms, all in one week. We knew that these firms communicated with each other regularly. They would quickly find out what other firms we were meeting with. It was in the interest of these friendly competitors to regularly communicate with each other about new deals. In order to keep their top-tier status, these firms needed some form of the tacit consensus as to what was hot and what was not. This way, unpopular deals—those that might have difficulty receiving top-tier money in the future—could be delegated to the lower tiers.

Alexander and JP coached us extensively on how we were expected to behave. We would only meet with the venture firms after they had expressed serious interest in funding us and had set up a presentation to at least one key partner in the firm. We would then give a concise presentation and answer questions about the business. We were not to discuss the deal. All of the crucial details of a funding deal would be done by Alexander and JP. To keep us out of this area they played to our egos. "You have much too much to do as it is just running the business. You do what you do best and let us do what we do best. Your time is too important to be mixed up in funding issues."

These presentations did take up quite a bit of our time though. We went through endless revisions to our investor presentation. Alexander and JP were never happy. We always had too many slides about the product. We'd take out slides. Then we didn't have enough financial information. They'd give us some new things to add. Then we had too many slides again. We'd take out some more. They'd add some in. In the end, there was very little information about what we were doing. We could have been anybody doing just about anything. But we *were* showing that our market was *very* large.

While Alexander and JP were trying to make us presentable, they were working the phones, leveraging their extensive network to carefully orchestrate a week of meetings. They gave us upbeat assessments of their progress, but offered few details. We figured that, with their prestige and our business model, they would have no problem getting us in front of KP.

But that was not to be. For some reason they were not interested in our *space*. We didn't fit into the kind of market they wished to pursue. Or so Alexander and JP told us. Jeff and I shared a hard-to-justify belief that there was something more at work here—that perhaps Alexander and JP were not as well-connected as we had thought. We got a bit nervous. However, they did successfully schedule meetings with several well- known, top-tier firms.

The big week had come. The show was on.

Jeff and I showed up at each meeting. We talked the talk. We walked the walk. We acted confident. We confidently acted.

But in each debriefing with Alexander and JP, we became less confident. While our story was well-received, our *space* was — well, unproven. Like it or not, healthcare wasn't a very exciting market. Ideas targeting consumers were much more familiar to investors. While there was indeed much buzz about the potential of business-to-business companies, there hadn't been any successful B2B IPOs yet.

Alexander and JP played to each firm's sense of domination. "Now, we are only raising a few million dollars, so we need to know whether you would lead the round with the largest investment, or if you simply want to follow another top-tier firm with a smaller investment."

So no firm, except KP, was outright dismissing us. Most of the firms expressed an interest in taking part in a round. They just wanted someone else to take the lead. They needed more time to think about a deal like ours.

It became clear that, while several firms were considering us, nobody was willing to quickly commit to take the lead. This was a common problem for young companies. VCs love the idea of leading investment rounds—once another firm has said that they are willing to lead it.

Alexander and JP wanted to make sure that word did not have time to spread that Neoforma wasn't likely to be immediately grabbed by one of these prestigious firms. So they implemented phase two of their plan.

They called Venrock.

They implied that this hot Valley company was about to be funded, but since Bret had been in the previous round, we wanted to let them look at the deal before closing it with someone else. They'd have to act fast though. We expected our first term sheet that week. (A term sheet is what VCs give you as a serious expression of their interest.)

Suitably stirred up by the idea of losing a great deal to a Valley firm, Venrock quickly decided to take an unprecedented action. They would have us present to their entire partner team in a single meeting. It just so happened that the New York partners were meeting at their Sand Hill office the following week. Alexander told them, "Well, we can't guarantee where we'd be in the process with other firms, but we can make sure that we don't sign with anyone else until you look at this. Since this would require a quick decision, it would be best if your team met in the Neoforma offices, so that we can make sure that anyone you need to speak with will be immediately available."

To ensure that their statement about expecting a term sheet from another firm was accurate, Alexander and JP went back to the VCs we had met with and let them know that the potential for them to lead a deal was nearly gone. In fact, Venrock had a reputation for funding large deals, so it was probable that they would take the entire deal. It wasn't likely there would be room left for any other VC to participate.

Under this pressure, one of the firms decided to rush a term sheet to us after all.

At this point, the Neoforma offices were buzzing with energy. We were growing into an increasing number of rooms in the office suite. Each room was hot and muggy from hosting more people and computers than the air conditioning was designed to handle. Everyone was busy and excited about what they were doing.

Alexander and JP knew this. They knew how contagious the start-up environment could be. That's why they staged the meeting with Venrock to be held in the small, glass-enclosed conference room that we shared with other companies in the suite. We met the conservatively suited partners in our shared lobby, gave them a quick tour of our cramped offices, and sat them down in the unadorned conference room.

Playing the part of a company in a hurry to get to the point, we gave a much less formal presentation of Neoforma than we had been giving. Somehow the contrast between the formality of their dress and the informality of our presentation and offices spawned an atmosphere of candor. They were open with us, to a degree. We were open with them, to a degree. Unlike our other presentations, Jeff and I were truly comfortable in the meeting.

Maybe it was the brilliant staging by JP and Alexander. Maybe it was the rare presence of all of the decision-makers in one room. Maybe it was the electric sensation of a start-up, created by our energetic staff, buzzing past the conference room windows. Maybe it was some odd compatibility between their conservative East Coast nature and the conservative nature of healthcare. Maybe Jeff was being more charming than ever. Maybe my hair wasn't sticking up as much as usual. For whatever reason, the meeting was a success. And everyone knew it.

The meeting went on far longer than planned. When it was clear that it had accomplished its objective, JP and Alexander exchanged a subtle signal. Alexander said, "Okay. So now that we are all in love with each other, let's get on to the next step."

Ray, the lead Venrock partner said, "Well, this deal looks very good to us. We'll discuss it between us in our offices this afternoon and get back to you."

Alexander displayed exasperation and said, "Who else needs to be part of this decision besides all of you?"

Ray said, "Nobody."

Alexander quickly said, "Then you have everything you need right here. We thought you came here to seriously evaluate this deal . . ."

He glanced at JP, as if to say, *Wasn't that what you thought they were here for?* "Come on, guys. What's it going to be? Are you going to do this deal or not? Let's not waste anyone's time on this. We'll just step out of the room and you let us know when you've made a decision."

Ray paused, clearly stunned by this tactic. He looked at his team with an expression that said, *Sheesh! These Silicon Valley boys sure don't play by the rules.* But he said aloud, "Okay. Give us some time to talk about this."

Jeff and I walked out of the room flabbergasted. This took some nerve. After all, our other offer was by no means assured. What would we do if this fell through? We paced in our offices, listening to Alexander and JP discuss our position. They were optimistic. They felt that their move to force a decision had a fair chance of working. I could see that they were nervous, but I could also see that this kind of moment was what they lived for. They were high on buzz.

Not ten minutes after leaving the room, Bret came to call us back to the room. Because of the short duration of their meeting, we figured we were about to be dismissed.

Ray said, "Well, we have never made a decision about any deal in a week . . . much less ten minutes." His team laughed. A quick consensus was clearly something of an oxymoron for this group. "So it is quite startling for me to be here saying, Yes indeed. We would like to do a deal with you . . . pending due diligence. We feel very good about this company. We'll get you a term sheet tomorrow."

And just like that Neoforma became a Player. With a name like Venrock behind us, we would be a formidable company. And another three-and-a-half-million dollars could take us to previously unimagined places.

We were excited to tell our early investors about the deal, now that we had doubled the value of their investments since the previous round, completed just two months ago.

Jack, our lawyer and first investor, was even more effusive than usual. He acted like a proud papa, telling us that we wouldn't need him any more now that we were in the big leagues.

To our surprise, our angel investors, Wally and Denis, were less enthusiastic.

They were happy to see their investments grow, but they were unhappy that we hadn't included them in more of the VC selection process. They hadn't told us they wanted to play a part there, but they clearly hadn't expected things to move so quickly past them. They emphasized our need to be cautious. "Alexander and JP are impressive fundraisers," they warned us again. "But they are not working for you the way we have been. If you are not careful, they will eat you up and spit you out of your own firm."

We had been so transfixed by the magic of Alexander and JP—and so thrilled by the investment—that we were stunned to think that Wally and Denis might not think their results were so great. We told them not to worry, we could take care of ourselves.

As the details contained in the final paperwork for the funding round were revealed and discussed, Wally and Denis became increasingly agitated. Just five months earlier, they had decided to invest in Neoforma. They had each joined our Board with the idea that they would play an active and primary role in the company's growth for some time to come. Now things were different. When a VC invests in a company, it is assumed that they will appoint someone to represent them on the company's Board of Directors. They selected Bret Emery. They also insisted that, since Alexander and JP brought the deal to Venrock, one of them needed to have a Board position to represent the previous investors. Everyone agreed that a board larger than five members for a company as small as ours didn't make sense. So, if Jeff and I were both going to remain on the Board, that left only one position for our early investors. Of Wally, Denis and Jack, only one could remain on the Board. Two would have to step down.

Jack had already made it clear that he was ready to step down, but Wally and Denis were not so compliant. Wally was inherently wary of quick decisions. And Denis didn't trust the motives of Alexander and JP. He still mourned the fact that he had given up control of the Board of a company he had co-founded long ago.

Denis expressed his concerns in a message to the Board.

Questions: Just who is the new Board member Bret Emery?
What other boards does he serve on? What is his reputation?
He was a senior VP at Oracle (known for a heartless manage-

ment style), worked at another company known for its sloppy management style, and another company known as a top-quality firm of decisive, but somewhat arrogant and opinionated consultants to senior management.

There should be a frank discussion about CEO position and surprisingly there has not been (and should be soon). On paper, Jeff's background is not what VC's are looking for—they may like him so much that is no problem, or there may be another agenda.

If new CEO comes in, then CEO gets position and Board cannot have 3 management members on board, so Wayne or Jeff loses a seat. The founders would be down to 1 vote out of 5.

Bret Emery would be in full control when this happens.

Alexander made it clear to Jeff and me that he did not want Denis to remain on the Board. He used the excuse that it looked better to have an M.D. on the Board (which meant Wally), but it was clear that he did not particularly value Denis's previous accomplishments and conservative style. He had founded a company, yes, but what use was that to us now? He wasn't a Player.

So Jack and Denis left the Board. Wally, Jeff and I remained on the Board. And JP and Bret joined the Board. Sadly, we didn't hear much from Denis after that. JP was active off and on, advising us in certain issues.

And Bret didn't really pay much attention to us until the IPO heat awoke him a year later. We were generally happy about that, since we had heard horror stories about overly intrusive VCs. We figured that he just trusted us to do what needed to be done. Later, we would get to know him very well.

June 1998

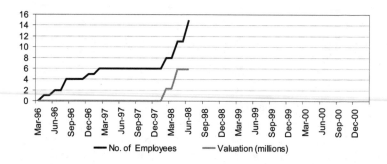

No. of Employees — Valuation (millions)

Walla

Letting go felt very good—until I lost my grip.

Jeff and I were getting tired. Tired of wearing so many hats to work each day. I fantasized what it would be like to focus on only a few jobs at a time. Independent middle managers, that's what we needed. Just a few talented people who could relieve our burden in several areas. We were much too picky to ignore the little things. There were many parts of the company neither Jeff nor I had time to run as well as we believed they should be run—like managing the software development process.

I had been searching for someone to run a programming group. Most of the dozens of people I interviewed had high expectations, but showed little promise. Most of them had nowhere near the management experience that I had. Yet they expected salaries that were half again or double mine. I wanted someone more experienced than me at managing technology personnel, not someone just out of school.

The headhunters sympathized, "That's just the way the market is right now. These are the most sought-after people in the Valley. Most of the good ones have already been hired by the consumer-oriented Internet start-ups. And we can't get their attention because they're vesting their options that are worth a small fortune. When they cash out, they'll probably retire. If you change your mind and decide you're willing to pay a quarter to a half million, we might be able to find some candidates with more than a couple of years of experience."

I had this momentary vision of putting my own résumé out there, getting a job making so much money without the daily fear of going broke, or the constant worry over what was not getting done. It hadn't really occurred to me how much experience I had gained in the last two years. I was a veritable veteran of the Internet boom. Scary thought, because I felt that I knew so little about the frontier I was heading into.

I was trying to hire guides, only to find that they didn't know much more about the territory than I. I didn't want to become a technologist. I wanted to hire one. Candidates with just a moderate knowledge of the Internet and people management skills would do fine, but I couldn't even find those.

Typically, I tended to gravitate toward unconventional résumés. So, when I saw on Larry's résumé that he had experience as a software team manager and was a part-time Olympic gymnastics coach, I was intrigued. Really, that *was* what I was looking for—a coach—someone to guide a bunch of smart, quirky programmers with social skills even worse than mine and egos as large as the Valley.

When I interviewed Larry, a tall, matter-of-fact man with a large smile, I thought he would fit the task nicely. He seemed to have many of the characteristics I was looking for. So I hired him.

In addition to the priority I set on hiring someone to run our programming group, I was looking for someone to improve and expand the use of words on our website. The challenge was to find someone who had both the skills of a liberal arts major and the ability to understand and thrive in the wake of the collision between technology, healthcare, business and investment.

Emma was one of the most promising candidates for the job. One reason that Emma said she wanted to leave her middle management job as an editor of the Oracle website was the ruthless nature of the corporate culture. Yet, I could see that she was clearly a product of that environment too. She was aggressive and opinionated. She talked fast and conveyed a desire to take control of something new. I couldn't help but think of the dire warnings by Denis about the heartless management style at Oracle. But I needed managers who were willing to take control of key parts of this evolving company.

It looked like Larry and Emma would be able to take complete control of their areas. And it was a welcome relief to me. At last I could get further down my endless list of things to do.

But as the months went by, I became concerned about how infrequently they consulted with me for direction. Eventually, I realized that they had taken it quite literally when I said I wanted to hire people who would come into the company and take control. They had been treating the assorted requests and directions I sent them on an almost hourly basis as if they were simply "suggestions."

I was confident that I could easily clarify things by discussing it with them. They both said they knew I was very busy and were simply following my request to get things done, but said they'd consult with me more often in the future.

This eased my mind—until I found out from Jeff that Larry and Emma had immediately gone to his office and complained that I was meddling in their affairs. If I had really hired them to run their parts of the company, I should give them the authority to do so. If not, then maybe they should go somewhere else.

Jeff did not like to get involved in conflicts between me and other employees. He told them what they wanted to hear—that I had been running these parts of the company for years, so it was only natural for me to want to continue to influence the direction of the website and that he'd have a talk with me.

Jeff encouraged me to give them a bit more room to do their jobs. I told him it was a bad sign that they had smiled in my face, then run to him to complain about me. They seemed to have decided that I was simply an obstruction to be worked around.

It reminded me of my days at Varian, where battles between middle managers inundated the company with inefficiency and mediocrity. I sensed that they cared more about their power than their product. Jeff disagreed. Since nobody else was complaining about them, I hesitantly ascribed my concerns to my need for control. The last thing I wanted to do was to let my personal insecurities affect the company.

At first Todd, who was still in charge of the look and feel of the website, liked the idea of having allies at a management level. He was emboldened by their increasing agreement with him on some of the issues he and I had disagreed on over the last year and a half. I noticed a change in him too. He included me in fewer decisions and instead chose to run things by Jeff. Jeff was focused primarily on investors and key business partners. He was used to me handling detail-oriented issues and assumed that I would work these conflicts out on my own. Todd, and others, considered the absence of negative feedback an endorsement for whatever they wanted to do.

This was working great for Todd, until Larry and Emma turned on him and began to dispute some of his decisions. Suddenly, he was the incensed one. He had taken the Neoforma website from an obscure, rather plain destination and turned it into an international attraction, and a thing of beauty. Who were they to question his judgment?

Seeking an ally, Todd came to me complaining about their under-handedness and lack of respect. He said that when he'd told them I had already directed him on a major design issue, they'd said, "Wayne doesn't run the company, Jeff does." It created the desired effect. I was very upset.

I ranted at Jeff, "I hired these two. How could they be so disrespect-ful, so disloyal? They're both competent, but they're sneaky and under-handed. They constantly whisper behind closed doors. We are not a culture of closed doors. These aren't the kind of people we want to build out our company. They are creating a culture of division. We have never tolerated that before. Why should we put up with it now?"

Jeff listened respectfully to my tirade, then responded gently. He knew that I was overworked and he knew I was a control freak. "Come on Wayne. They are just trying to do the job you hired them to do. Let's give them time to prove themselves. Right now there is too much work to do."

In all matters except money, Jeff and I had always been able to agree to disagree. Many of our arguments had been heated, to say the least. But we had always been able to make difficult decisions, one way or another.

And over the years, we'd developed a fallback plan. Whenever we couldn't resolve an issue by talking it out, we referred to the last disagreement. Whoever had conceded on that one got the right to decide on this one. I don't remember what the last disagreement had been, but I must have won that one because I gave in on this one.

We would keep Larry and Emma, at least until the new website was released. I would be nice to them and exert my influence less directly. Jeff had always been able to depend on me in the past and assumed that this crisis was no different than previous ones. Unfortunately, his confidence in me would prove to be overly optimistic.

On movie sets, they have a great word to describe the indecipherable background conversation over which the main characters are communicating. They call this necessary, but empty noise, *walla*.

Sometimes the walla can distract us from the main story.

July 1998

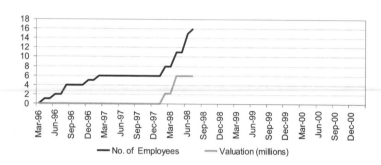

Chart legend: — No. of Employees   — Valuation (millions)

(X-axis: Mar-96, Jun-96, Sep-96, Dec-96, Mar-97, Jun-97, Sep-97, Dec-97, Mar-98, Jun-98, Sep-98, Dec-98, Mar-99, Jun-99, Sep-99, Dec-99, Mar-00, Jun-00, Sep-00, Dec-00. Y-axis: 0, 2, 4, 6, 8, 10, 12, 14, 16, 18)

Neoforma Uses Immersive Imaging from Be Here for Groundbreaking Medical Facility Planning Application

Neoforma, Inc. and Be Here Corporation today launched the first-of-its-kind, state-of-the-art virtual reality tour of a medical facility at neoforma.com. Healthcare professionals and medical facility architects around the world can now tour the real world, 1000-room University of Chicago Duchossois Center for Advanced Medicine (CAM) from the convenience of their desktop with Be Here's immersive images . . .

Neoforma Press Release
July 1998

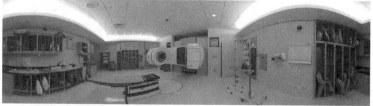

Photo: Attainia, Inc.
Panographic image of a medical linear accelerator room

Spinning Rooms

Spinning rooms and not much more.

That was the description that one of our competitors would later use to belittle us. However, I was quite flattered by this characterization. In a time when none of the companies that competed with Neoforma had offered anything original or substantial, we had something quite grand.

In July 1998, we were only excited by the beauty and value of what we had created. Our competitors would not show up for many months.

I worked for more than a year at Varian before I actually saw one of their cancer therapy machines in a hospital. It was my job to support the customers who purchased these complex machines. I was supposed to help them figure out how to design their hospital to accommodate this big, heavy, radiation-producing equipment and I didn't have a clue what the rooms *really* looked like, or how patients and staff interacted in them. Sure, I had seen drawings and photographs of the equipment positioned in a room, but that had given me very little information about what was really in the rooms or what went on in them. This bothered me. And it gave me an idea.

At Neoforma, we had been trying to figure out how to convert the substantial quantity of traffic at our website into higher quality traffic. That is to say, we wanted to turn our visitors' activities into revenue opportunities. We wanted people to come to our website every time they were selecting medical equipment. We wanted their experience to be worth the visit. We wanted it to be *good.*

When a facility is being constructed or remodeled, the vast majority of medical equipment is predetermined. I believed that the best way to service the people who were looking for stuff to put into the rooms of a hospital would be to present our listings of equipment in a hospital setting—not a physical hospital, but a virtual one.

Since early days, when we were producing our CD, we had organized a large database of healthcare equipment, using photographs and three-dimensional drawings of rooms, as well as lists of equipment that went into some of the more complex rooms in a hospital. On the scale we were doing it, this had never been done before. This information was very popular with our customers. If anything, they wanted us to include a broader range of rooms. But there wasn't any room left on the CD, so we were limited in what we could add.

When we moved this room information to our website, it opened up all sorts of opportunities for improvement. For one thing, since there was no longer a space limit, we could actually present an entire hospital, not just a few departments. And we didn't have to limit ourselves to one picture per room. It took a lot more information to properly convey what these rooms really looked like.

The problem was that this kind of content was very difficult to get. We had to create the list of products found in each room by commissioning people with experience in each type of room. This was expensive and time consuming.

At first, I created three-dimensional computer renderings of a few key rooms. Then we had to commission someone else to do more— also very expensive and time-consuming. It would have been much less expensive to take photos of actual rooms—except a photo couldn't show as much of the room as a three-dimensional model could. It was while I was searching for a better way to publish this information that I stumbled upon the technology that would give me everything I wanted.

While the presentation stretched the limits of the limited bandwidth and computing power of most Web surfers at the time, panoramic images are really quite simple in concept. They consist of regular photographs with overlapping views of a single scene, electronically stitched together in some way or another and displayed in a window on a computer screen. By moving the mouse around the window, the viewer can pan left, right, up, down and even completely around the scene, giving a very three-dimensional feeling to this two-dimensional window.

The technology was straightforward enough that I was able to mock-up a few Web pages in a couple of days. I was even able to find a way to allow high-quality drawings to be panned and zoomed on the same Web page, using only an Internet browser.

Once I had established the feasibility of these technologies, I was ready to present my idea to the key members of our team.

The idea was that we would select a hospital that demonstrated some of the latest and greatest equipment and design ideas, panoramically photograph every room and hallway, survey every item in every room, gather computer plans of the entire facility, and present it on our website. Every category of every item in about a thousand rooms would be linked to detailed information about the products available and the manufacturers that made them. It would give website unprecedented depth, utility and quality.

There was some resistance at first, primarily because this seemed like a very ambitious undertaking for a company that employed only sixteen people. Alexander was particularly adamant that all of our efforts should be focused on e-commerce. I expressed my belief that e-commerce functionality wouldn't do us any good if nobody was using the site as their primary source of information for selecting hospital equipment. When everyone turned to Neoforma for this information, we could support the content by adding contextual advertising too.

The facility I considered to be ideal was the Center for Advanced Medicine (CAM) in Chicago. I had visited it a year earlier and been very impressed by its quality and breadth of services. It was a place that felt more hospitable than most medical facilities I had visited.

CAM wasn't actually a hospital. It was an ambulatory care center, which means that nobody stayed there longer than twenty-three hours. I thought this was an ideal project because the Center was new, it looked good, it had just about everything a hospital had except the beds, and it was closed most of the weekend. I had calculated that it would take us about forty-eight hours to photograph.

It would be tough to do this while a facility was bustling with staff and patients. At least, I knew I would be uncomfortable if I were a patient—seated in a gown in a waiting room, under stress, in my most introspective and vulnerable moment—if a crew of five obviously-not-from-around-here individuals walked in carrying cameras and clipboards, scurrying this way and that, straightening the furniture and magazines, avoiding eye contact. That could certainly make anybody's bad day worse.

At CAM, unlike most hospital settings, we could avoid making patients miserable by coming in on the weekend. I figured we could do it with two twelve-hour shifts on two weekends.

After much persistence, I achieved a reluctant consensus on the project.

To do the job in forty-eight hours, we would need four Neoformites: one to set up rooms ahead of us, one to assist the camera person, and two to survey the items in each room. I knew that it would be unfair to expect any of our overworked employees to volunteer to lose two weekends of time with their families, so I volunteered Jeff, Anil and Stephen to join me for duty. After all, they had the most experience with the workings of a hospital. They were thrilled to help out, or so I assumed, since I refused to hear any reason why they might not be able to go.

I had based my time estimate on the use of a specific type of camera to create the panoramic images. Since this technology was quite new and obscure, there were very few choices available for capturing the photos.

One option was to simply stand in the middle of each room and take a bunch of overlapping pictures with a film or digital camera. There was software that could then stitch the images together. However, the number of steps in each room and the difficulty of assembling everything afterward made this option impractical on this scale.

There were a couple of other cameras that spun around and took a single shot for each room, but they didn't capture a wide enough view for small rooms. We needed the floors and ceilings too.

There was one company that did seem to have what we needed. A venture-backed start-up called Be Here had created a parabolic mirror that fit over a conventional camera. The mirror, which looked like a robot when mounted on its tripod, facilitated the ability to create a single photo which could be converted digitally to an almost spherical view of any room.

I contacted the head of business development at Be Here and told him about what I had in mind. Their primary business model at that point was to sell their cameras for a substantial amount of money. I didn't intend to spend that kind of money. So in conventional Silicon Valley style, I impressed upon them how groundbreaking our use of their technology would be. I told them that I had been thinking that we should partner to create this first virtual hospital. The PR value to them would be substantial.

I don't think they entirely bought my argument, but they could tell that I wasn't going to buy a camera, so they lined up a photographer they had worked with before. She could borrow one of their cameras and we would simply pay for her time and receive a discount on the fees for turning the film images into panoramic images.

This worked fine for me, though I was a bit nervous about the photographer. Most of the photographers I had worked with were very meticulous. I needed someone who could take one image every three minutes, for twelve hours. The Be Here guy assured me that Nancy would be just right for the job.

Now, all I had to do was get permission from CAM and from the architects. I had a great contact at CAM, so I figured it would be an easy task. *Who wouldn't want their facility featured—as a premier example of the best of the best—in way-cool three-dimensional photography?*

My contact was Chet Szerlag, who headed up one of the largest departments. I'd met him in my Varian days and had been very impressed with his sincerity, affability and intelligence. I knew that it had been his hard work—before, during and after CAM's construction — that had been instrumental in making this facility as wonderful as it was. He had become a valued advisor to Jeff and me at Neoforma.

Chet introduced me to the powers that be with his endorsement. But I did not receive the type of reception I had expected.

The first group I spoke with was responsible for hosting visitors to CAM. As one of the newest and most comprehensive ambulatory care facilities in the world, CAM was a very popular destination for hospital executives planning their own new facility or expansion. Pairing tours with educational seminars had become a very profitable enterprise. When I walked in with this idea to publish a tour of their facility online so that anyone in the world could experience their great facility, most of the administrative department members loved the idea. However, the head of the department didn't. He flatly said no.

He didn't like the idea of us showing the world what was in each of their rooms. "What if someone saw that we had only three of something and believed that six were required for safety? The liability is unacceptable."

I told him that we wouldn't publish the quantities of any item found in the rooms, or even the brand, just what kind of item it was.

Without pause, he moved on to his next argument, "And the way we lay out our rooms . . . what is in them . . . that's our proprietary information. It's a big part of how we deliver quality care."

I made the point that he was already sharing that level of information with anyone who visited their facility in person. But his biggest issue was that he felt that it might dilute the value of their onsite tour programs. I pointed out that our virtual tour could never replace a physical tour, but it would make more people aware of the facility. And it would deliver the next best thing to those would never be able to visit in person. I thought this argument was persuasive, but his answer was still no.

I was stunned. *How could they squelch such a great service to the community? After all, we were going to do almost all of the work.* I had been so convinced of the value that this tour would deliver that I had not even considered the possibility that I would be turned down.

I was upset for a few days. Once I had that out of my system, I was set to try another avenue.

I figured that the architects would have very high contacts into CAM, since the executives tend to be fairly active in at least the early stages of projects of this scope. *Who would be more eager to get their project published than the architect?* Most architects spend a substantial amount of their revenue on marketing activities, particularly on getting their projects published in various periodicals.

I tracked down and contacted Jane, the large architectural firm's

PR person. I gave her my spiel and waited for her enthusiasm. She hesitated, then said, "So, let me get this straight . . . You want to show our building on your website using some new kind of photography? That sounds interesting. And how much are you going to pay us for this?"

I waited for her laugh, indicating that she had only been joking. She didn't laugh. I could see that things were only getting worse down this path.

But I was getting desperate. And sometimes, when I get desperate, I get pretty good at talking. Luckily, this was one of those times. I took a different tack, explaining to Jane that getting published on our site was indeed an honor, not much different than taking out an ad in a glossy magazine with a large, national circulation. Only, this would be much cooler, reach a much broader audience—and she wouldn't have to pay thousands of dollars for the photographs.

My expressed desperation had worked. Jane changed her mind. Tentatively, at first, and then with more enthusiasm, she speculated aloud—maybe this would be a good thing, even if they didn't get paid what they were used to getting paid for. But she had to get the approval of a few people in the local Chicago office. She set up a meeting for me to present the idea to two of the healthcare specialists and the head of the office.

As Jane led me into the appropriately lush, contemporary conference room, she apologized, "Tom, our president, won't be able to join us. He's on an important call that he thinks will last for longer than this meeting. The rest of us should be able to work through this, though."

I was disappointed, since I assumed that he was the final decision-maker, but what could I do?

We were soon joined by two men who did not look happy to be wasting their time with me. They had that rushed, distracted look that almost always predicts an unproductive meeting.

It looked like things were taking a bad turn. And then I learned that these were the people primarily responsible for specifying what type of medical equipment would be needed for healthcare projects. When I heard this, my optimism returned. These were exactly the type of people who would benefit from our website.

I gave them a comprehensive briefing and demonstration. Each time I presented the prototypes, I got very excited. This was really cool stuff. I figured that my excitement would be contagious, so I didn't hold it back.

After I had covered everything, I paused for their comments. One said, "How can you publish all of that information . . . those lists of equipment? We make our living by providing those lists." The other guy was nodding his head vigorously.

This was not a good sign. I said, "You have to understand. We've been publishing this information for years. There is nothing proprietary about lists of what equipment goes in which rooms. Every architect has lists like this. If they don't, they create them the same way we do— by visiting an actual site.

"Our goal is to make sure that everybody benefits from having complete lists and saves time creating and maintaining them — including you. The value you bring to your clients is the education and experience you use to make the best decisions you can for a particular project—not to republish the list from your last project!"

I had run into this mentality—and been frustrated by it—many times before. *It's my data that makes me so special* is an obvious fallacy. As I struggled to make them see that, I know I came on a bit strong. I kept my cool, but refused to yield. They were less cool, but also refused to yield. Jane actually came to my defense several times, but she had little influence with these guys. We were going nowhere.

Just when I assumed all was lost, the president walked in. He fit the part of the senior partner perfectly: grey hair, good suit and a confident, outgoing manner to match. He introduced himself, shook hands with me and sat at the table. "Sorry to be late. I didn't think I'd ever get off that call! So . . . tell me what this is all about."

Jane gave him a brief summary of my proposal and voiced her support for it. The specialists voiced their concerns in tense, strained voices. The president listened politely, attentively. When he had heard enough he said, "Okay, let me get this straight. Wayne wants to publish one of our projects on this website of his. If he doesn't publish one of our projects, he'll publish one of our competitor's projects. Is that right, Wayne?"

"Yes, that's true."

He stood up, with a look that said how nice it was to have such a short meeting, for a change. "Well, that's all we need to know." Turning to Jane, he said, "Give Wayne whatever he needs. Wayne, call Tom at CAM. He's in charge of their marketing. He'll make sure you get the approvals you need on their end. Thanks for coming."

The specialists did not make eye contact with me as I shook their hands and left.

After receiving the permission we needed to photograph the facility, I scheduled two weekend trips to Chicago for our crew. I arranged for us to meet Nancy, the photographer, at our hotel. She would fly directly from her home town in Southern California.

I'm not sure what I expected, but Nancy was definitely not it. A bubbly, casual woman in her thirties, Nancy did not match my stereotype of the neat, serious, professional photographer. That's probably because she wasn't. Photography was one of her many hobbies and semi-professions. She ran several websites, one dedicated to the study of UFOs, one to animal rescue, and another to frog memorabilia. She dabbled in Web page design and was taking classes in advanced computer graphics. But most of her notoriety and character had resulted from her position as the host of Zola's Pleasure Palace, a computer bulletin board dedicated to stretching the boundaries of sexual expression.

We asked Nancy if she preferred to be called Zola. She said that either name was fine, but we could tell she preferred the name of her alter ego. Calling her Zola felt quite natural. She was the last person a casual acquaintance would associate with Zola's Pleasure Palace. And yet, when you got to know her, the association seemed obvious in some inexplicable way.

I was a bit nervous that she might not be enthusiastic about racing through four 12-hour days. She wasn't thrilled by the idea of getting up at 4:00 on a Saturday morning, but said she was up for the challenge. And she certainly was.

We arrived at the large, nearly empty facility at 6:00 the next morning. We were greeted by the curious, *are-these-guys-nuts?!* gaze of sleepy security guards. When I told them why we were there with several cases of equipment, the guard in charge eyed us suspiciously, but acknowledged that he had a note regarding a film crew arriving today. He was clearly nervous about the idea of a group of strangers wandering for hours through rooms filled with all sorts of very expensive equipment. I assured him that we knew what we were doing and wouldn't disrupt anything.

At first, the security guards had the idea that someone should watch us the entire time, but after an hour or so they realized that we seemed to know our way around a hospital, were terribly boring, and appeared quite focused on our harmless task. So they decided that we would only need a guard around when we entered locked areas. We could just call them on the house phone, they said. But then that happened often enough that they gave up and just let us have a key to get in everywhere, except the pharmacy. Not even the security guards could get into the pharmacy.

So with free access to the entire facility, we methodically documented every room in every department. We wandered through radiology suites, even photographing the MRI rooms — where one false move could send the camera flying toward the magnets, causing tens of thousands of dollars' worth of damages.

We photographed restrooms and janitors' closets. We captured the sterile surgical suites wearing booties and hats. Jeff and I couldn't find the chic, masculine surgeon's caps we wanted and had to wear slightly embarrassing, blue, muffin-shaped paper bouffants. They did their bit to add to the surreal atmosphere of the empty rooms and corridors.

As we wandered purposefully, hour after hour, we became increasingly aware of the enormity and importance of our task.

In each department, we found the large shelves containing the catalogs of supplies and equipment that each department ordered from. The catalogs were mostly years out of date and represented a very small segment of the current choices in each category. We realized that our site could free up that space and provide so much more current information.

Even though we had all worked in healthcare to varying degrees, we had only an abstract idea of the potential impact Neoforma could have on real people in real hospitals. The creation of this virtual tour solidified our connection to the real thing and gave us a renewed sense that what we were doing wasn't just good for business, it might actually be *important*.

As our weariness grew from the grueling work, so did our excitement. There was new meaning and urgency to our work at Neoforma. We really were going to make the world a better place.

We produced many other online tours at notable facilities over the next year, each more interesting and of better quality than the last. The tours became very popular with healthcare providers, designers, and suppliers. They even made some money.

It was ironic, telling, and sad that our competitors would later choose to pick this service to bear the brunt of their criticism. They acted as if adding valuable, educational content to our website was a silly premise for a business, as if it were a sign of weakness.

August 1998

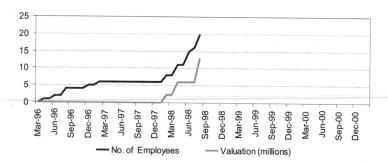

No. of Employees — Valuation (millions)

Online bookseller Amazon.com said Tuesday it agreed to buy Junglee, a software company that makes it easy to comparison shop on the Web, and PlanetAll, a Web-based address book and reminder service.

Under terms of the transactions, Amazon will issue 1.6 million of its shares—worth $173.2 million based on Monday's closing stock price of $108.25—for all shares and options of Junglee . . .

Wired News Report
August 4, 1998

A Flashback

A company's psyche develops slowly, imperceptibly. Old patterns merge with new traditions to form an entirely new cultural tapestry.

Just before graduating from architectural college, I burned out of school in spectacular fashion. I used the excuse that I had run out of money and jumped into a chaotic cycle of exploration. I was convinced that the key to discovering life's internal mysteries and potential was buried under the comfortable assumptions I had come to rely on. I broke up a long relationship with the woman I had lived with. I drifted from job to job. I spent every spare moment reading, thinking, and drawing.

While I was very efficient at my day jobs, my real interest was in my evening explorations. Each new discovery brought renewed vigor to my pursuit of life's secrets. Work became increasingly distracting. In an attempt to break completely with my natural tendencies, I moved through a series of increasingly dire living situations, at times going for days without money or food.

While designing a restaurant in a Southern California tourist beach community, I met two quirky local craftspeople, a married couple. They liked the odd, and strangely controversial, wooden sign I had designed for the restaurant and asked them to build. We kind of hit it off.

Vern, the wood carver, was an edgy, evasive man, with a persistent skin condition that changed the way he looked from day to day. Mary, the painter, was a thin, effusive, New Age woman, with curly hair and desperate eyes. They lived with their seven-year-old son and two-year-old daughter.

When they learned that I was sleeping on the restaurant owner's living room floor with restaurant staff, they offered to rent me the empty room under their rented house. I knew that they lived near the beach and the idea of having an actual room of my own was very appealing. I asked to see the room.

When Mary and Vern guided me down the exterior path that led from their porch to the back side of the small hillside house, my first impression was quite positive. The view from the front door of the room *did* provide glimpses of water over an apartment building that fronted the ocean. The sound of waves was hypnotic.

The first thing I noticed was that the exterior door did not close completely, let alone lock. Entering the room I observed a dark, low-ceilinged, musty smelling crawl space that had been partially, and sloppily, enclosed with gypsum board. A sand-and-dirt-encrusted rug covered most of the concrete floor in the eight-by-ten-foot room. A tiny toilet and shower enclosure was wedged along one side wall. Shelves of rough lumber, filled with the odds and ends commonly stored in a garage, lined the other side wall. Carved, literally, into the back wall, was a nook containing a raised mattress.

I pulled up the mattress and confirmed what I had suspected—it had been placed directly on a bed of dirt. *Why bother with all of that extra excavation?* The entire back wall and ceiling over the bed were constructed of old sheets that had been tacked up to conceal the dirt, foundation and joists that supported the house above.

The ocean-facing wall, in addition to the entry door, was pierced by a small, square casement window with glazing divided into nine panes by peeling wood mullions. Three of the panes were missing. Another was broken. The window frame had warped such that it could only be pulled to within three inches of a closed position.

In short, the place was a dump. But it was better than sharing a living room with the restaurant's kitchen staff. And, oh, what a great, artistic way to suffer a bit more!

So I moved in. By this time, moving in meant hauling and stacking two small particleboard cabinets next to the bed. One contained my favorite records, the other contained my books and drawing supplies. On top of this cabinet went my turntable. Next to the cabinet went the duffle bag that contained my clothes.

Immediately above my quarters was the house's living room and kitchen. My hosts were night owls, which suited me just fine. I owned no clock or watch. I usually stayed awake until the sky began to lighten.

My landlords were very social. Almost every night, and well into the morning, anonymous, laughing and arguing crowds would gather a couple of feet above my head. The floors creaked with every footfall.

Often, after her guests had left, Mary would come down to my room, drunk, carrying a bottle of the two-dollar sparkling wine they consumed by the case. She didn't knock. The door was always open. She'd stagger over to my nook, sit uncomfortably close to me, her loose blouse gaping, and lament the state of her life. She knew she was an alcoholic. She knew her husband was unbalanced, even dangerous. She knew her children had grown more attached to me than to their father, even calling me dad occasionally. (The kids pretty much took care of themselves, cooked their own meals and followed their own routines.) She'd inevitably lament about how she didn't know if she was going to be able to pay this month's bills or not.

Broke as I was, I increased my own rent twice and even commissioned her to draw a portrait of a friend, which cost me my next two paychecks.

I didn't know what else to do as I listened to her convey her woes, spittle gathering at the corners of her mouth. I couldn't hug her, which I knew she needed, because inevitably Vern would come into the room soon after her, equally drunk. He would cast a friendly, jealous, and deeply menacing glance at me, smirk painfully, then firmly guide Mary, obliviously, off the bed, out the door, and up the stairs.

I'd return to my reading or drawing, listening to the floorboards squeak above me as they made love, wondering how they managed that in their inebriated state.

When I needed a break from my introspections, I would entertain myself by rolling up my pant legs and walking slowly across the carpet, which I ordinarily avoided. The fleas were so prolific that I could usually get ten to twenty of them to hop on me in a single pass. I'd kill as many of them as I could and repeat the process. It seemed entertaining at the time.

I had no television, and my radio only received a limited number of AM stations. The fleas and I had an agreement. Most of them stayed in the rug, only visiting my bed when their hunger became life-threatening. At least, that's what they told me.

However, I had been unable to reach such a truce with the four-legged occupants of the establishment.

They tacitly assumed that I was willing to share my space with them. After all, they *had* been there first. I kept my plate and cooking pan fastidiously clean. I hung my garbage bag from a rope attached to the ceiling and made sure not to put any food products in it. But the rodents watched me from the shadows and assumed that if I were putting so much effort into protecting this bag, it must be worth exploring.

Several times, I awoke to the sound of trash falling to the floor through the hole they chewed into the bottom of the bag. Somehow they had walked across the ceiling and crawled down the narrow rope to get to the bag.

Actually, trying to keep them out of my trash was more of a game than a concern. What really bugged me was that my bed was right in the middle of the primary access path from the underside of the house to my room, and through its window, to the outside world. At first, they were courteous, choosing the long way, around the edges of the bed. But once they saw that I wasn't a threat, they wasted no such effort.

Finally, exasperated by a night of being awakened several times by feet treading callously across me, I kidnapped Zoe, Mary and Vern's cat. It wasn't really their cat. They didn't feed it often enough. But it had hung around long enough to get a name.

I blocked the larger holes around the broken window, so Zoe couldn't get out, and closed her in for the night. She tried to get out for a while, but eventually settled on the bed with me. She was absolutely flea infested, but I could handle that.

Within minutes of turning the light off, Zoe caught her first victim, a small mouse. I let her torment her victim for a while, which seemed only fair. Then I tossed the carcass outside. She caught two more critters that night, another mouse and a rat. She caught at least one rat on each of the following three nights, and then nothing for several nights. Satisfied, I set her free to hunt elsewhere.

I had only occasional rodent visitors after that. I felt good. I had helped the cat. The cat had helped me. Now we no longer needed each other, so we parted ways. If only all relationships could be that simple.

A friend from high school visited me. When I showed him my living quarters, he was aghast, visibly disgusted. He asked, "How can you live like this?"

I told him, "It's not so bad. I don't have mice in my bed anymore." He suggested we walk down to the beach. He did not stay long and did not visit me again.

One evening, I was sitting on the bed, surrounded by the many books I was reading at the time. I was suffering dissociation vicariously through Raskolnikov in *Crime and Punishment*. The room was illuminated solely by a reading light that rested on the edge of the cabinet next to me. Gradually, at the edge of consciousness, I became aware that the record I was playing on the turntable didn't sound right.

I blearily glanced over the book, to where the turntable was. What I saw was so odd that I didn't react at first. Droplets of water were landing directly on the center of the record, snaking to the edge as the record continued to spin. The needle slid one way, then the other. Classical music had never sounded so, modern.

How bizarre. I though. *It's not raining outside. How can this be?* Almost immediately, the individual drops merged together, becoming a thin stream. My eyes followed the stream, dazzling in the glow of the single light, up to the ceiling. There I noted that the water was emanating from a dark spot on the fabric ceiling directly above the turntable. I also noticed that the fabric was bowing, expanding, getting steadily more taut.

I think I gasped or squawked. In any case, I know I made some exhalation of alarm, then jumped from the bed, scrambled to pull the electrical cord from the wall, ran out the door, stumbled up the stairs, threw open the house's unlocked front door, which opened into the kitchen, and gazed upon the eye of the storm.

Kneeling on a chair that had been pulled up to the kitchen sink, was James, the seven-year-old boy who had called me Dad. His sleeves pushed above the elbows, he moved his hands slowly and purposefully through the mounds of bubbles that floated in the sink. He had apparently been washing dishes and discovered that when large amounts of soap were distributed under a fully opened faucet copious bubbles were produced. Soft, delicate, beautiful, vulnerable bubbles.

He had become so entranced with the spectacle that he had failed to notice that the sink was completely full. Water was pursuing its freedom in all directions along the sink's edges, pouring onto the wood plank floor, down through the cracks between the boards, seeking safety as far from tomorrow's sun as possible.

His expression was so calm and rapt, I experienced a moment of joy. A brief moment. I tried to sound calm as I said, "Please turn off the water!"

I didn't have a chance to see the impact of my interruption on his revelry. I was already on my way down the stairs.

By the time I returned to my room, the trickle had become a torrent. Water was cascading off the turntable, onto and into the particleboard cabinets, pooling around my bag of clothes and sundries. With the exception of the books on the bed and the dishes in the main room, everything I owned was drenched.

I simply sat down and watched the fountain, until the torrent became a trickle, then a stream of drops, finally slowing to an occasional drip.

I laughed aloud, ignoring my moistening eyes.

As the flow subsided, my thoughts drifted backward, one event at a time—seeking an explanation for my current condition. It was clear to me that I had orchestrated this moment, or at least one like it. I had succumbed to unconscious forces, letting them drive me, one step at a time, to the point of complete surrender, of complete loss.

So here I was. Having given up conscious control over my actions, having freed myself of all material and social constraints, I had become addicted to the shadows. I had learned a great deal about the shadows, but what now? What good could these discoveries do if I stayed in this cave?

It was time to turn around, to regain control of, and take responsibility for, my decisions. I hoped that I would be able to rebuild my life with expanded vision.

Slowly, surely, I dug my way out of surrender. The lessons I had learned about releasing control would be more valuable to me than I could ever have imagined.

Ten years later, as Neoforma grew quickly from a company where I had complete control to a company where I had yielded much of my control, I was shocked by how often control issues came up and by how few people could cope with them.

The problem was most obvious in those individuals who assumed that any gap in control was theirs to exploit, regardless of their qualifications. But by far the most common, frustrating, and damaging issue I had to deal with in those days of frenzied growth was disempowerment.

As much as I had screened candidates for ability to cope with discontinuity and uncertainty, most had no experience with the tumult that they were about to encounter.

Everything was new or transient—technologies, tools, job titles, org charts, accounting processes, human resources policies, product priorities. Things were happening so fast that there was no time for documentation or formalization. Everybody was expected to wing it.

And we were hiring from the bottom up. First we hired the people doing the work—then, when the need was absolute, we hired the managers to organize the work, and so on.

This growth pattern was driven in part by economics—we were getting more money to be able to pay for more experienced employees.

Our development was also driven in part by the boisterous job market, in which candidates had the luxury of choosing the lowest risk opportunity—in other words, the one closest to IPO. As we approached that mark, the experience level of our candidates increased.

And most of all, our growth was driven by practicality. There was so much to do that we hired whoever could do the job. We'd figure out how to put it all together later.

Within this dynamic, unstable environment, employees were convinced that their voices were not being heard. No matter how much we tried to ensure that they were empowered and had access to me and other executives, many felt undervalued. They flooded into my office, yelling, crying, pleading.

Competent, intelligent, creative people were unwilling or unable to recognize that a young organism is focused on its growth, not its form. Each organ has to function individually before the organism can function. And, most importantly, every organ is critical. The brain is not more important than the heart.

Seemed simple to me, but the tendency of so many individuals to believe that their initiative was being restrained by forces adjacent to or above them drove me nuts. Their perception that they had limited power and importance within the company was completely out of sync with reality. We needed and listened to them all. It certainly wasn't a question of money. Jeff and I paid the vast majority of the staff substantially more than we paid ourselves.

Because we couldn't communicate an unwavering message, employees let their minds drift to fantasy. They imagined all sorts of obstacles, incompetence, and motivations.

I listened, guided, reminded, reasoned, advised, manipulated, motivated, scolded, flattered, and complimented. Whatever it took. And it took a lot.

My objective in those early days—what really thrilled me—was to assemble a bunch of bright, caring people together, and let them put their best into creating unprecedented solutions to a real-world problem. In our idyllic vision of the company, everyone mattered equally. It wasn't until we had twenty or thirty employees that Jeff and I gave in to an increasing demand for printed titles on business cards.

In the end I wondered, What was it that made so many people value themselves so little? I knew this wasn't a simple question, but I couldn't help but wonder, Had my past flirtation with abdicated personal responsibility somehow rubbed off on the corporate culture? Or was there a broader cultural influence? I hoped it was the latter, but that didn't make it any easier to accept or deal with.

September 1998

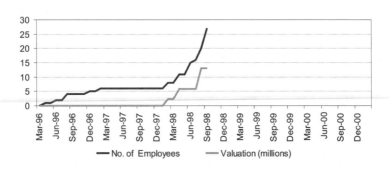

Legend: ── No. of Employees ── Valuation (millions)

Photo: Jamis MacNiven

Buck's Restaurant in Woodside, California

A Classic Scene

I am not one who can live in a stereotype without subconsciously fighting it.

Trapped as I was in the role of an aggressive, dotcom entrepreneur, I lacked many, if not most, of the habits of the natives.

Okay, to be honest, I did have mid-afternoon lunch meetings at Chinese and Indian restaurants. I did scamper from one Sand Hill Road meeting to another. I did wear sandals to work quite often. I did go to Fry's Electronics more often than would allow me to completely avoid the term *nerd*. I did have a couple of *South Park* figures on my desk (but I swear I didn't put them there!). I did experience frequent struggles to be verbally articulate. And I did stay up late.

On the other hand, I did not get up late. I did not wear shorts and a T-shirt to work (very often). Jeff bore this responsibility for me. I only got around to playing ping pong at work once. My office was relatively neat. I ate breakfast and dinner with my family almost every day. And, I was in my late thirties—which made me downright *old*, if not necessarily *mature*.

So when I ended up at Buck's Restaurant for a breakfast interview with a team of sought-after programmers from Netscape, I could not help but feel a bit disembodied.

I had read in several Internet periodicals about breakfast meetings at Buck's. It's a simple restaurant that its owner, Jamis MacNiven, modestly describes as "a Silicon Valley restaurant, tucked against the hills in the quiet village of Woodside, California where the venture-capital community and the Information Age execs conspire to bring you the 21st century." This was a place where myths were born.

Jeff had already been initiated to Buck's during an early round of fundraising. Alexander and JP had already convinced Robert to invest in Neoforma without meeting us, so Jeff's meeting with him was merely a formality. Robert had suggested breakfast at Buck's.

Jeff walked into the restaurant at the same time as another man. He and the other man surveyed the people in the waiting area. A couple of people waiting for their own breakfast partner surveyed Jeff and the other arrival. One pointed his finger at Jeff and said "John?" Jeff said "No," then the other new arrival pointed back and said "Brooke?" They exchanged handshakes and were seated at a table.

Jeff then pointed at the other man in the waiting area and said "Robert?" and Robert pointed back and acknowledged, "Jeff!" After the obligatory handshake, Jeff and Robert headed to a table.

Once seated, Robert commented that there was close to a billion dollars in personal wealth belonging to the occupants of the surrounding tables. Jeff didn't have a clue who these people were, but it was as good an ice-breaker as any. The discussion then transitioned into Robert and Jeff relating their interests and backgrounds.

As they methodically made their way to the topic for the meeting, they began to realize that something was wrong. Robert's face expressed confusion, and Jeff found himself feeling increasingly disoriented. Something occurred to Jeff that he had a hard time accepting. He interrupted the conversation and pointed his finger at Robert for the second time that morning. "Robert? Robert Wilson?"

Robert looked back at Jeff, and said "Jeff? Jeff Mason?"

It turned out that Robert was not the Robert Jeff had come to meet, and Jeff was not the Jeff Robert had come to meet. After seconds of disbelief and internal calculation of the odds against this happening, both laughed and stumbled through their goodbyes.

They stood up and walked back to the waiting area, where the real Robert and Jeff were waiting. This time Jeff and the wrong Robert called out the names "Robert" and "Jeff" in turn. The other Robert and Jeff responded by pointing back and saying "Jeff?" and "Robert?" As soon as each had responded, all of them knew something strange had just happened. They laughed, matched up the right Roberts with the right Jeffs and went to separate tables. That's just the kind of place Buck's was.

Now it was my turn. I don't know what I expected the place to feel like, but it seemed like a fairly conventional, semi-rural restaurant to me.

Wood-rimmed laminate tables and smooth naugahyde booths, wood-paneled wainscoting below table level, cluttered walls above. Assorted quirky novelties and large models were hung from the ceiling. The food was mostly standard fare, with some California cuisine highlights. A few tables had small groups of well-dressed people straining to read papers scattered amongst the dishes, but I didn't notice anything going on that looked particularly noteworthy. *Maybe it was a slow morning.*

I was the first to arrive, which made me a bit nervous since Alexander was the matchmaker here. As our company momentum increased, Alexander was becoming more involved in Neoforma. He was winding down his assistance to the company he and JP had invested in just before us. Initially, they had told us that they didn't think we would need much operational help because we had far more management experience than most of the entrepreneurs that they helped out. However, with the quick Venrock investment and the sudden spotlight shining on B2B Internet companies, they had decided it would be best if we had some daily help managing our growth. As the operational guy of the pair, Alexander would be helping us out in a number of areas. Jeff and I were happy for any help we could get.

Alexander is not a patient man. As he jumped into the detailed operations of Neoforma, he vacillated between admiring compliments and expressions of exasperation—with an emphasis on the latter. He liked some of the processes we had set up. He liked, for instance, that our customer and website databases were completely integrated with our business processes. Anyone could easily retrieve the current status of every customer. That was unusual for a business as young as ours.

But he believed that our sales and marketing efforts were much too modest, being based on simplicity and cost-effectiveness rather than reach and company branding. We had to GROW . . . FAST! And our website conversion, to hear Alexander tell it, was a *disaster*. Everything was improving much too slowly for Alexander's taste.

Speaking about the engineers I had hired, he told me, "These are good guys you have, but come on—they have no idea how to take you into the big leagues. They don't have experience building a world-class e-commerce system. You need the best of the best, if you are going to compete in this race!"

And naturally, Alexander had someone in mind. Three someones, actually. There was this team of three guys he knew. They were among the pioneers of e-commerce. They might be convinced to move to Neoforma. The company they were working for had been acquired a year ago by Netscape, then one of the hottest public Internet companies. They were not happy with how they had been treated during the acquisition. They believed that they had been left out of much of the process and the gains.

Alexander had tried to hire this all-star team to the company he was working with before us. They had politely turned him down. It was not a big enough market play. Alexander believed that they could be sold on the idea of Neoforma, though. Healthcare was such a huge industry, how could they find anything larger? And, if we could get a team as high-powered as they were behind us, our next funding round would be a cinch.

With Alexander, everything was always about the next funding round. Every decision was measured in units of investor return. That still bothered me.

Alexander was right about our development group, though. I liked the team we had in place, but they seemed a bit overwhelmed by the scope of our development needs. And rewriting the website was only the first of many planned steps. The next priority would be the addition of e-commerce to our site. We had completely abandoned our profitable supplier advertising model and would need to have some new revenue mechanism in place before another funding round. E-commerce, with its potential returns—not to mention the buzz it had in the press and the investment community—seemed to be the most important next target. We needed someone who had experience in this domain.

So, many conversations and much posturing had led to this breakfast meeting. Alexander was very excited and, uncharacteristically, nervous. He had kept me out of the early conversations with the all-star team. Now he believed that there was a good chance we could get these guys! He wanted me to meet them. He could see his investment swelling, if only I wouldn't screw things up. He knew I would focus on operational and cultural issues. He feared that I would downplay the scale of the Neoforma mission and opportunity.

He coached me incessantly on the importance of painting a portrait of what the company *could be*, not what it was. I was a bit hurt by his implication that we were still small fry, but I knew what he meant. He was nervous because he hadn't spent a lot of time with me in my role as motivator and employer. He had seen me only in my investor role, where I was largely deferential to Jeff. I assured him that I was perfectly able to play the part I needed to play here. After all, we had convinced him and JP to invest hadn't we?

Soon after I had sat down in the restaurant, feeling quite small and alone in the large booth, two unfamiliar men approached my table. They asked if I was Wayne. I said that I was. So they joined me and introduced themselves as Mitch and Apar. To fill the awkward moments before the whole group was assembled, Mitch and Apar exchanged gossip about several of the people who were at the restaurant. There was an Internet executive here, a well-known headhunter there, a prominent venture capitalist over there. They speculated on the purpose of their meetings. The seeds of the company they worked for were said to have been planted right here in this restaurant.

I tried to play along, as if I knew who they were talking about. I read all of the Internet industry periodicals, but I always focused on the business models, not the names of the *Players*. We made small talk.

Mitch was a tall, slightly rounded man, with functional glasses, functional clothing, functional hair. He wore a white T-shirt under his plain, short-sleeved cotton shirt (another of the stereotypical things I didn't do.) Mitch had an unsharpened pencil over his ear—also classic, but this was one of the very few times I would see the pencil over his ear. Usually, it ended up in his hand, spinning nervously between his fingers — during meetings, during conversations, while he worked, while he walked, pretty much all the time. I had no difficulty visualizing Mitch in front of a computer.

Apar was another matter. Of medium height and medium build, sharply dressed and edgily calm, his gaze took everything in. He didn't look like a programmer to me.

Alexander phoned me on my cell to tell me that he was stuck in the middle of some crisis with another company. I'd have to start without him. I could tell he was nervous about that. He had staged the meeting so carefully, coaching me on which areas he would address and which ones I would cover. I was a bit relieved though. Now I could just be me.

The purported leader of the group, Dave, was still due to arrive. We continued with small talk, since I assumed that Dave was the key guy I had to convince. I didn't want him to miss any of the preliminaries. Alexander had been working on him for two months. I had met Dave a couple of times and been impressed. He was a rarity in the industry, being several years older than I. Though he was tall and thin, his purely functional attire and inclination to stoop diluted any impression of physical dominance.

His intellectual presence was another matter. Even during the most mundane conversation, nervous energy seemed to flare from every pore. Sharp spikes of intellect and creativity would burst energetically at seemingly random intervals.

Dave arrived a half-hour late. I learned that he tended to arrive late to meetings. Actually, he tended to arrive late to everything. An avid time traveler, Dave always lived in multiple dimensions at once. The past, present and future existed simultaneously. With so many things going on inside him at once, time was just not a constant to him.

Anything that could be, should be—*now*. The slightest suggestion that something was not practical to produce *now* could send him into an all-night frenzy to prove the suggestion wrong. He would usually succeed, on the schematic level at least. The energy he directed at the improbable and the impractical was breathtaking. He didn't seem to sleep. He talked and worked so quickly and disjointedly that I could not follow him most of the time.

As part of evaluating the idea of working for Neoforma, he had produced poster-sized diagrams of the healthcare industry and our role in it. They were so extensive and complex that we could have spent decades connecting all the pieces. To him, the diagrams were illustrations of the present as he would have it. He had no inhibitions at all regarding his capabilities. He gave limits not the slightest attention.

Anything that had been, still was, happening now. The past was a major presence in the present. Any flaw exposed to him, any mistake that had been made, would flood into any decision he was about to make, creating an inner turbulence that was at times frightening to observe.

Since anything going on now had happened before and would happen again, he believed that if he had been screwed before, he was going to get screwed again. We wanted to hire him first, then have him help us recruit a team. Because he had been burned before, he told us that he wouldn't join us unless Mitch and Apar joined at the same time to reduce his risk.

Anyway, I was glad that he had finally arrived so we could get things started for real.

I asked each of them to give a summary of themselves and I gave them a description of Jeff and me. Then I moved on to an outline of Neoforma's history and development. I conveyed my enthusiasm. I played up our accomplishments. I did not exaggerate, but neither did I display my usual modesty, as Alexander had feared.

They asked very intelligent questions. Dave took us off track at every opportunity. Apar tactfully brought things back into focus. I quickly realized that Apar was actually the key decision-maker. He asked the most critical questions without the slightest hint of aggression. He clearly wanted to know what he was really getting this gang into and would have no patience with evasion or incompetence. This worked well with my natural tendency toward frankness in situations where I am asking for someone else to share some of my risk.

The only issue with which I had to be evasive was the area of compensation. Alexander had made it clear to me that I should not discuss this in any way. I was uncomfortable leaving these details to someone else. I was impressed with these guys and knew they would not only be expensive, but they would want a substantial amount of equity. I had always handled the negotiation over compensation myself, but I knew Alexander had more experience with people at this level. So I told them that any issue regarding salary or options would be handled by Alexander.

Dave made it clear that he just wanted to be compensated fairly. That's all that mattered, that we were fair. He did not want to be screwed again. Of course, I had no idea what he thought was fair. I hoped Alexander would.

Mitch seemed to like, or at least accept, most of what I said. He had one major concern: "Will I be able to have time with my wife and baby? I have put in so many hours for so many companies for so long that my family life has really suffered. Not that I won't work hard wherever I am. It's just that I don't want to continue at a burn-out pace."

This was an issue I could certainly relate to. So I responded from my heart. It would come back to haunt me almost immediately.

I told them that I firmly believed in quality and efficiency, rather than quantity and regularity. I was proud of the fact that, while we did work long hours around deadlines, the office was empty most evenings. We did not have the stereotypical office with people working every night. I told them truthfully that I ate breakfast and dinner with my family almost every day. I told Mitch that I believed that family comes first and that I hoped Neoforma would be a company that continued to value family commitment. As long as employees worked well and hard, their outside life would be accepted, if not embraced. Nobody would be ostracized for taking a vacation, as long as they didn't take it during a deadline.

I truly believed this, so I was convincing as I said it. What I did not, could not, tell them is that I wasn't the only one driving the culture anymore. It was too early for me to admit that to myself, let alone this group of relative strangers.

Alexander arrived just as we finished up the meeting. He apologized profusely and told them that he would meet with them the following week whenever and wherever they wanted. They didn't seem upset by his absence. I took this as a good sign.

After they left the meeting, Alexander asked me how I thought it went. I told him that I liked them and that, while I couldn't accurately gauge their current interest level, I thought it went well. If they didn't want the job, then they weren't the right ones for us.

So ended my first meal at Buck's. Over the next few years, I would have breakfast, lunch and dinner meetings at many of the best known haunts in the Valley, but I would never again be quite so self-conscious about playing the stereotypical role of the Valley dotcom entrepreneur. The mystique was fading. It was starting to be just another part of the job.

After a rough month-and-a-half of on-and-off negotiations, we did hire Dave, Mitch and Apar. I was proud to have a group as talented and skeptical as they were join Neoforma. They would indeed help carry us to the next level, but not without a few bumps along the way.

October 1998

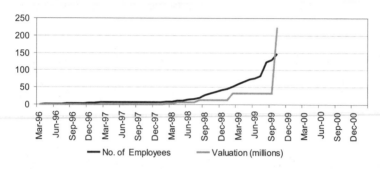

250			
200			
150			
100			
50			
0			

—— No. of Employees   —— Valuation (millions)

Neoforma Designs Website to Offer Medical Search Engine.

Online matchmaker. A website takes a page from amazon.com by linking healthcare professionals to medical products, hardware and services . . .

American Medical News
October 19, 1998

Healthcare Goes Online

Neoforma brings medical community closer via the Web. Until now, the healthcare industry has been slow to move its business processes to the Internet—but that's changing. Neoforma Inc. is joining VHA Inc. and other companies building online trading communities for the healthcare industry . . .

Information Week
October 19, 1998

Neoforma Makes Itself Indispensable to Buyers and Sellers

The reactions of some of the first buyers and sellers to Neoforma, a new market targeted at hospitals, are the kind that any infomediary could envy. These guys are doing several things right . . .

Net Market Makers
October 26, 1998

Focus

So much that hadn't been possible before suddenly seemed inevitable. We passionately came to believe that it was our responsibility to pursue every opportunity.

The Chief Medical Officer of one of the world's largest aid organizations was going to be quoted in an upcoming article saying that Neoforma was *the—sort of—"medical Yahoo" of search engines.*

We were being repeatedly compared to Yahoo and Amazon in the press, two of the most successful online businesses with a market value of more than $20 billion. And the new theory was that businesses that served businesses would be much larger than businesses that served consumers.

So there was great pressure on us to stake out as large a territory as possible. We had no credible competitors at the time, but everyone knew that some well-funded start-up would come after us soon. Rumors regarding the B2B land-rush were flying around the venture community. We were instructed to move very quickly. The process of raising our next funding round was already beginning. Alexander and JP made it clear that the more ambitious our reach, the higher our valuation would be, and the more money we could raise.

Following the *first mover* directive—the idea that the bulk of the spoils would go to the first player in a market—we were lulled into thinking of our markets *subtractively.* That is, we saw the world's healthcare markets as consisting of customers to *lose* rather than customers to *gain.* We were the clear market leader, but that did not mean that we had actually captured these scattered and complex markets at all.

At the time, projection of potential seemed more important than projection of success. *Certainly our investors didn't want us to lose any potential growth opportunity, right?*

The robust rewrite and upgrade of our website seemed like a great opportunity to add a few new features too. Our new and expanded development team was the best there was. Certainly they could handle some modest additions to the design specifications.

Denis gave me a copy of *Net Gain*, one of the latest business fad books. He told me that I had to read it, that it had great ideas on how we could monetize the value of the substantial traffic at our site. It was a book about the importance of customer participation to the success of an Internet venture. It was filled with phrases like *virtual community, member loyalty, fractal depth*, and *value extraction*.

I enjoyed the book. Even though it was focused on the consumer markets, it seemed to be talking about us. It did not provide me with any particularly new insights. We had founded Neoforma on the importance of leveraging and listening to our visitors. What the book succeeded in doing was greatly enhancing and validating the language we had used to describe what we were doing.

Many of our investors had evolved from simply being interested in the financial potential of our business to being thoroughly engaged in the intellectual challenges of predicting what would work and what wouldn't work in this new world. Other investors saw a moderately lucrative investment turning into a potential windfall. But whatever our motivations, we all began to speak a common language for the first time. And we all felt the electric energy created by knowing that we were in the middle of a spectacularly unique place and time.

Everyone's dreams were awakened. We each entertained the possibility of fulfilling previously unattainable fantasies. The problem was that we did not share common fantasies.

I wanted to improve our already-effective, supplier-messaging system and our already-cool, virtual-tours interface. I also wanted more links to other websites offering valuable content, like books on Amazon, and reports from ECRI.

Jeff wanted us to offer our own branded email addresses. (For us, *branded* meant that we used technology from other companies and put our name on it.) Hard as it would be to imagine only a couple of years later, one barrier to our growth was that a large percentage of our potential customers did not have email at work yet.

Several investors felt that we should offer connections to healthcare job listings. Alexander believed that offering space to allow healthcare aid organizations to match needs with donations would provide a valuable service and great PR. Emma wanted to implement a state-of-the-art search engine. We all wanted a simple user interface.

Each of these tasks seemed manageable for our growing staff of thirty-three. However, the sum of these tasks could have kept five times that number of people busy.

But we were special people. With proper motivation and creative energy a team like ours could achieve miracles.

That was the theory anyway.

What actually happened instead was—well, everything went wrong. Absolutely everything.

For our email system, Bret, our VC guy, wanted us to use a company he had invested in. At first, they seemed fine. They promised that they could do anything we needed. Our deadline had been determined by a major trade show.

As the date approached I realized that we would never get what we needed. I was being duped. The company didn't want to tell me bad news because of my connection to Bret. In spite of resistance from Bret, I switched to Critical Path, who would need a miracle to succeed in getting us up and running by deadline, but they would try.

Monster.com was great to work with when it came to connections for healthcare job listings, but it would really stretch them to create customized links to our system in time to meet our deadline. They said they would try.

We had endless arguments over the user interface. Everyone's level of intuition must be radically different, because we could get no agreement on what constituted an "intuitive" interface. At Alexander's insistence, we contracted an expensive *human interface* firm to help us out. They told us we needed a better user interface. They then showed us their suggestions, which clearly indicated that they didn't have a clue what was on our website or how it was used. That wasted a good month of everyone's time.

And then there was the question of *search* or *browse?* It is amazing how much time and energy can go into the simple decision on how best to lead site visitors from the home page to their destination. Should we offer them a search box to type their query into (which could lead to results that were too broad) or should we offer a complete directory of categories (which would require that they know exactly what they were looking for)? For a site that had more than a thousand kinds of forceps alone, this would've been a challenge.

Our product catalog had to be completely reformatted and integrated with ECRI and other information. This could have kept content teams with dozens of people busy for a long time. We had six people.

We were adding so much stuff at once that simply keeping track of everything taxed our development team. And we were changing all of our hardware and software applications at the same time.

Then there was the fact that the team building this new site had not worked together long. Everyone was busy being human—staking out territory, testing boundaries, establishing a pecking order. We couldn't just raise our voice and let everyone in the company know what was going on. We had grown past that stage — in size — but hadn't caught up with it in organization.

Teams would arbitrarily form to address an issue, but fail to consult with key people who were working on the same issue from another angle in a separate team.

I was still the architect of the site. I was responsible for figuring out what it should contain and how it should work. But for the first time, I didn't know every detail of the technology. I had to rely on others.

As Alexander reviewed our progress by meeting with various groups, he began to panic about the development side of the process. Nobody seemed to be reaching consensus on key technology decisions. Factions were forming. One afternoon, a livid Alexander walked into my office, closed the door and said, "I just sat in this meeting for three hours. And I'll tell you, Wayne . . . NOTHING HAPPENED! I wanted to fire everyone on the spot! Nobody takes responsibility for anything. They complain about every little petty thing! They drive me nuts, these people. We have to do something—*now!*"

Alexander reluctantly agreed to take on the daily supervision of the group. Alexander couldn't limit himself to one area. The key to getting the development effort optimized was to ensure that the connections between them and the rest of the company were efficient. So he became involved in more and more parts of the process.

In addition to my attempts to keep pieces of the site coordinated, I was busy developing particular areas of the site and running much of the company. I was so busy that, sometimes, it would be several days before I was updated about how various parts of the site were coming together. Invariably, I would be shocked when I heard about the current status of the site.

I had laid out prototypes for the entire site on walls in our development area. As each page was developed in code, a printout would replace the prototype. More often than not, there was very little resemblance between the two. Instructions I left were ignored. Critical interface issues remained unaddressed. Decisions were made that completely failed to make use of the lessons we'd learned in our earlier days.

Whenever I presented my list of corrections to Dave and Emma, who were responsible for coordinating the development and content for the site, they'd say that I was being too picky, that changes had been decided in meetings I hadn't attended, or that either Alexander or Jeff had approved the changes. Then, since Jeff was traveling much of the time, they'd complain to Alexander about how intrusive I was. They wanted to be left to do the job they felt they were hired to do. They told him, "It isn't just Wayne's site anymore!"

Alexander expressed sympathy for my dilemma, but gently insisted that I be more selective in my suggestions to the development team. We could address my other issues later. I had designed the site, now I should trust the people I had hired to build it.

This advice was contrary to an important lesson I'd learned in the past. When I designed my second restaurant in my spare time while working at Varian, it was an outside project that was more difficult than the first one. I had far more responsibility. But since it was a local project, I believed I could manage it. I struggled a bit during the design phases, just barely managing to keep up with an aggressive schedule. When the drawings were approved and the construction had begun, I was terribly relieved. It meant I could get by with far less time dedicated to the restaurant project and catch up on my Varian work.

But my distraction with my daytime job allowed the contractors to make onsite decisions and revisions without my review or supervision. The owner's bad taste, which I had so carefully restrained during the design phases, flourished in my neglect. My clear and clever design ended enshrouded in mud and mundanity. I vowed never to let this happen again.

But here I was again. It felt like a nightmare, where I was driving down a steep, bumpy dirt road without brakes, steering with a six-inch-diameter wheel. All I could do was to hold on tight and try to maintain control.

By the end of the ordeal, everyone was overworked, exhausted, grumpy, disgruntled. The one thing I couldn't complain about, the one thing that gave me hope, was that every member of the team had worked hard. Very, very hard. There were people in the office nearly every moment of every day.

As a gesture of support, I often tried to be the last one out the door at night, but I seldom succeeded. I could not stop thinking about my confident statements to Dave, Apar and Mitch, about how we were a family friendly company, providing flexibility and time with the family. Just one more thing for me to feel bad about.

In the wee hours of the morning, a week or so after our original deadline, the site was officially launched. There had been a few tense false starts where the developers had had to roll back to the original site, due to serious problems, but this time, it seemed like the site would stay live.

The next morning, I received lukewarm compliments, via email, from a handful of customers and investors regarding the site, but everyone else was furious.

In spite of the heroic efforts of the quality assurance team, our shiny new search engine could take up to a full minute—which felt like eternity—and then return irrelevant results. The pages were a muddled mess of mixed fonts and other formatting nightmares. The user interface didn't interface well at all with human users.

Our pride and joy—the catalog and supplier messaging system— was nearly impossible to find and, often, didn't deliver messages properly for those few people who did manage to find it.

To make matters worse, the colors we had selected for our navigation system made text illegible on nearly half of the computers that viewed them. Of course, all of this was true only when the site was functioning. The only consolation over how bad the site looked was that only a relatively small percent of visitors *could* visit. It was down more than it was up.

Our traffic dropped precipitously overnight from tens of thousands of visitors per day to hundreds.

I didn't go into work that day. Although my body was relatively healthy, I was feeling too sick to go anywhere. I knew that, for the first time, I would not have been able to hide my growing despair.

We had tried to be everything to everyone. All at once. In the process we turned our innocent, obedient child into an adolescent monster. On the surface, it looked much larger and more grown-up than it had been before, but it was raw and unstable underneath.

I was pissed at everyone, but could only blame myself.

November 1998

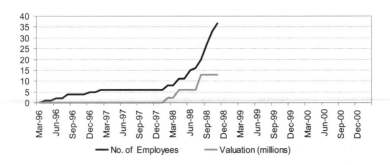

No. of Employees ——— Valuation (millions)

The Web Hotlist – Web sites worth checking out

Neoforma provides a Web-based community for healthcare professionals that showcases panoramic, 3-D photographic technology.

InfoWorld
November 23, 1998

Forget Disintermediation, Portals: There's a New Buzzword in Town

Another emerging vortex site is Neoforma.com, a Santa Clara, Calif., purveyor of health-care technology and equipment information online . . .

The Wall Street Journal Interactive Edition
November 24, 1998

One-Stop Shop

Billed as the world's largest resource on medical products, services and information, Neoforma.com . . . provides online access to an inventory of 13,000 suppliers in 8,000 different product categories . . .

Healthcare Informatics
November 1998

Make-up and Hair

As our audience grew, we had to put our best face before the cameras.

Two months earlier, in September, Junglee, which had been founded three months after Neoforma, had been sold to Amazon.com for nearly two hundred million dollars in stock. This was nearly one hundred times their annual revenue. Junglee sold software that captured information from multiple Internet sources and republished it on other websites for various uses.

This event officially launched Alexander and JP into the league of Silicon Valley Players. They were credited by their peers as having raised Junglee from obscurity to riches in less than a year. I knew that they, and those who had invested with them in Junglee, would receive a huge return on their investment.

Neoforma was to be their next success story. Alexander and JP needed to make sure that everyone knew this.

That's when Alexander brought in Lori. She was the first key employee who had been hired without my review. He brought her in to get us some exposure. Lori had worked the public relations (PR) for Junglee. Now that Junglee had been absorbed by Amazon, Lori had been put out of a job. That suited her fine.

Lori was credited—particularly by Lori—with having been the key reason Alexander and JP had been successful at making Junglee successful. She had managed the all-important flow of information between the company and the press. Beyond that, she had certainly influenced the message. It had been her idea to dress the somewhat hairy and masculine CEO of Junglee in a shapely black dress, photograph him, and use the photo in an advertising campaign.

This might have been amusing at any time, but it was particularly so because it came on the heels of an almost identical photograph that was used in an almost identical ad campaign. The other ad had featured the carefully maintained, and very feminine body, of the CEO of another software company that was trying to climb from obscurity. That other CEO just happened to be Christy Emery, wife of Bret Emery, our newest board member.

Ms. Emery's very effective ad was controversial in the community because of its blatant use of her physical, rather than her professional, characteristics. Lori's very effective parody of the ad was only controversial to the Emerys. It was quite funny to everyone else. Junglee achieved buzz. Big buzz.

In the face of possible objection by Bret, Alexander hired Lori for a repeat performance. Apparently Jeff had interviewed her and liked her, so Alexander went ahead and closed a deal with her. When he introduced her to me, during a chance encounter in an aisle, he seemed a bit awkward, "Hey . . . Wayne, this is Lori Peters. Lori ran PR at Junglee. She's brilliant at this PR stuff. Jeff interviewed her and we agreed that she is just who we need to get Neoforma the attention it deserves."

I wasn't particularly bothered by the fact that Alexander had hired a key position without including me, but I was bothered by the fact that he seemed nervous about how I might take the subtle affront to my area of focus—hiring key employees.

Lori was still riding high on her success at Junglee. Her ad campaign had been given an award by an association of her peers. She had a tough reputation to live up to now. She jumped into Neoforma with a tornado on her heels.

One of her first pet peeves was like deja vu: "The name, the name, we have to change the name . . . Neoforma doesn't *mean* anything . . . and it has at least one . . . two . . . maybe three too many syllables. It doesn't sound hip enough."

When we made it clear that the name was far too entrenched to be changed, she said, "Well, at least you have to add .com to the name. We'll get three or four times the valuation as a .com company."

I didn't like this idea at all. We had always professed that we were a company that delivered specific solutions to specific problems. The Internet was a great medium to deliver those solutions through, but it did not define us. We had been doing the same stuff before the Internet and we could do it again without the Internet.

However, the other managers and investors seemed unconcerned with my objections, and it wasn't a big enough deal to me to fight everyone. So at significant expense, we changed the official company name to Neoforma.com. *Hey, maybe it would increase our valuation. Who knows?*

Lori saw everything through the eyes of the press. And she did not like what she saw when it came to Neoforma. We weren't sexy enough. Sure, we had been covered by a few niche publications, but not the *right* publications. Not the *major* publications. Lori's two defining characteristics of a successful company were (1) being written about in the *Wall Street Journal*, and (2) being funded by Kleiner Perkins (KP).

She had made her disapproval very clear regarding the fact that KP had not funded us in our first venture round, but she still held out some hope for us. She knew we were already beginning the process of raising another venture round at the beginning of next year. She wanted very much to have an open channel to John Doerr, the legendary partner at KP. In Lori's world, that would be the pinnacle of success.

She figured the best thing she could do to get us in the target of KP would be to get Neoforma in the *Wall Street Journal*. In spite of the fact that Lori came close to getting us covered by the *Journal* several times, we were always bumped at the last second by breaking news. To her frustration, the *Journal* didn't cover us for almost a year. However, through Lori's work, Neoforma did get covered by an increasing array of minor and major periodicals. They liked our big market and our spinning rooms.

Early in her initiation into the company, Lori often came into my office to brief me on a few of her contacts with the press, dropping names that I was supposed to recognize, but didn't. Then she would begin chatting. About everything.

I always liked the first minute of her briefing. After that, well, I had many things to do, so I would tune her out and avoid any suggestion of interest, like a shrug or accidental raised eyebrow, hoping she'd take the hint. When that didn't work, I'd say something like, "Well, thanks for the update, Lori. I really need to get back to this report I'm working on."

After awhile, she spent far more time with Jeff. He was much more inclined to listen to her talk. His natural amiability made it difficult for him to send someone away.

So I suppose it was inevitable that one day Lori would walk into my office and say, "You know, Alexander and I have been talking . . . and we both agree that Neoforma needs to be associated with a single individual. I know that previous articles have focused on both of you as founders, but now the company is getting bigger, and the symbolic role of the CEO is becoming more important. We need to convey that this is not just some start-up company anymore. Neoforma has been around a long time. That will become a major difference between us and the inevitable competitors that will appear."

Lori was a star-maker. And she liked Jeff. He had charm and good credentials. She believed that Jeff could be made into something of a celebrity, like the CEO at Junglee. It's even possible that, at this point, she actually believed that Jeff was the only one running the company.

It is one of my biggest fears to be recognized in some public place by someone I don't know. So I thought, let Jeff be the front man. Let him be the one to wear the shapely black dress in the photos. I had to admit that I'd much rather be the guy behind the scenes.

Now that the VCs were in the picture, I even liked the fact that Jeff, as CEO, had to go to all of the investor networking meetings. I didn't want to go and he was much better at it than I was anyway. So I really couldn't complain about her desire to groom him for a role in the public eye. But I was uneasily aware that the warnings from Wally and Denis were gradually coming true. This was clearly one more step toward losing my grip on the company we had created and nurtured for so long.

December 1998

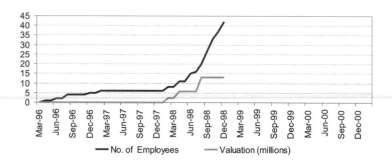

— No. of Employees   — Valuation (millions)

Net Sites Take Liaison Role in Biz-to-Biz Transactions

. . . Neoforma Inc., for instance, provides information on hospital supplies . . . Infomediaries are gaining in popularity. Since its founding two years ago, Neoforma, a Santa Clara, Calif.–based company, has brought in more than 15,000 hospital product suppliers on its Web site . . .

Investor's Business Daily
December 14, 1998

Bluescreen

Partitions, earlier erected for protection, now imprisoned the architect.

Since the day that we had enabled our website visitors to communicate with manufacturers of medical equipment, we had been receiving email from people who couldn't find what they were looking for on our site. We displayed a huge directory of products and manufacturers, so I can imagine what visitors might have imagined Neoforma to be. They probably pictured rooms full of dedicated employees, busily chatting on the phone with all sorts of people in the healthcare industry.

Actually, that is pretty much what it was like, only on a much smaller scale than people imagined. There were only a few of us interacting with customers. The rest of the employees were busy keeping the website running and growing. Much of my interaction with customers was with those outside the Unihted States. This was very satisfying because international visitors were effusively grateful for the resources we had made available to them. Due to time zone and language disparities, they had been accustomed to the slow and frustrating process of sending faxes to request information on products. A simple question might take a week of iteration to get an answer. In most cases, we could cut that to a day or less.

As Neoforma grew and we established a department dedicated to assisting customers, I received fewer and fewer new messages. However, to maintain at least some connection with the customers, there were a few visitors I kept in contact with. They'd send me requests for information regarding who made this gadget or that, not knowing that I was the president of the company and usually delegated such inquiries. I'd spend whatever time it took to dig up any tidbits of information I could find in order to service them. This connection to our original purpose was very important to me.

At a moment when I was at the peak of frustration over the company's growing pains, I received a Christmas greeting from Anton. It cheered me up immediately.

Anton was one of my favorite visitors. He was a distributor of medical equipment in Moscow. Whenever he was trying to find medical equipment for a hospital in his region, he used Neoforma. When he discovered that some piece of information on our site was out-of-date, he would send me the updated information. When he couldn't find something, he would send a message to notify me.

His messages were always polite, intelligent and grateful. He would send messages just to say hello and tell me that he hadn't sent any messages lately because he had been finding everything he needed on the site. And when he sent me that holiday message, he helped me through a tough time without ever knowing it.

Since founding Neoforma, I had not looked forward to the end-of-year holidays. We always seemed to be running low on money in November and December, which coincided with a time when almost all investment activity ceases for six weeks or so.

This was the first year that Neoforma had enough money to survive through the holidays, but I felt worse than ever. I had an intense case of the holiday blues.

For the first time in many years, I actually had a few weeks with very little that I *had* to do. I spent some time helping the programmers with their frantic website repairs. Hiring slowed down during the holidays. I wouldn't be involved in fundraising activities until January. New development was postponed until the new website was stabilized, which also wouldn't be until January.

This respite might have been pleasant had there not been several years of unrelieved stress waiting for an opportunity to break out.

Rushing to fill the lull, my postponed feelings poured in, bursting partitions and flooding crevices. The sediment was washed away, leaving exposed areas of raw emotion.

I didn't want to let go, but knew I had to let go. I suddenly became vividly aware of my overwhelming personal financial risk and dwindling control over that risk, of my pride over the value I had helped create and my anxiety over losing that value, of my failure to cheer others up and the failure to cheer myself up as well. To put it another way—I was depressed.

Everything that I had helped create was staring back at me from a computer screen—in the form of a page on the Neoforma website. It was frozen introspection.

Logging on, I attempted a search.

When the site entered its third minute, searching for a response to my simple query, I peered over the screen, through the window of my darkened office. I saw tired engineers in their cubicles, struggling to bring order to chaos. And felt helpless to assist them.

In the absence of productive activity, I could only focus on my increasing sense of failure. Trying to shake my sense of unease, I got up and wandered the aisles, struggling to smile, to offer compliments, encouragement and suggestions. Then I returned to my office and closed my door, which I had seldom done before. I stared blankly at the screen again, my thoughts and feelings washing over me, unabated.

One day, I found myself thinking about the call I had received a couple of weeks earlier from a woman who was reviewing a credit application I had filled out. She expressed concern over what she was reading. My income-to-debt ratio was not good. She said, "Don't you have some other kind of investments . . . you know, stocks or bonds . . . that sort of thing?"

I said, "No, I really haven't had time to focus on outside investments." Then, after a pause I said, "Well, there is the stock I have in Neoforma. Based on the last funding round, that would be worth . . . um . . . about two million dollars. Now . . . just be clear . . . this is a private company and that stock is not liquid at all."

She told me that she understood the risk factors, but said it still counted as a two million dollar investment. I was startled by her matter-of-fact acceptance of the monetary value that had been assigned to Neoforma.

As I typed in one fruitless search after another on the Neoforma website, it seemed absurd to think of Neoforma having this kind of value. On the other hand, I could not give up hope that someday it would again deliver amazing value to customers like Anton, who had come to rely on us in our early days.

Without that hope, I would have been completely lost.

I was feeling an increasing sense of dread. I even dreaded facing the fact that I needed to escape my increasing sense of dread. I was not unfamiliar with depression, but this time I did not have the luxury to indulge it. Because I had so much invested, financially and emotionally, into Neoforma, I was anxious that the company depended so much on me. I felt that if I dropped my guard for a moment, the increasing pressures on the company would overwhelm me. And, if I were overwhelmed, the threat to the company would increase—which would make me even more anxious. If that was the risk of introspection, I couldn't afford it.

In my struggle to relieve the pressure, I chose to delegate control at almost every juncture where I could, to make the company less dependent on me. From my point of view, almost every time I let go of a task, a whirlwind of chaos and disaster had resulted. In attempting to hold things together, my panicked grip became tighter and more painful. But gripping so tightly only increased the tendency for control and composure to escape under the pressure. I was losing myself.

And then there was the deteriorating relationship with my wife.

As the complexity and intensity of my work at Neoforma increased, my ability to communicate with Anni had decreased. In my hours off work, I had difficulty slowing the frenetic journey from problem to solution. My thoughts and speech patterns became terribly efficient—not the best for intimate conversation. I had shifted into a mode of solving problems, not talking about them. The tension this created between us was inevitable.

As the enormity of risk I had placed upon my family increased, so did my desire to separate the pressures I experienced at work from the time I spent at home. The last thing I wanted to do was scare Anni and the kids with the reality that our entire lifestyle was balanced on a knife-edge.

I had been tucking this stress into this compartment and that stress into that compartment, all nicely controlled by a central load-balancing system. At work, the system worked pretty well. There, I was able to hide my emotions with relative ease. My tendency to keep everyone at a safe distance helped me maintain a fairly consistent composure.

At home, that was a bit more difficult. Most successful relationships are built upon a foundation of beliefs and feelings that have been shared at very intimate levels. Mine and Anni's certainly was. We both needed and craved the rejuvenation of our intimacy. It was what made us more than two.

But, increasingly, our pursuit of intimacy was interrupted by the grip that Neoforma had over me. Any time we breached the surface tension, dangerous hairline cracks would appear in my carefully constructed compartments. A kiss could release the memory of a sad or stressful interview or the most recent incident of someone crying in my office — an almost daily occurrence now. A needy hug might trigger a jolting moment of panic that I had forgotten to pay a bill or communicate some key instruction.

My ability to connect was dissolving. My libido had dwindled to a dull flatness for extended periods. The fear of letting go had become my survival mechanism. I couldn't risk it.

In the earlier days of Neoforma, Jeff and I had been able to talk about nearly anything that was bugging us. We had vented our stress on each other nearly every day, arguing aggressively, holding nothing back, knowing that once one of us had exhausted his opinions or complaints, we would each go back to our business, still friends.

As the pressures on us increased, Jeff and I spoke with decreasing frequency. We'd go a week or so without talking. When we did meet, we had little to share beyond a cursory acknowledgment of the feeling that we were being increasingly entangled in a web of our own creation.

His role was focusing outside the company. My role was focusing inside the company. Alexander's presence had driven a stake right down the middle. Once Jeff and I stopped regularly venting our emotions with each other, our simple disagreements tended to explode into nearly violent incidents. Of course, thick-skinned guys that we were, we did not take the time to look at why we'd get so pissed off at each other. We each just assumed that the other was becoming increasingly irrational. It became easier for us to simply avoid each other.

There were many people at Neoforma that I liked very much. Many that I might have become friends with under other circumstances. However, Jeff and I had learned early on — through Cassandra and others — that there was, that there had to be, a solid wall between the two of us and the employees. If either of us were to display the slightest indecision or weakness due to a personal friendship with an employee, the entire company would suffer. So I couldn't turn to anyone at Neoforma for help.

Of course, I didn't believe I needed help, exactly. But Anni disagreed. As patient as she had been with me over the last several years, she became increasingly insistent that I get some outside help. It was that, or learn to deal with being single again.

So, although I was definitely not comfortable with the idea of asking for help, I figured that I might be okay with asking for advice. I was having a natural reaction to an unfamiliar, but not entirely unique situation. I thought that there must be people out there who specialized in advising company executives on how to handle the stresses associated with chaotic growth.

I asked a human resources manager whom I respected if there were anyone who specialized in this situation. She recommended someone who said, "Oh, you're looking for an executive coach. Well, I have a couple of great recommendations for you. One is a woman who I have had great feedback on. The other is an extraordinary man named Greg. He certainly isn't right for everyone and he won't work with everyone. But if you are able to connect with him, he's the best."

Executive coach. That sounded okay. I could ask for some coaching. After all, I hadn't founded a large company before. This was all new. I wouldn't be admitting personal weakness. I'd just be bringing in another consultant. We had certainly hired plenty of those.

Once I had bought into my rationalization for hiring someone, I interviewed the two recommended coaches. The first interview was not memorable. The second interview was something else entirely.

The man I met did not fit my image of the suited business consultant. Greg Brodsky was dressed casually and appeared to be in his forties. He sported a shiny bald head, sparkling eyes and a knowing smile. He was of average height, but moved with a confidence that projected a larger presence. I'd later learn that he was actually in his sixties.

Greg relied less on his college education and business experience than on his forty years of practice with assorted martial arts and his study of neurolinguistic programming. He was not a psychologist, but he knew a lot about people. His unconventional background and style were very appealing to me. I found him very easy to communicate with, though I could see why he wouldn't be right for everyone. He did not waste words. He had no preferred theory of human behavior. Whatever worked was the right thing to do. And he had no shortage of things to try. So, I agreed to meet with him and try a few things.

Since Greg was not a psychologist, I thought I might be able to avoid digging into my emotions and focus instead on behaviors to improve my stress management. I figured some good advice on how to make me more efficient would reduce the stress to a manageable level. It didn't work out that way.

No matter how superficial I tried to keep an issue I discussed with him, Greg managed to get me to expose the roots of my response to the issue. Some of those roots went very deep.

I met with Greg for about a year, with dwindling frequency. We did "good work", as he called it. He gave me the tools to better manage my stress. He helped me and I accepted that help. It was a big deal for me to accept help.

I had felt very alone in my inability to inwardly cope with my stress and inadequacies. It was not until years later that I would read disclosures by several well-known executives describing the bouts of extreme depression they had suffered. I didn't hide under my desk for hours at a time, as one had, but I certainly would have welcomed the idea that such an escape was possible. It would have helped to know earlier that I wasn't alone after all, that it is okay to admit limitations and seek help.

January 1999

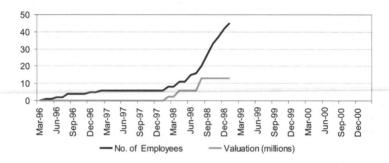

| | No. of Employees | Valuation (millions) |

The Magistrate

Many of industry's renowned mavericks and iconoclasts do not convey their depth and complexity during routine encounters. But some do.

Our software developers had worked almost nonstop for two months—and straight through the holiday season—to get our new website under control. Fortunately, our customers and investors had been largely quiet during the end-of-the-year holidays.

In addition to the fact that there was a lull in my responsibilities, I had finally found someone to help build and maintain the shell that contained and protected Neoforma. This was a huge relief to me.

Roy had been one of my toughest hires. He had a challenging, well-paying job in a large software company. He was about to take a long-delayed sabbatical. An operations job at a healthcare software company was a poor fit to his vision of the future.

About halfway through 1998, Jeff and I finally admitted that the company couldn't survive in our cramped quarters for much longer.

Neoforma's presence in our building had grown from a single small office to six offices of assorted sizes, scattered disjointedly about the building. We had twenty employees, along with servers and file cabinets, in an area that could uncomfortably accommodate ten. We had three or four people jammed into offices meant for one. Jeff and I shared one of the smaller offices with Steve. If we leaned back in our chairs, we bumped heads. To make matters worse, Steve had one of the loudest voices I had ever heard. And he liked to use it.

At first, these tight quarters were invigorating. We fed off of each other's energy. Communication was very efficient, since everyone could hear what was going on everywhere.

But not everyone could get along with everyone else in such tight quarters. As our activities became more frenzied, tensions began to build. And these small rooms had not been designed for such high heat loads. Tempers got shorter as the temperature rose each day.

The premium price we had paid at the office suite had been very cost effective when we had only had one or two offices. Now the costs were very high compared with other locations.

Then there was another small detail: we planned to fill thirty job openings by year's end.

Had I envisioned this situation years before, I would have seen myself as the empowered architect, preparing to modify or construct the ideal space to house, nurture and express the company I had helped create. In reality, this was just one more distracting thing to do.

I calculated that we needed about ten thousand square feet of space to accommodate our projected growth for the next two years.

We contacted a pair of commercial real estate brokers who had been recommended to us. Ron and Brad were trim, clean-cut youths. They were clearly basking in the glow of an increasingly robust economy.

They informed us that we should not set our expectations very high, considering how little we were willing to pay and how narrow an area we were willing to consider. Our employees were scattered equally north, south, east and west from our current office. We wanted to minimize the disruption that a move would cause, so we drew a seven-mile circle around our building and defined it as our search area.

It turned out that the type and size of space we were looking for was exactly the one that was most popular at the time. Just a month earlier there had been a glut of such spaces on the market, but the sudden rise in venture-funded start-ups had snapped up most of the desirable starter-size spaces.

Prepared for the worst, Jeff and I hopped into Ron's Mercedes and viewed an assortment of available spaces. I had definitely not lowered my expectations adequately. What they showed us was dramatically below what we'd expected.

Seeing our reactions, Ron and Brad encouraged us to look at slightly pricier locations or expand our search radius. During several tours, we caught sight of the vapor trails of companies ahead of us on the dotcom path. We walked through the dark, vacated offices of

WebTV, which had been acquired by Microsoft. We visited the buzzing, soon-to-be-vacated offices of Hotmail, which had been acquired by Microsoft.

We did see a couple of buildings we liked in the higher price range, but they had already been leased by the time we agreed to pursue them the following day.

The way I figured it, I'd rather have forty-nine employees sharing a pleasant space than have fifty employees sharing a dark, uncomfortable space. That was the financial difference between the desirable and the undesirable spaces we had seen.

JP, Alexander and Bret from Venrock saw it quite differently. In my scenario there would be one less person working toward a return on their investment. Bret was indignant, "We need to spend every possible penny of our money on *people*—not space!"

I briefly visualized an idyllic office space with happy, fulfilled employees skipping around with youthful energy. It was a brief moment of weakness. But, measured against our other priorities, I realized that the minimum space would have to do. There were more important things for me to focus my attention on.

During a rare visit by Bret, Jeff and I summarized our frustration to him, as well as JP and Alexander, at not being able to find a suitable home for Neoforma. Bret said, "What about Arrillaga? He must have some space available that would suit you."

"Who is Arrillaga?"

Alexander frowned. "He has more than fifty million square feet of office space in the Valley."

I wasn't sure, but I thought I saw something unfamiliar in Alexander's eyes—something beyond respect, something like intimidation. Alexander was never intimidated.

I did some research.

The Top 25 Power Brokers in Silicon Valley
JOHN ARRILLAGA, 60

As dealmaker for one of the area's top landowners, the secretive developer calls the shots when it comes to doling out precious office space. Normally, he only provides facilities to companies

that can pay cash. But if Arrillaga senses a winner, as he did
when Sun Microsystems and Quantum were start-ups, he gives
lenient terms — and then collects rents as they grow . . .

BusinessWeek
August 25, 1997

Apparently, Arrillaga was something of a local legend, a magistrate
whose empire had grown with every Silicon Valley boom. By pairing
himself with successful companies, he had turned land into gold. His
net worth was reported to be quickly approaching a billion dollars.

Jeff had been told by Ron and Brad that Arrillaga was an avid and
dedicated supporter of Stanford University. So Jeff called Arrillaga and
chatted about various things, including the fact that since receiving
his MBA at Stanford, Jeff had continued to be active in the Engineering
department. He was able to up an appointment for us to meet with
Arrillaga.

Alexander cautioned us, "If Mr. Arrillaga likes you, he'll be able to
get you just about anything you want. If he doesn't like you, he will
have nothing available."

Beyond that, he did not coach us, which was quite uncharacteristic.
He usually had VERY specific advice about everything. But this time,
he was restrained. And I had never heard him refer to anyone else as
"Mister." My curiosity was piqued.

We had an obligation to contact our brokers, Ron and Brad, and
tell them that we were meeting with Arrillaga. After bringing them up
to date, we asked, "Why didn't you tell us about Arrillaga?"

They paused, looked at each other, and said, "Um . . . Mr. Arrillaga
does not get along well with brokers, but we'd like to come along to
the meeting . . . so that we can help you negotiate with him."

Jeff and I thought it made sense for them to come along. After all,
they *had* put a lot of time into showing us various buildings.

Ron and Brad drove us to Arrillaga's non descript, tilt-up, concrete
industrial office building. We walked into a small, simple reception
room and announced ourselves.

Ron and Brad seemed very nervous. That made Jeff and me nervous.
We were perplexed that a man of Arrillaga's stature would be meeting
with us simple folk on short notice, without our being screened by

someone else. I guessed dropping the Venrock name had some influence on that.

After a short wait, the receptionist led us into a large, elongated office. At one end, facing the door, was a large wooden desk. Stacks of files and papers were scattered on and around the desk. Apart from the fact that the room was decorated in rich, dark wood, there was little formality about the office.

Behind the desk was a large man who wore his sixty years comfortably. He was speaking loudly into a phone, gesticulating wildly. He was expressing his displeasure about something. His tone was firm and polite. I thought I sensed viciousness under the surface, but maybe it was just confidence, as if he knew that he was holding all of the best cards.

Mr. Arrillaga waved us to his desk, smiling. Ron, Brad, Jeff and I stood awkwardly in front of his desk. There were only two chairs.

Arrillaga spoke into the phone for a few minutes longer, seemingly oblivious to us. After hanging up the phone, he stood and vigorously shook hands with Jeff and me. He did not acknowledge Ron or Brad.

"Jeff. Wayne. Sit down." He nodded his head toward Ron and Brad and, keeping his focus entirely on us, said, "Oh, and those two can sit in the chairs over there. They won't be participating in this conversation."

He pointed to chairs in a nook at the far end of the room, at least fifteen feet behind Jeff and me. Ron and Brad obeyed, but I knew they were seething at the indignity. Gone was their fantasy of using this visit as an opportunity to get tight with the infamous Arrillaga.

He sat down, leaned forward and said, "So, tell me about yourselves and this company you've started."

Jeff and I took turns giving our well-practiced biographies and company description. Arrillaga was the first person of position who seemed genuinely pleased when I said I was an architect.

He asked us a few pointed questions about Neoforma. "I suppose you've put a bunch of money you don't have into your company, rather than simply relying on those venture guys."

We said, "Well, yes. We have a great deal of our own skin in this game."

He said, "You know, it's people like you that make this Valley so great . . . not useless predators, like those guys in the back of the room." Ron and Brad, who could easily hear us from their exile, squirmed some more, avoiding eye contact.

He paused, leaned back in his chair and looked each of us deeply in the eyes. His manner changed entirely from charming interviewer to efficient problem-solver. Then he said, "Okay. What kind of space are you looking for?" I described the type and size we needed. He said, "Oh. There aren't very many places that size available."

I said, "We know."

He called in an assistant and asked her about the status of several of his buildings. He said to us, "I have some great buildings just being completed in San Mateo. I can give you a good deal on those." I told him that San Mateo was outside of our search area. He was disappointed. "You're sure? They beat anything you'll find around here."

I said, "Yes, we're sure."

Then he told us about the Scott building, which he thought would best suit us. It was just across the freeway in the very heart of the Valley. There were a couple of other buildings he wanted us to see. He described the buildings to Ron and Brad, acknowledging them for the first time in awhile. He said, "And show them the Menlo space. It might just appeal to these guys."

Ron protested that he didn't think the Menlo space was a fit. Arrillaga interrupted him and issued a stern order: "SHOW THEM THE SPACE."

That afternoon, we saw the buildings Arrillaga had suggested. As we parked in front of the Menlo space, Brad apologized for taking us there. "Arrillaga has been trying to lease this space forever. You'll see why when we go inside."

The building, a particularly poorly designed, single-story, tilt-up building, didn't look promising from the outside, but the location was good. I remember thinking that we could live with it. But we didn't enter the front door. Instead, we walked up some stairs in a vestibule at the corner of the building and entered through an unlabeled doorway.

The building's attic had been converted into office space. Since it was not designed to be a two-story building, the ceiling was about seven feet high. The only light that entered the warren of arbitrarily placed walls came from the top two feet of the widely spaced narrow windows that protruded through the floor at the edges of the building. The acoustic tiles that had been glued to the ceiling were chipped and discolored.

Much to the chagrin of Ron and Brad, Jeff and I kind of liked the space. I saw why Arrillaga had directed us here. It was so bad, and so cheap, that it appealed to the sensibilities of our pre-funding days. It reminded me of my old beachfront nook.

Our consideration of the space was short-lived, though. Once we left the building, we realized that our new crop of employees might not appreciate our eccentricities.

The last building that we saw was the one that Arrillaga had considered the best fit. He was right. It was very middle-of-the-road. Neither opulent nor dilapidated. With a little work, it would do just fine. We were very tired of the distraction of looking at buildings and we were approaching thirty employees. Several people had to work from home. The rest were getting grumpier by the day.

I met Arrillaga alone the second time. "The Scott building looks okay. But $2.95 per foot is a bit over our target price."

He paused, took a deep breath, and said, "What do you want to pay?"

I tried to sound firm as I said, "$2.50."

He glared at me with an expression that could have been irritation or admiration. I held his gaze, with great effort. He said, "Okay. I can do $2.50 . . . under one condition. When you grow out of the building, you come to me for your next building. If I can give you what you need, I'll give it to you at a fair price and you will not go elsewhere. If I don't have what you need, then you can look anywhere."

Because he seemed to be the only guy in the Valley that had space available and because I felt that I could trust his word, I accepted these terms. We shook hands. I told him, "We need it as soon as possible. We have already spent far too much time finding a place."

"Don't worry about that." He called in his assistant. "Get me the plans for the Scott building." While she was locating the plans, he swept the clutter on his desk toward the edges.

After the assistant handed him the plans, he unrolled them on his desk, pulled a pencil and an architectural scale from a drawer, and said, "Okay. So you say you need about fifteen offices, three conference rooms, a server room and a lunchroom. You'll need about half of this building."

As he spoke, he efficiently drew lines on the plans. I liked his hands-on approach. I was in very comfortable territory. I knew the applicable building codes and how to efficiently share aisles and such. We worked well together.

I told him, "We need to have adequate space in the lunchroom for a ping-pong table." This was one Silicon Valley stereotype I was determined to fulfill. I justified it by pointing out that we would need extra space for larger gatherings and presentations.

Within fifteen minutes, we had a floor plan. He asked me, "Will this suit your needs?"

"Yes, it will."

He picked up the phone and dialed a number from memory. "Mark, get a crew to the Scott building. Have them clean it up. I'll get you some plans on the tenant improvements later today."

He made a copy of the plan for me to take. "Alright, we're done. Let me know soon if you need any changes to the layout. They'll start new construction tomorrow. You should be able to move in about three weeks."

I was stunned. This type of project usually took months. I asked him how he could get permits that quickly. He shrugged, smiled, and said, "Let me worry about that. You have a business to run."

I asked about the paperwork. "Don't you need some kind of application and financial statement from us?"

He said, "Our handshake is enough to get things going. Let the brokers take care of the lease papers. They should earn at least a small portion of their commission. You'll find our terms to be very fair."

In my excitement, I drove straight from Arrillaga's office to Neoforma's new home. I wanted to visualize how it would look based on the plans we had just drawn up. When I arrived there, not fifteen minutes after parting with Arrillaga, several construction crews were already busy doing demolition work. When I walked inside the foreman greeted me, "Hi. Are you the new tenant?"

"Um . . . Yes, I guess I am."

We started with half of that building. Later, we would take over the entire building. And then the one next door.

I was stunned by how easy the process was. Since the inception of Neoforma, Jeff and I had been required to submit our personal financial statements with every credit or lease application and personally offer our assets as collateral. This time, a whisper from one of our investors had been enough. Things were changing. One more fiber connecting me, the individual, to Neoforma, the organization, had been severed.

And with that, my need to take full responsibility for Neoforma's protection had been eased. I pursued our open positions for people to take over our operations with renewed vigor. By the time I'd found Roy, his position was so important, so personal to me that I threw every hiring technique I had learned at him. He didn't have a chance. My efforts were handsomely rewarded. He was very good at what he did. I never worried about Neoforma's home again.

February 1999

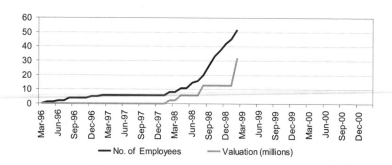

Shadows

We were surprised by how long it took for the imitators to arrive. We were even more surprised by how large their flock was.

Nearly three years after starting Neoforma we caught our first glimpse of real, potential competition — mere shadows of shapes, moving along the periphery.

Almost from the beginning, there had been one company with a website trying to do something like ours, but, of course it was nothing like ours. We were ambitious, smart and experienced. They were — well, we didn't know anything about them, but we figured they were probably a couple of medical equipment service guys trying out a few ideas in their spare time. We didn't feel threatened by them, but we did pay attention to them. You never know when someone else might stumble onto a good idea.

They paid attention to us too. When we changed the design of the pages we created to direct traffic to us from the search engines, a week or so later, they duplicated our techniques. When we switched our site background from white to black, sure enough, theirs became black within a couple of weeks. It was irritating, but quite flattering.

That anonymous group of fellow pioneers eventually wandered off the trail, never to be seen again. I sometimes wonder if they continued to watch Neoforma. I imagine them sitting together, and occasionally setting down their beers, to say, "That could have been us. Those guys didn't have shit on us . . . and just look at what happened to them. Bastards!"

But the whiff of competition was different this time. We weren't the only Internet healthcare company getting attention.

At the beginning of February, we hired our first celebrity. Well, he wasn't really a celebrity. We just thought of him that way because we were celebrating the arrival of a guy who would later come to be known simply as "Sonic."

Alexander, JP and Jeff had hired him. Through some of his connections to the software industry, JP knew of Sonic and his reputation. Sonic was a well-known, high-level salesperson from one of the largest software companies in the area. He was the kind of guy who received daily calls from headhunters offering lucrative jobs. He had choices. And he had chosen Neoforma.

I first met Sonic after he had been hired. He walked into my office, rolled the extra chair to my side of the desk, straddled it casually, tinkered with some trinkets on the credenza, glanced smoothly up at me and said, in a slightly Southern, good ol' boy accent, "So, I'm told you're the guy who's running quite a few things around here. Tell me what you think Neoforma is about."

Sonic was a big guy, well-groomed, but not over dressed. He wasn't yet known as Sonic, but would be soon because of his always close-cut hair, which resembled the spiky coat of a hedgehog. There was a computer game with a character named Sonic the Hedgehog. The character didn't actually have close-cut hair or resemble a hedgehog, but the moniker seemed to stick.

Sonic was smooth. He was charming. His first phrase was carefully constructed to stroke my ego. And so was every other phrase. He used a very effective, self-deprecating style — *I don't know anything about this, but I sure want to learn all about it from you.* He was a relationship guy, used to discussing large deals over expensive lunches. That's why we hired him. Sonic was the guy who would later ensure that he could always get a table at a prestigious Palo Alto restaurant by putting the maitre d' on the list of people who would be able to buy early Neoforma IPO stock.

After getting to know the company, Sonic went on the road, wandering the halls of many venerable hospitals for about three weeks, then returned to give us his first summary of where he thought Neoforma was in the eyes of hospital executives.

He had some good things to say. We had fairly good name recognition. Nobody had anything really bad to say about us. The executives *did* consider their supply chain process to be a major candidate for improvement.

But the most interesting information of all was that he heard people in healthcare talking about a new company called Medibuy. They were talking about how much Medibuy was saying bad things about Neoforma. Medibuy was telling anyone who would listen how much better they were than Neoforma. Medibuy was picking a fight. This was not necessarily a bad thing. In a business focused on fighting microscopic bugs and invisible diseases, everyone loved to see fights play out on a grander scale. Healthcare execs were getting excited about us for the first time.

At that point, Medibuy had a very simple website, consisting primarily of a list of categories of hospital equipment. Each category name was a link that, when selected, would send an email message to Medibuy. Medibuy's entire business consisted of a couple of materials managers picking up the phone and contacting manufacturers to ask them for money in exchange for a customer lead. That's it.

I have to admit that it was a clever ploy. We had yet to solve the problem of how to force manufacturers to actually respond to the customer requests we forwarded to them. We sent them faxes if they didn't use email and we called them if they didn't respond to the faxes, but we still held true to the idea of not becoming another hurdle in the communication process. We insisted that manufacturers respond directly to their customers.

By sending false messages through our messaging system, the low-tech materials manager who had founded Medibuy discovered that many manufacturers were slow to respond to customers, or didn't respond at all. They decided to exploit this weakness in our system. Instead of dealing with the inadequate resolution of a percentage of the tens of thousands of messages per month we had, Medibuy chose to carefully hand-carry a small number of messages to manufacturers. Almost overnight, they were able to look like us.

A little research on our end revealed that Medibuy was funded by second-tier venture money. It wasn't top-tier money, but money was money. Using us as the measure of their potential, they had been given more money in their first few months of existence than we had received in our first few years.

For awhile, we were indignant that a company had stepped into our spotlight with such ease, instantly benefiting from our efforts in defining a new industry. But soon, we realized that, as long as we were ahead—and we were still very far ahead—the efforts of competitors would simply enhance and validate our standing.

Hospital personnel became more enthusiastic and attentive. Manufacturers and distributors became more polite and cautious. Venture firms began calling us. Our employees became a bit less complacent, a bit more nervous and a bit more focused.

A few months later, we discovered that another competitor was being formed at about the same time as Sonic's first presentation to us. A team of well-connected techies who had just sold their previous company were looking for their next big thing. They had narrowed in on the healthcare supply chain because of its huge financial potential.

They were supposed to be a big secret, but we knew about them— who they were, what their strategy was, who they were courting. They spent months studying us and then our limited competitors. They gave each other presentations about how they could do things so much better than Neoforma by embracing the distributors rather than threatening them. These undoubtedly bright minds thought this was an original idea.

We had dealt with the distributors many times over the last couple of years. We knew that their idea wouldn't work and we knew why it wouldn't work. We had already tried it. They could have asked us. We would have been happy to tell them, but they didn't ask.

Instead, they found some fresh investors and hustled thirty million dollars or so to go after us, calling us "the 800 pound gorilla." A few carefully presented statements by us at investor and customer conferences were all that was required to squelch their plans, but not all of the competitors were so easy to deal with.

Over the next two years, we would document the steady increase in our number of competitors, until the list included more than one hundred legitimate companies. Dozens of these companies received substantial investment, from millions to hundreds of millions of dollars.

All targeted at us. From that February on we were constantly distracted by the need to glance over our shoulder, ready to duck as each shadow enlarged over our head, wondering if this one would be the one to strike hard enough to cause damage.

March 1999

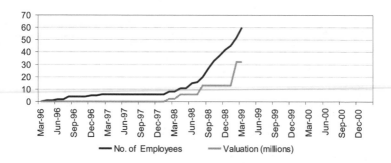

Legend: No. of Employees — Valuation (millions)

Neoforma, Inc., the online leader in the business-to-business global electronic healthcare marketplace, today announced it has completed a $12 million third round of equity funding led by Delphi Ventures. The round also included investments by TCW/ICICI Investment Partners, Venrock Associates, Amerindo Investment Advisors, MedVenture Associates, TTC Ventures, and Comdisco Ventures.

Neoforma Press Release
March 9, 1999

The Coup

I was feeling much better about things. Experience should have warned me that this was a bad sign.

The website had steadily improved over the previous couple of months. I still wasn't happy with it as a whole, but I was very happy with parts of it.

I focused most of my time on the capital equipment planning portion of the website. I was glad to have the luxury of having my hands on the product again. I was helping to create something *and* I was able to attend trade shows and meet with the customers who were benefiting from our work.

I was getting better at releasing things, without letting go, and at subtly guiding others, without infringing upon their need to control their own outcomes. I was getting better at accepting the choices of others, even when I disagreed with them. I was learning that I could trust others to get it right—if not the first time, then at least by the second or third.

In other words, I was backing off, giving everyone else — and myself—a break. My drive to do more and better, *right now*, was dissipating into a desire to do more and better, *eventually*. My newly relaxed work style provided me with a better perspective on what a pain-in-the-butt I could be.

And now, only the capital planning group had to deal with my fussy side. But even there, I had delegated much of my authority to someone I trusted. So I would only irritate people here and there, now and then.

I was becoming an active observer rather than a central force and the break was nice. It gave me the opportunity to release some of the last three years' stress.

When I'd stare out of my office window at the cubicles beyond, I'd notice an argument or bit of celebratory distraction and enjoy the momentary equilibrium between my need to interfere and my need to let it go. I wasn't disengaged. I was simply more balanced.

Neoforma was back in the fundraising mode. I wasn't much involved in it. Alexander and JP were setting up meetings with name-brand VCs. Jeff was attending them. Well, actually, he was doing more than just attending them. Since the close of our first venture round and this upcoming second one, Jeff had educated himself in the nature of the venture capital world. He was paying attention to the details and motivations that had been irrelevant in our money-starved days.

As I stepped back from power, Jeff stepped forward. He was certainly charismatic and intelligent enough to lead, but he wasn't enjoying himself. He liked the challenge, but he had less patience for unmotivated or dependent personalities than I did.

As he became increasingly embroiled in the world of venture capitalists, Jeff began to express to me his concerns about the true motivations of some of our investors.

Even though I only attended a few of the key VC meetings, Jeff and I spoke nearly every day, discussing the various pros and cons of each option Neoforma faced. Jeff knew that his vote alone was not enough to direct any decision. He had to convince me to look out for myself too. He became increasingly angry when I wouldn't accept the idea that there were some who would, without a thought, screw us for personal gain.

Jeff had become convinced that a possible objective of the outside investors was to separate the founders — Jeff and me — and earliest angel investors, from of our share of the company in order to increase their returns. As our next funding round approached, Jeff became more concerned about protecting our investment in Neoforma. Rising to the occasion, he proceeded to learn the workings and language of venture capital with lightning speed and admirable proficiency.

Now that we were backed by a tier-one venture firm, blossoming press coverage and a stimulated financial market, we had many options to choose from.

Jeff learned that some of the investment terms favored outside investors rather than the founders. One distinguishing factor was the valuation of the company. Jeff had been able to solicit a term sheet at an attractive valuation from one of the tier-one firms. He felt that the long-term benefit of strong, active partners was more important than a higher valuation. Bret and JP, in particular, insisted that we could get perfectly good money, at a higher valuation, from slightly less renowned VCs.

Jeff's fears were confirmed when each of the term sheets arrived. These documents outlined the details of a deal. Mostly they covered who gets to keep what in the event of liquidation—either through the failure, sale or public offering of the company. Somehow, in the details of the high valuation deals, a clause dealing with participating preferred stock had been inserted. These provisions addressed what would happen in the event of the sale of the company before an IPO.

The term *participating preferred* meant that if the company were sold, the most recent investors would get their money first. Not only that, but they would be guaranteed a multiple of their original investments before any remaining money was distributed to earlier investors. So in some scenarios, the latest investors could get two or three times their money back, while early investors could potentially get nothing.

Foolishly, this idea didn't bother me much at the time. After all, we were talking about large amounts of money. The investors deserved a fair chance at a good return. I didn't like the idea of them getting three times their investment, but one-and-a-half or two times didn't seem unreasonable. And when it came down to it, I refused to consider the possibility that the company would be sold for less than the amount that would yield Jeff and me a good return.

Jeff didn't see things this way at all. How dare these investors think that their money was somehow worth more than our years of labor? This just confirmed his belief that, as soon as they owned more of the company than Jeff and I combined, these investors would be quite content to sell the company for a quick return to them, independent of the value to us or to the employees. Under the terms of these agreements, the company could be sold for $60 million or more and Jeff and I wouldn't get a penny. Most of all, he wondered how these terms got in deals anyway. It turns out that their insertion had been suggested to the new VCs by our own friendly investors as a means to assure future them that their money was safe at a higher valuation. This was fine for them—they would be included in the preferred group. But Jeff and I and the early angels wouldn't.

I thought we should be able to negotiate some kind of compromise. Jeff was furious at me for my naïveté and disloyalty.

To the chagrin of Bret, JP and Alexander, Jeff adamantly refused to accept these clauses. He was confident that he could secure an attractive deal without the preferred clause. Bret and company did not want to wait.

Playing the role of a tough negotiator, he simply refused to work with the deals that favored our recent investors over our early investors.

About a week before the deciding Board meeting, while enjoying a moment of my newly balanced contemplation at my desk, I was suddenly interrupted by a fiery Greek storming into my office and firmly closing the door. Alexander was hyperventilating—pacing two steps forward and two steps back, two steps forward, two steps back. His arms were tense, his muscles quivering. He held his hands outstretched in front of him, palms up. It was as if he were lifting a heavy box—getting ready to throw it, then calming himself, lowering the box—then getting angry again, lifting it to throw it—and so on.

I waited while he tried to compose himself enough to tell me what was on his mind. He eventually managed to say, "WAYNE, WE'VE GOT TO TALK. JEFF IS DRIVING ME NUTS. HE IS POSITIVELY INSANE. HE'S GOING TO KEEP US FROM GETTING THIS FUNDING ROUND CLOSED. YOU HAVE TO BE PREPARED TO TAKE OVER. THE REST OF THE BOARD WANTS YOU TO TAKE OVER AT THE NEXT BOARD MEETING."

By now, Jeff had become sufficiently hostile to me and everyone else that I was not particularly surprised by this request. But that didn't make me any more comfortable with it. Since founding Neoforma, Jeff and I had disagreed on many issues, big and small. But we had always managed to compromise. And in spite of our differences, we had always displayed a unified face to the rest of the world.

Now I had been asked to not only disagree with him, but to throw him out of the company. Putting aside my feelings of loyalty for a moment, I couldn't help but go along with Alexander's point. Jeff had told me that he would quit before he would accept the proposed deals.

Everything we had built was suddenly at risk. Unless I was able to calm Jeff down, he was in danger of severely injuring the company.

As if awakened from a dream, I jumped out of my finely balanced retreat and surveyed the environment. I called some of the most recent investors. They too were frustrated by Jeff's seemingly intractable position. They were telling me that my moderate voice was what the company needed right now. In the face of a one-sided advantage to a few, Jeff did not appear to be open to moderation. Of course, what they were really doing was massaging my ego and telling me that I was the only one who could legitimately take over without upsetting the potential new investors.

So I called a few of our early angel investors. I needed their advice and I felt a duty to inform them that Alexander, JP, led by Bret thought I might need to take over the company. Instead of jumping on the bandwagon with the others, they acknowledged the merits of Jeff's argument.

As early investors, they would be only one level above Jeff and me from the bottom of the list if the company were sold. And they didn't necessarily trust the motivations of the later investors either.

None of them liked the participating preferred clauses, but they had come to accept them as a necessary evil. They weren't happy with the situation, but they were also afraid what Jeff might do and gave me their support should I get left holding the bag. They liked Jeff, but they had enough experience with him to fear his stubbornness. They had to protect their investments.

That's how I felt too. I hated the idea of going against Jeff in favor of largely unknown future investors, but I couldn't let him jeopardize the company. I put my deeper feelings on hold. I had a job to do.

On the day before I was to take the reins, I made a last-ditch effort to bring Jeff and Bret to a state of compromise. Bret indicated a little flexibility, but he was so upset with Jeff that he dismissed the idea of even considering a compromise.

For his part, Jeff was barely willing to speak with me. He was disgusted with me, convinced that I was being led to the slaughter by the vicious VCs. But I was able to discuss the issue with him. That was progress.

He unhappily said that at this point he was willing to consider a compromise position on the participating preferred clause. *If* we could get the new investors to accept a significantly smaller multiple in their preference—meaning they would only get a little bit more than us in the event of a sale of the company—then he might be able to accept it. He'd think about it, anyway, and let us know at the Board meeting tomorrow. I allowed myself a moment of hope.

Because of the number of legal issues that might need to be dealt with at a meeting—both about approving a funding round and changing a CEO—this Board meeting was held in a conference room at our attorney's office.

It was a breezy, overcast morning. I walked into the building in a daze. I did not want to see any of the attendees before the meeting, so I arrived exactly on time. I silently nibbled on sweet rolls and sipped coffee, while the other attendees trickled into the room and greeted each other quietly. The somber mood in the room was not typical of a meeting about closing a twelve million dollar funding round.

I was the only one who had any hope that Jeff would still be in his job the next day. I knew that Jeff would often take extreme positions as a negotiating tactic, but I wasn't sure what he'd do this time. Jeff was out of town and would only be calling in to the meeting. This would make it very difficult to read Jeff's intent. Bret was also calling in from his vacation in Europe. Before Jeff got on the line, I told the Board that I thought Jeff might accept a suitable compromise position. They didn't believe me.

When Jeff did get on the phone, he acted curt and indignant, but he did accept the compromise position *for the sake of the company.* Then he hung up.

It looked like I was off the hook for the time being. However, my short-lived peace of mind had been irrevocably jolted. I knew now that, even when things looked okay, I had to be ready for anything. Doing my job would never be enough.

Jeff and I didn't speak much for many months. I had always thought of him as a business partner. No more. Now I felt the absence of a friend.

And as much as I had disagreed with the inflexibility of Jeff's position on the funding round, I did agree with him on one thing—my new partners, the VCs, were certainly not my friends. I had allowed them to manipulate me into putting my fear of losing everything above my loyalty to a friend.

April 1999

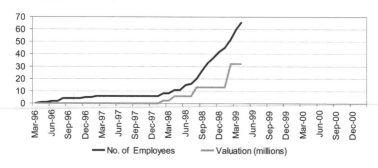

No. of Employees — Valuation (millions)

Cool Company
A Site Where Hospitals Can Click to Shop

Today hospitals and suppliers checking into Neoforma.com
swap 10,000 to 20,000 emails a month about products . . .

Fortune Magazine
April 12, 1999

E-Commerce Poised to Impact Healthcare Supply Industry Significantly

Several companies are lining up to cash in on what looks like
the purest form of healthcare e-business . . . Probably one of
the most visionary, and by far the best financed, of the medical
product e-commerce companies is Neoforma . . .

IDN Strategies
April 1999

The Trillion-Dollar Opportunity

One of the Internet's great conceits is that it changes everything.
In the Internet Economy, you can buy anything from Furbys to
furniture online . . . But swallowing the trillion-dollar dinosaur
that is the U.S. healthcare industry could give Net entrepreneurs
a serious case of indigestion . . .

The Industry Standard
April 5, 1999

Discontinuity

Balance is not always found in the middle.

In moments of stress or confusion, I often catch myself looking back in time to similar situations. One such moment occurred as I was leading a meeting in a crowded conference room in April, 1999. I was thinking about a meeting that happened long ago. The context of that meeting had been quite similar to this one, but had turned out very differently.

About fifteen years earlier I had been working seven days and nights a week helping a friend, Andy, design and build a restaurant that he wanted to open in Southern California. Things were not going well. The contractor had used all of the money we paid him to buy a sporty new car, then he promptly disappeared without paying any of his subcontractors.

I had brought in a few friends from architecture school to help out at almost no cost. They were not getting along with each other nor with Andy. Then a series of unexpected accidents happened.

Foolishly, I took one day off to go water skiing with a friend. I had been so tired that I severely pulled a hamstring, leaving me almost unable to walk. A few days later, I had fallen twenty feet from a ladder that had broken under me. I landed hard. Nothing was broken, but everything was strained and bruised. I could have used an excuse to take a day or so off, but I was still able to hobble around, so I kept working. I was a mess, but the project was even more of a mess.

On the day of my return, Andy was in a particularly bad mood. He was in the middle of a nightmare project and could see no end to his misery. Andy was standing inside the dark and dusty restaurant, yelling at one of the guys I had brought in. He was pointing out his distaste for the way this guy had constructed one of the walls. Another guy I had hired had stopped working and was listening, disgusted by the incessant arguing. When I stepped in to intervene, both workers told me that they were quitting, right there and then. Andy snapped back that if they quit it just fine with him—maybe he would just quit too.

I don't know why, but I was so upset at the way he said this that I did something I had never done before and have never done since— I lurched forward, raising my arm to strike him. I caught myself just before completing the act — stopped cold by the startled look on Andy's face.

I immediately escorted my tense body past the rest of the crew who had witnessed the incident and into the bright sunlight. I staggered like Quasimodo, which was the only way my injuries allowed me to move, aimlessly, around the beachside community for several hours.

I seemed to be the only one left. Everyone wanted to quit—even the owner. What is it to me? I asked myself. I am not even getting paid for this job. I'm working for room, board and experience. I'm doing this for the fun of it. And it's no fun at all. I should just pack it up and go.

On the other hand, what will I accomplish if I quit? Failure, nothing else. All of the good stuff that we had been working on until now would be gone, obliterated by my moment of weakness.

As my mind cleared in the fresh air, my conviction returned. I would get this project built. It would be up to Andy to run the business after that. I couldn't quit. I had little to lose and everything to gain.

I assembled Andy and the crew together that afternoon. They were reluctant to sit around the same table, but finally agreed to humor me.

I began speaking to the slouching, frowning, sighing group. In the past, Andy and I had shared duties. This day, I took control of the group. I would get the building built. He would fill it with food, utensils and people. As I spoke, I became aware of the changing attitude of the individuals around the table. They sat up, became attentive, even smiled, as I carefully acknowledged each individual's feelings, frustrations *and* infractions. I told it as I saw it. I held nothing back. I was decisive.

Afterward, a woman who was coordinating orders and deliveries came up to me and said, dreamily, "Wow . . . that was amazing. I sure wish I could talk like you do."

I wasn't sure what I had said or where the words had come from, but that didn't matter. I gained the confidence that day that I would be able to handle similar situations in the future, as long as I presented my beliefs with conviction and compassion. This proved to be true during many leadership challenges I would face in the future.

The restaurant was built. It was opened. The food was very good. It turned out to be a very successful venture.

Now, fifteen years later, I was sitting at the end of a much larger table in front of a much larger group of people. Other than that, the situation was strikingly similar.

For the first time in nearly a year, I was running the company's weekly staff meeting. The stress and frustration over the previous funding round had left Jeff tired and discouraged. His energy was almost exclusively focused on getting the Board to find a new CEO. Alexander was out of the picture too. He had moved on to a new company.

So without any convincing explanation, I informed this group of about twenty managers that I was going to be in charge of these meetings for awhile. I told them that Jeff was busy with some special projects.

Most of the people in the room had been hired by me, but had become used to taking their direction from Jeff or Alexander. Although I had remained active in many parts of the company, I had been careful to ensure that everyone saw Jeff as the one in control. For now, that had to change.

Each manager gave a brief update on his or her group's progress and problems over the last week. As they made their presentations, a clear pattern began to emerge.

If the manager had been reporting to Jeff, he or she was focusing on Jeff's priorities. If the manager had been reporting to Alexander, then Alexander's priorities were dominant. If he or she had been still working under my influence, my very different priorities had come into play.

There was clearly a crisis of leadership. And for the time being, I was the one who needed to provide focus.

But that was a temporary situation. Neoforma was about to begin a formal, high-profile search for a new CEO. Jeff and I had always known that we weren't the right guys to run Neoforma in the long run. We preferred to design and build rather than to operate. Neither of us savored power over others.

Once we filled the company's current job openings Neoforma would have more than a hundred employees. We wanted to hire someone with experience running a larger company. And whoever that was would direct the company's operations. I would be out of that role.

So after everyone had completed their status report, all eyes were on me. Decisions had to be made. There were too many projects under way. Some had to be postponed. Others had to be cut. Some of the decisions were easy, some were not.

Everyone knew my bias. They knew that I was obsessively focused on the capital equipment solution we were building. This project was code-named *Picasso*. I knew that many, if not most, of the managers believed that Picasso should be cut. I knew that I was biased.

Working privately in my office, I could indulge my biases. But in the role of the leader, I was uncomfortable with my bias, so I polled various people in the room, seeking some kind of consensus on how we should proceed. But consensus was impossible.

I either had to make the more popular decision to cut Picasso and alienate the people who had remained loyal to my original vision for the company, or I had to make the less popular decision to keep Picasso alive and alienate the others. If I made the former decision, I would reveal my weakness as a leader. If I made the latter decision, I would be showing my disregard for the advice of the majority of the managers I had hired. It was a classic leadership problem.

My concern for doing the right thing clouded my ability to see the real issue. I was going to disappoint people with either decision, but *which* decision I made was unimportant. What was important was that I make a prompt and clear decision.

This was a group of intelligent, driven people who wanted to do the best they could do. I had hired them for this reason. If I made an unpopular decision, they might grumble, but they would implement it with a passion. If I wavered or made no decision, they would lose their passion.

In my similar crisis of leadership fifteen years earlier, I had nothing to lose. This time I had everything to lose. I was afraid that the wrong decision might lead to failure—not just mine, but that of everybody in the room. I was afraid of losing my house and my family. And I was not used to being afraid. The fear obscured my sense of purpose and, ultimately, my projection of leadership.

I'd like to say that I rose to the occasion this time, as I had when there was nothing on the line. But, in an attempt to be fair to everyone, I came up with a weak compromise that satisfied and inspired no one. We'd keep the Picasso program going, but only allocate it just enough resources to stay alive. Sadly, my half-hearted decision conveyed uncertainty. The effect was immediate and deeply disheartening.

I stayed in the room after everyone had left. As I sat at the end of the now-empty table, I buried my head in my hands and contemplated the dreadful mistake I had just made. Instead of seizing this moment as a great opportunity for rejuvenation, I had turned it into a catalyst for disenchantment.

When I attempted to correct the errors I made that day, I made some progress, but there was no way to undo the damage. I might remain a spiritual leader in the company, but I could never again be its executive leader. My only consolation was that I had certainly set the stage for a new leader to come in and save the day.

May 1999

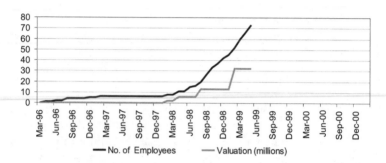

Chart legend: —— No. of Employees   —— Valuation (millions)

x-axis: Mar-96, Jun-96, Sep-96, Dec-96, Mar-97, Jun-97, Sep-97, Dec-97, Mar-98, Jun-98, Sep-98, Dec-98, Mar-99, Jun-99, Sep-99, Dec-99, Mar-00, Jun-00, Sep-00, Dec-00

y-axis: 0, 10, 20, 30, 40, 50, 60, 70, 80

Sleeping Giants

Large tracts of online economic terrain remain unconquered. But not for long. Business-to-business e-commerce will draw 90 percent of the projected $1.4 trillion in total Internet-based business by 2003 . . . While Jim Clark's Healtheon mines the online possibilities in healthcare admin and benefits, Neoforma wants the first bite in the $30 billion market for medical equipment and supplies . . .

Business 2.0
May 1999

Healtheon, Neoforma Join Forces

Healtheon Corp., a leading online healthcare site formed by Netscape co-founder James Clark, has entered a partnership with Neoforma Inc., an e-commerce site for the health care marketplace. The two Santa Clara–based companies will offer health care professionals free, convenient access to Neoforma's online database of medical products . . .

Silicon Valley / San Jose Business Journal
May 19, 1999

The Masters

Motivation and intelligence in the absence of experience yields dazzling inertia.

I hadn't thought about Sharon for more than a decade.

That Sharon and I ever shared words at all was a fluke. I was all dressed up in new clothes for a job interview, looking uncharacteristically dapper. I had just returned from Southern California and was staying with my mother for a few weeks until I found a job and place to live. My mid-twenties wanderings were behind me. I was ready to face the world with new energy and focus. I even cut my hair to the same length on both sides.

The doorbell rang. I opened the door, curious who would be calling on this suburban house in the middle of the day. Facing me was a tall, attractive brunette, a few years my junior. She was all dressed up too. We shared one of those *this-is-not-what-I-was-expecting* moments. It was pleasurable. Then she introduced herself. She was delivering some documents to my mother as a favor for her mother. Before I could say anything clever, or even intelligent, she handed me the papers and walked to her BMW in the driveway. I thought that was that.

But it wasn't. I couldn't get the image of her smile out of my mind. There was something so simple and direct about it.

I tracked down her number and called her the following day. I asked her out.

When I picked her up in my car, which used to be sporty and now was just beat up, she seemed a bit startled at my transportation—and at my appearance. I was no longer dressed up for an interview. All of my normal clothes were well-worn and tinged with remnants of my seventies punk sensibilities. She asked if we should take her car instead of mine. I said, "No, that's okay. This car hasn't broken down in weeks."

She was still dressed up. I deduced that this was how she always dressed and became quite conscious of the tattered hems on my pant legs.

She told me that she had known I would call her and added, "I'm glad you did." Well, maybe things weren't going as poorly as I thought. Still, I readily assumed that this would be our only date, so I was able to relax completely.

As we exchanged brief life summaries, I became very comfortable with her. She had just completed her undergraduate degree and was staying at her parent's house until she started her Masters in Business Administration.

After I presented a heavily edited summary of my life story, she asked how much money architects make. Her impression was that architecture was a very respectable and well-rewarded profession. I confidently said, "Oh, between thirty and seventy thousand . . . depending on seniority and such. Maybe a bit more, once you become a principal." I thought that was pretty good money.

"Oh, I could never marry anyone who made less than a hundred thousand." She said this casually, without the slightest bit of malice, so I didn't take it hard. But, I did feel the need to point out that there was more to life than money. After all, this was my chosen career she was dismissing.

I asked, "How about creativity . . . and exploration?"

She responded, "It's a simple matter of lifestyle. I know what I need. I mean, you're educated and you're tall enough . . . just barely (I couldn't go out with someone shorter than me), but you'd never make enough money to support the lifestyle I need."

Fair enough. I could certainly respect, even envy, someone who was that certain about her goals in life. She knew what she wanted and deserved.

I came out of my reverie and focused back on the young woman sitting across from me in my office. She had exactly the same quality. Karen was the first of a crop of young MBAs I was scheduled to interview.

Alexander had told me, "Look, you need to focus on running the business. What we need to do is hire a bunch of bright MBAs . . . just a couple years out of school . . . and send them out to do deals."

This was his polite way of saying that I had neither the personality nor credentials to forge the plethora of business partnerships that would be required for Neoforma to play in the big leagues.

I knew that my clumsiness with casual conversation inhibited my ability to open the doors to new partnerships. I had relied on Jeff's social skills for that. And I knew that I couldn't share in the inevitable boasts about alma mater sports teams. But I wasn't convinced that some youngsters just out of school could bring us much value. Our investors and Board disagreed. So we opened up a few business development positions.

When I received my first stack of résumés for these positions, I consulted with Lori in PR. Unlike the other positions I had filled, I had no idea what I was looking for. But Lori had made it very clear that the school the applicants had attended was very important. She went through the stack, "This one is good, this one isn't. Oh, you have to talk to this one . . ."

She read off the names of the schools. They didn't mean anything at all to me. I paid great attention to the type of secondary education that each applicant had pursued, but my experience indicated that any individual could get a lot or very little from almost any college. It was up to them.

Apparently, my view was naïve. I was told that the world did not work that way. Only the best were accepted into certain schools. If I wanted the best, then I had to hire those who had attended the best schools.

So that is how I ended up interviewing Karen. I was just as comfortable with Karen as I had been with Sharon. She was so—clear. She projected none of the ambiguity I was so used to in interviews. She had heard about Neoforma and was considering it.

She walked right into my office and told me her story. She had been working in an investment bank on Wall Street for a year. She said, "I made a few hundred grand." So she obviously wasn't coming to the Valley for the money. "I've saved enough that I can work on the smaller salary that start-ups can afford. I want some real-world experience, so I can increase my options down the road."

Then she asked me questions about the company.

I was glad that she had taken control of the interview because I was very distracted by my own observations.

How can her skin be so smooth? And her hair, it's simple—yet it looks perfect. She is casually dressed, but her clothes look—well, just right somehow.

Don't get me wrong, I was not attracted to her. I was awed by her. I don't think that she was naturally beautiful, but she would attract attention wherever she went.

She was so confident, so certain about what she was looking for. She summarized the pros and cons of choosing Neoforma over her other primary choice, a sports-and-fitness Internet start-up. She was very athletic, so that subject matter was more interesting to her. Yet Neoforma was further along. She would get more advanced experience.

I didn't realize it immediately, but she was indirectly asking my opinion on which job she should take. I was so flattered by her respect for my position as a founder that I told her the truth—she should take the other job. It was a better match to her objectives. I made her an attractive offer. She didn't accept it.

Without exception, the young MBAs I interviewed were eerily similar. Whatever their gender or ethnicity, they all had the same charm, handsomeness, intelligence and confidence. They all had many choices. They knew that Neoforma would be privileged to have their attention.

We hired several of them and paid them a bundle. We sent them out to forage and they found things. But they had no idea what to do with what they found.

When it came down to it, they were just kids, very smart kids. And they wanted to have a good time. Their expense accounts were astronomical.

They had no experience to call upon when it came down to the details of a business deal—which might have been okay, except that they were so used to the path of least resistance that they simply switched to something else when something didn't go easily. They were far more interested in rewriting a business plan than implementing it. It was easier that way.

Despite their confidence and poise, they were the first to go, when the time came to trim the fat. Wherever they are, I am sure they're doing fine—they have Neoforma on their credentials.

June 1999

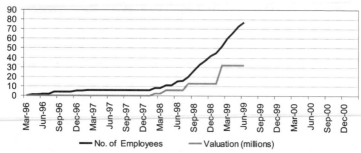

No. of Employees   Valuation (millions)

UPSIDE's 1999 Hot 100

. . . They won because we believe they are the hottest private high-tech companies of 1999 . . . Neoforma, founded in 1996, operates an online marketplace linking buyers and sellers of all kinds of medical products. The company is a rising star in the lucrative business-to-business market . . .

UPSIDE Magazine
June 1999

Ariba IPO Goes Through the Roof

It looks like the Internet IPO market is still alive and well. Shares of e-commerce software provider Ariba went through the roof on their first day of trading on Wednesday . . . Ariba stock priced at $23 and closed at $90, a remarkable gain of 291 percent . . . E-commerce software looks hot, hot, hot.

E-Commerce Times
June 24, 1999

Web Firm Neoforma Names to Top Post Zollars From Cardinal

Neoforma Inc., in another example of an Internet company recruiting top management from traditional industries, said it is hiring a senior official of Cardinal Health Inc. to be chairman, president and chief executive . . .

Wall Street Journal
June 28, 1999

The Star

Jeff and I started Neoforma.

We had provided its first monetary food. We had reared the company, nurtured it, guided it, imposed our will and ingrained our personal ethics. But we did not control Neoforma. We did not control Neoforma because we did not *want* to control Neoforma. There are those who seek control for its own sake. We knew we weren't that type at all.

Jeff and I were much better at creating diversions than avoiding them. Our primary motivation was the release of outside control over us rather than the imposition of control over others. Both of us found ourselves increasingly fighting the need to direct others.

Our roles were still much too significant to ensure that our diversions didn't disrupt, or even destroy, the company. We needed to hire someone to keep the company on course for the long run. Someone who cared more about the business than the *idea* of the business. The sooner the better.

I have dabbled in and been transfixed by the workings of power, but in the end I get uncomfortable with its trappings and its unit of measure—money. I like money, but I don't like the pursuit of money. It is not satisfying. I like to design things. I get a thrill out of helping people create something beautiful, something useful, something original. However, in most cases the pursuit of beauty, usefulness and originality is not enough to run a company. A small company, maybe, but not a large one.

To me, Neoforma was like a child. I had loved it and nurtured it, but now it was growing up. I still loved it, but I didn't necessarily like everything about it. It wasn't quite as cute anymore. That is the nature of growing up. I was a part of Neoforma, but Neoforma was becoming a much smaller part of me. I increasingly resented any display by Neoforma of dependency on me.

Jeff was pretty much the same way. His response was not quite as extreme as mine, but he didn't like the constraint of keeping so many people content. It kept him from pursuing what he really liked to do —he loved to tinker.

When Jeff and I originally became friends, it had been because, not only was I willing to listen to his ideas, but I was able to take them to the next level. Once I did, he'd fiddle with them for awhile. Then I'd receive the dreaded, middle-of-dinner, or seven-in-the-morning phone call. "I have a brilliant idea!"

No hello, no niceties, just out with the idea. He'd call from his kid's soccer practice. He'd call from an airline counter, interrupting his call with me to yell at the unfortunate messenger of his latest luggage mishap. He'd call from a restaurant restroom, nearly dropping the phone after each plumbing fixture activation.

For cheap entertainment I would sometimes hang up immediately after he said: "*I have a brilliant idea!*" Then I'd wait to see how long it took him to call me back.

I knew that he wanted to express his displeasure at my rudeness by withholding his wisdom from me, but he found it physically impossible to bear the weight of one of his own brilliant ideas alone.

So he'd always call back. He learned to give the niceties a try, "Wayne ... uh ... how's it going ... hey I have a brilliant idea!" No pause for me to answer the question. But he was trying.

This year, Jeff hadn't been calling me as much. He was not himself.

Until Jeff's rebellion during the last funding round, most of our investors and Board members believed that finding a professional CEO was important, but not critical. In spite of the fact that Jeff and I had both made it clear from the beginning that we did not think we were the right kind of people to run Neoforma in the long run, they had believed that Jeff could do the job for as long as necessary. Now they were finally listening to Jeff's advice to pursue hiring an experienced CEO.

The investors smelled an IPO. Hints of possible big returns were everywhere. They panicked at the idea that this rare opportunity could slip away. They fished every day, but only caught an IPO once in a great while.

The investors also knew that the placement of a very well-known CEO could substantially amplify their returns. Earlier, they had been unwilling to give up a large part of Neoforma to get a top CEO. Now, they were willing to give up a bigger percentage of a much larger pie.

They hired the best recruiter they could find.

The Top 25 Power Brokers in Silicon Valley
JOHN T. THOMPSON, 49

Top dog in Silicon Valley for high tech's key headhunting firm, he is the one that troubled companies call to find that executive savior . . . Thompson's latest job may be the toughest: finding a replacement for Gilbert F. Amelio, who was ousted as CEO of Apple Computer in early July.

BusinessWeek
August 25, 1997

It was a privilege to hire John Thompson. That was made very clear to me by our investors. And to attain that privilege, a company had to make a very strong case for the company's pending—and preferably, huge—success. Once that difficult task was accomplished, the company was obligated to express its appreciation through the generous contribution of a significant amount of cash and substantial amount of equity to John.

I was aghast when I learned how much equity he would receive. "How could anyone be worth that much?" I argued.

"You'll see," was the reply.

I was even more concerned when I met John. He was a bespeckled man of average stature. He seemed neither strikingly charming nor particularly engaging. He seemed to be far too self-conscious to be the kind of powerful communicator I had imagined. I couldn't visualize him relating on a first-name basis to the country's top executives. But I was told that was exactly what he did for a living.

I was skeptical, but I'd have to put some trust in our investors. They had a lot to lose too.

About a month after we officially hired John, he was ready to present his list of candidates. He hadn't communicated with us much during the process, so we had no idea what to expect.

On the morning of the day we were scheduled to meet with John, we received an email link to a private website that contained biographies of his proposed candidates. The moment I read the list of candidates I knew why we had hired John. These candidates for the top job at a little company like Neoforma were of a much higher caliber than I had expected. And many of them had already expressed some degree of interest. Reading through the biographies, I knew that Neoforma was about to change completely. Or, maybe it already had and I had simply chosen this moment to accept it.

Included on the list were a few heads or seconds-in-command of large logistics companies. There were even a couple of candidates from the executive suite of Fed Ex, which I would later find out was typical of a high-level search.

There was the legendary head of one of the largest healthcare software companies, the previous head of a large hospital GPO, and the number-two guy at one of the big accounting firms. There were senior executives in the number-two or -three positions of some of the largest healthcare product distributors. And there were a few other candidates too.

What surprised me was that these executives were running businesses with tens of thousands of employees. We didn't even have a hundred yet.

Everyone on the Board had a slightly different opinion of what we should be looking for in a candidate. Jeff and I believed that healthcare experience was crucial. So did Wally. Others believed that a technology background was most important. Still others believed that aggressive management skills were all that was necessary.

But I can say that, when we viewed the candidate list, all of us would have been thrilled to get almost any of the candidates.

When we met with John we complimented him on his list. He could barely conceal his pleasure. He knew he had a special talent and he knew this was the moment when everyone always recognized it. He'd learned to savor it.

John presented a summary of each candidate, going into details regarding their level of interest and any personal issues that might affect their availability. We were able to eliminate a few and prioritize the others.

We were disappointed, but not surprised, to see that there was only one woman on the list. We had been trying to balance our executive team with a woman for a long time. It had proven difficult to cull experienced women from the male-dominated healthcare and technology industries.

Our last attempt to hire a woman in a top role had ended poorly. At the beginning of the year, as Alexander and JP had been gearing up for the next funding round, they had seen a huge hole in our management team. We did not have a VP of Marketing. We did not have someone whose job it was to build our *brand*. Todd and I had been casually sharing this role for a couple of years. During the previous year we had been interviewing people to head up our marketing efforts, but had not run across anyone we thought could do a better job than we already did.

Alexander and JP had told us that it was time to get serious. If we wanted world-class funding, we needed a world-class marketing VP. And if we really wanted to project the image of a progressive Internet company, we needed to have a woman on the team. Jeff and I both agreed that a woman would be ideal to balance our team. Since we didn't consider healthcare or technology experience crucial to a marketing position, we hoped we'd have a large pool of woman candidates.

We hired a high-end recruiter and sent her to work looking for a VP of Marketing, then the most sought-after position in the Valley. A flock of start-ups had been gearing up ahead of us, filling in their management teams for their next, larger funding rounds or IPOs. There was a severe shortage of supply.

After a number of bland interviews, we found what we thought was the perfect candidate. A woman of superb intelligence, creativity and communication skills. Jeff and I liked everything about her. However, after thinking long and hard, she chose another position, running an Internet site for women. We were very disappointed.

We also interviewed a man that Jeff and I liked very much. Lou had been an early employee at eBay and had just left to avoid the upcoming madness preceding their IPO. He was articulate and smart. He definitely understood what we were doing. And, on top of that, we were unusually comfortable around him.

Alexander and JP, however, felt that he lacked the aggressiveness they wanted to bring to the marketing position. They couldn't accept the idea that anyone would leave a company just before an IPO. Plus, he wasn't a woman. As a compromise, Jeff and I insisted that we hire Lou as a consultant while we sought a candidate that everyone could reach consensus on. This worked for Lou, since he wasn't quite sure what he wanted to do next anyway.

Our secret hope was that he would do such a good job that he would become the Marketing VP by default. It didn't work out that way. (And it's just as well because Lou had a lot of eBay stock and would soon spend most of his time managing his own private family foundation.)

When we had almost given up on finding an acceptable female candidate, Mara appeared. She was not quite as polished as the earlier woman, but she made up for it in enthusiasm and assertiveness. Her aggressive style was a little too much for me and I was concerned that she had worked at a lot of different places over the previous two years, but I didn't veto her, because I believed that she was competent and displayed the leadership skills we needed to build a marketing organization. We were about to discuss pricing with investors in our next funding round. We needed to fill the position now. So we hired her.

Mara, a tall, fast-talking woman who seemed perpetually one step ahead of herself and ready to fall forward at any moment, could never be accused of inaction. She plowed through the rows of cubicles in our offices with gusto, created meetings about meetings, brought every flaw she could find to our attention, wondering aloud why these people or those people shouldn't be part of the marketing organization. Marketing was *everything* to her.

In her view, a moment's pause to contemplate why something was the way it was would be a moment lost. It was much easier for her to tell everyone the way it should be. My office door became perpetually closed, as I calmed one after another of her furious victims. The only people who weren't complaining were a couple of rather bland people she had immediately hired.

When word got back to Mara that I had spoken with some of the employees in her department, she stormed into my office and screeched at me: "When my employees have something to say, they need to have the courage to say it to me. I don't need you coming in to muddy things up!"

I pointed out that *they* had come to *me* and that I had started this company. I also observed that she seldom consulted with me or anyone else about anything. She said, "Well, you didn't hire me. The Board of this company did and I am working for them. If you have any issue with me, you need to talk to them!"

Now, I couldn't help but be amused. I even smiled at her naïveté until I realized that I was being rude. I had given up a great deal of control of the company, but I was still on the Board and I was still a pretty important guy around there, relatively speaking. She didn't have a clue that she had just gotten herself fired.

But the company got to it before me. Adversaries on all fronts united against her. They simply refused to tolerate her any longer. While Jeff and I were busy documenting her many infractions and quietly informing key investors that she would be leaving, making sure everyone knew why, Mara was finding all doors in the company closed to her. In a matter of days, she had become unwelcome everywhere. The Neoforma culture had rejected her.

While I was never happy when emotional conflict disrupted the office, I must admit that I was rather proud of Neoforma that day. Without the slightest direction by Jeff or me, the company had coalesced to make a unified decision. A good decision.

Now here we were a month later, and we were reviewing the recruiter's CEO list. We were eager to interview the female candidate first, even though she had the least applicable experience of the bunch. This time we would favor her gender, but not give it quite so much weight.

Jo Ann headed a very large division of a major financial company. When the time came to begin interviews, we were lucky. She was able to fit a visit with us into a previously scheduled trip to California. Jeff and I met her for dinner at a trendy restaurant in Palo Alto. Jo Ann fit the image of a stereotypical Southern businesswoman. Confident, yet self-effacing; tough, yet personable; serious, yet sassy. Jeff's Texas drawl and good ol' boy charm surfaced immediately. They got along well.

Interviews with this level of executive were mostly about the executive interviewing us. We had been expecting that. We were the ones in need. They were the ones in demand. But we did manage to ask Jo Ann a number of questions that told us what we needed to know.

We liked her. She was very smart, very capable and very passionate. However, she knew neither the healthcare nor technology industries, and she didn't quite understand what we were doing, even after having researched the company and speaking with us. She wasn't right for us. Based on their own interviews with her, the investors concurred.

Jeff and I met most of the candidates separately from the other Board members. We wanted to ensure that candidates didn't hold anything back from us because the investors were around. We wanted to make it very clear that the investors would not have undue influence on the future direction of the company. The investors wanted to ensure that candidates weren't holding anything back from them because the founders were present. They wanted to make it very clear that the founder's opinions on how to run the company in the future were irrelevant. So separate interviews worked for everybody.

Our next interviews were with the accounting guy, the GPO guy and a logistics guy. Jeff and I were impressed by each of them, but none of them left us with the feeling that our company would be in great hands. None of them lived up to their biographies. None of them felt like a cultural fit.

Jeff visited and interviewed the healthcare software guy. Richard's company had just been purchased by a major healthcare distributor, so this previously unattainable person might be available soon. His shrewdness and aggressiveness were legendary in the industry. When Jeff met with him, it was very clear that Richard *got it.* He understood the healthcare industry, he understood the technology side and he understood the investor perspective. But, Jeff said that Richard was not a very good cultural match. He was much too slick for Neoforma.

Richard made it clear that he knew he was hot property, informing us that he was in discussions with many well-known companies. He also told Jeff that he had recently turned down the top job at a major consumer dotcom before their recent IPO. Had he accepted the job, his share of that company would have been worth nearly a billion dollars, on paper. He made it clear that he would expect to be compensated with a very large share of Neoforma. We decided to keep him on our list, but that we'd review all other candidates before pursuing him further.

Before we could contact Richard again, he became entangled in accusations of fraud relating to the sale of his previous company. He would eventually be indicted on accounting fraud. I shiver at the thought of what might have happened had we hired him.

As our list of candidates dwindled, our initial elation began to fade. When a couple of additional candidates dropped out of the running for various reasons, we began to panic. A few of the remaining candidates were okay and still available, but they just weren't *right*. And we were running out of new options.

From the day we initially reviewed the list, the candidate who struck Jeff and I as the most perfect fit was Bob Zollars. We already knew of him, because he was in charge of the team that his company, Cardinal, a huge healthcare distributor, had recently sent to evaluate a technology partnership with Neoforma.

This partnership would be a big deal for Neoforma because it could turn a number of previously hostile distributors into potentially profitable partners. It could strengthen Neoforma's position against increasing competition. Bob was one of the top four executives at Cardinal. Ironically, it had been two divisions of his at Cardinal that we were close to partnering with a year previously, until that trivial third-party lawsuit screwed everything up.

While I had not personally met Bob, I was told that the discussions with Bob and his team at their headquarters had been refreshing. He was straightforward, enthusiastic, professional and courteous. This was not how we were used to being treated by the increasingly wary large distributors and manufacturers. When his name showed up on the list, we were ecstatic.

However, when John got to Bob's name in his summary of the candidates, he curbed our enthusiasm quickly. Bob was a long shot. He had been included on the list because of his stellar reputation, but he was not likely to go anywhere. First of all, Bob was the likely successor to the number-one spot at Cardinal. Cardinal was an established company worth tens of billions of dollars, with forty thousand employees, several corporate jets and generous executive compensation packages. Neoforma was a $30 million start-up company with less than a hundred employees, a ping-pong table and free snacks.

Also, Bob's family was just about to complete their dream house in Ohio. His wife and school-age children would not likely be thrilled by the idea of leaving friends, family and a new house behind and moving to Silicon Valley, where they knew almost nobody and the equivalent house would probably cost five times as much.

When I had gone to ECRI to close that deal a while back, I had been dogged and stubborn. I had gotten it in my head that the deal had to be done and, thus, I would get it done. Simple as that. *That's how Jeff was about getting Bob to join Neoforma. He said, "Wayne, I'm telling you, I'm tired of being CEO and the right guy for the job is Bob Zollars. He doesn't know it yet, but he is going to work for us!"

Jeff could be scary sometimes. When he got something in his head like this, he wasn't kidding around or exaggerating his conviction.

Bret, our VC Board member, had taken a lead role in the candidate-screening process. We knew that he leaned away from hiring someone from the healthcare industry. He believed that it was essential to convey the impression that Neoforma would target other industries after dominating healthcare. Hiring someone outside healthcare would increase the perceived long-term potential of Neoforma. Our IPO valuation should then reflect that larger potential.

Because we had only seen glimpses of Bret's darker side, we generally trusted him to take the first pass at a candidate. But this time, Jeff was adamant, "I have to be there when we first meet with Bob! I know that Bob wants to hear a healthcare story, not some Internet tale."

When John called Bob to convey our interest in him, he turned us down out-of-hand. While he was intrigued by the Neoforma story, he did not want to disrupt his job and family at this time. John knew that we thought Bob should be our guy, so he continued to pursue Bob anyway.

After many weeks of dogged persistence, Bob agreed to meet with us, but only if we could accommodate his very busy schedule. He was on the road about seventy-five percent of the time and never seemed to pause anywhere for long.

After some frantic coordination of schedules, a meeting was set up for a couple of weeks later. Jeff first met Bob in New Orleans. The meeting went so well that Jeff was able to coordinate another meeting, this time with Bret. To ensure maximum privacy and discretion for Bob, we reserved a hotel room near the Denver airport for the meeting. Jeff and Bret flew into the airport and drove to the hotel to meet Bob. As the three of them checked in, they could not help but recognize that it probably did not look altogether wholesome for three men who seemed unfamiliar with each other to be checking into a hotel room without luggage.

The meeting went well. Bob sent a positive summary of it to John. In it, he expressed his excitement, but made it clear that he still had a lot of ground to cover financially and emotionally. However, he was now open to visiting our offices and meeting more of the team.

By this time, our other candidates were out of the picture, either by their choice or ours. Bob was our only serious candidate and he was a long shot. I was continuing to panic, but Jeff assured me that he believed that Bob would eventually be convinced. Jeff was giving it his all.

It took another couple of weeks to schedule Bob's visit to Neoforma. The visit itself would be two weeks after that.

By this time, we were three months into our search. While everyone was busily building new products and services, the stress at Neoforma was palpable. We had not been able to keep our CEO search a secret for this long. It was obvious that Jeff was focused on hiring a replacement. He wasn't giving speeches at company luncheons or showing up at many meetings. I was making myself more visible, but everyone knew I was a lame duck. Neoforma was running without a long-term leader.

On the same day that we finally scheduled Bob's visit, John sent our CEO recruitment team a startling message. He had surfaced another candidate for us. This candidate, Joe Galli, was currently the most sought-after executive in the country and he wanted to meet with us at our offices later that week.

Joe had built a reputation for himself on Wall Street as the thirty-eight-year-old wunderkind who had engineered a spectacular turnaround of a large division of an even larger public company.

Somehow, everyone knew that he had wanted to move from the top position in that division to the top position in the company. Everyone knew that he had been turned down. Everyone knew that he was now looking for another job.

The Wall Street Journal and assorted business periodicals were following rumors of Joe's options with the eagerness of a *National Enquirer* gossip journalist. It was rumored that he was being courted by one of the largest food companies to take over the top job at the largest division of their huge corporation. He was also rumored to be the top choice for the number-two position at the Internet retailing giant, Amazon.com.

These were, indeed, two of the options Joe was pursuing, but nobody in the press knew that his third option was a little company called Neoforma.

When our Board heard that Joe had expressed interest in Neoforma, they became as ecstatic and hyperactive as kids at an amusement park. Imagining what Neoforma's valuation would be if we were able to recruit Joe was as exciting and gut-wrenching to them as the first downhill section of a roller coaster. The PR value was awe-inspiring. They were star-struck.

JP, Alexander and Bret buzzed into the Neoforma offices that day to make preparations for Joe's visit. Joe would be visiting on the following Saturday only, so about a dozen Neoforma managers would need to break any previous plans they had and spend the remainder of the week preparing presentations for Joe. Bret was uncharacteristically engaged. He made it clear to Jeff and me that we only had one shot at Joe. Everything had to be perfect.

Jeff had several long phone calls with Joe during that week. Jeff turned on his charm and developed a good rapport with Joe in preparation for his visit. Jeff told me that Joe seemed to be incredibly astute, that he might even be able to overcome his deficit in health-care experience. He'd be a good second choice after Bob.

JP and Bret had a different perspective. Without even meeting Joe, they believed that Joe was the clear first choice. Wall Street would love the story of Joe turning down the other companies for a relatively obscure start-up. They would gain bragging rights for years to come.

Our team spent all day Saturday with Joe. The meeting was very focused and intense. Joe impressed everyone with his thorough research, quick grasp of difficult concepts and boundless aggressive energy. He had many ideas and freely expressed them. Recognizing that our biggest obstacle was user adoption, Joe declared that this was a simple problem to solve. "Hire a thousand MBAs right out of school and plant them in the country's top hospitals. That will get their attention."

While I must admit that I was thrilled by Joe's optimism and the grand scale of his vision, I had been working at this start-up thing for long enough to know that the economics and logistics of this idea were questionable at best.

At the end of the day, Joe told Jeff and me that he was very impressed with the team we had built and the opportunity Neoforma represented. He'd improved his opinion of us. He'd have to give this a great deal of thought — and soon — because he was under extreme pressure to take one of the other two jobs.

When I debriefed our team, everyone expressed admiration for his amazing intelligence and energy, but several people expressed concern over Joe's lack of healthcare and technology experience. They said that he seemed a bit naïve about the challenges inherent in the healthcare industry. And almost everyone expressed concern over Joe's cultural fit. He was unabashedly aggressive and ruthless in his view of business objectives. That wasn't the approach Neoforma had been built on.

Alexander surprised me by expressing the same concern. He had lived inside the Neoforma culture for long enough that he had come to care about it.

But JP and Bret were adamant: Joe was our man. There was a ferocity in their insistence that I had not seen before. Their charming smiles were a bit strained, quivering just enough that I imagined glimpses of fangs.

A few days later, we heard from Joe. He'd like to come by again in a couple of weeks. This time, he wanted to bring along his girlfriend and one of his children. He liked our story, but had personal issues with moving to California. He'd recently been divorced and had several children. He wasn't sure he wanted to live in California at this time in his life.

A few days before Joe was due back on his second visit, Bob was scheduled for his first visit to Neoforma. Jeff was as insistent as ever that we
would be able to recruit Bob. Bret and John were both adamant that
Bob was a long shot, at best.

Bob's visit was a bit more casual than Joe's had been. We did not have
rehearsals. Bret and JP did not coach us. Bob saw us pretty much as we
were. The fact that we did not feel the need to put on a show should have
told us everything. We instinctively knew that Bob was so connected
to the industry that any inflation or deception wouldn't fool him. We
hoped that this meant he would be equally forthright with us.

Because I wanted to gauge Bob's reaction to our team, I was last on
his schedule. By the time he had finished with the rest of Neoforma's
key players, our one-and-a-half hour meeting needed to be cut to a
half-hour. Bob was due to fly out early that evening.

I had been seeing Bob through Jeff's eyes for so long that I had lost
any true recollection of what I imagined Bob to be like in person.
Whatever fragments of association or stereotype that I harbored about
Bob were shattered when I finally met him. As I'd been told, Bob was a
full head taller than Jeff and I. But he did not project the aura of control
and power I had expected. In fact, he seemed a bit nervous.

After shaking hands, we each took seats on opposite sides of Neoforma's Board room conference table. Because there was no time for
preliminaries, biographies or prepared speeches, we each jumped right
into the heart of our concerns. I wanted to know how he had gotten
along with our team. He told me that he had been impressed by our
team and, most of all, by our team's passion. Usually I dismissed such
niceties as perfunctory, but something about the way Bob said this
made me believe him. He asked me a few questions about the origins
of the company. He asked how I felt about giving up control to someone else. I told him the truth, that Jeff and I knew there were better
people for the job of running the company during its next phase, but
that I cared very much that we handed control to the right person.

He then summarized his criteria for making a decision to join
Neoforma.

First of all, he had to believe in the company's vision and management team. He told me that, after his meetings that day, he was
mostly convinced that Neoforma was the real thing.

Second of all, he had to believe in the business prospect. More specifically, he had to believe that he would professionally grow with the opportunity. He said the reason he was sitting here with me, in spite of his initial rejection of our inquiry, was because of a recent Young Presidents' Organization meeting he'd attended. At that meeting, he had shared the nature of the opportunity with a group of similar young business leaders whose opinions he valued. They had asked him to review the pros and cons of accepting the position.

All of the rational, risk-avoidance reasons went into the *cons* column. He had a safe, challenging job. He had substantial compensation. And he was next in line to run a huge corporation. Neoforma was completely uncertain.

Every prospect for emotional and professional fulfillment went into the *pros* column. He would have the opportunity to impact an industry he was passionate about in ways that he had never imagined. Neoforma was completely uncertain.

In the end, everyone agreed that there was no rational reason to take the new job—and he would be foolish not to take it. It was clear to all of these business leaders who knew Bob that he had more to offer the world than his management skills.

So, here he was.

The third criterion was not so simple. He had spent most of his professional career climbing the corporate ladder. He had moved his family from one opportunity to the next. He had been on the road most of the time. Now that he was almost at the top, now that his wife and children were just about to settle into a new dream house, now that he was ensured a stable, lucrative position with decreased travel and early retirement, he was considering something completely different.

Well, he had a point.

While our time together was short, I left the meeting with a feeling of great confidence that Bob was the right guy to take Neoforma to the next level and an equally intense feeling of disappointment that there was no way that Bob would accept the job. How could anyone have that enough courage and self-confidence to do so, under the circumstances he'd described?

I started to think that Joe might be our only hope and I didn't put much hope in Joe accepting.

The weekend after Bob visited, we were due to host Joe again. This time our Board was going to do everything possible to smother Joe, his girlfriend and his son with artificial love and affection.

First, there was the Saturday night dinner — a positively grand affair, Silicon Valley style. It was all in the hands of Bret and JP. They reserved the private cottage at a very trendy and expensive Palo Alto restaurant. They requested the attendance of the members of the Neoforma Board and a couple of other key investors. We were all expected to bring our spouses.

Other than Jeff's family, I had not met the spouses of any of the Board members, let alone socialized with them. Investors are usually very cautious about keeping their family life shielded from those they invest in. They know that the investor/investee relationship is likely to undergo extreme stress. Nobody wants that stress to overflow into their personal life.

But, for that evening, we were one big happy family. Everyone dressed up. We met Bret's wife, the infamous Christy Emery, the woman who had posed provocatively for her company's magazine ad. After the introductions, she ignored me and adored Joe. In fact, she not only ignored me, but also Jeff and both of our wives. Maybe she was just shy. Everyone else seemed to make an effort to get along. Anni and I especially enjoyed our conversations with Alexander and his wife.

The food was good. Joe and his girlfriend seemed to be having a good time with Bret and Christy. Everyone drank enough wine to loosen up. Nobody said anything nasty to each other. I guess we *were* a happy family. Joe seemed to think so.

Next was the Sunday dinner. This time it was going to be even more intimate. Wally had volunteered to host a dinner the following day at his house. The same crowd was invited, except that this time we were to bring our children along. Joe's grade-school-aged son would be there. It was the responsibility of all of our kids to make him feel comfortable at Wally's house. This would be a bit tricky, since they had not met each other and had not been to Wally's house before, but, hey, there'd be food, a swimming pool and movies.

I hadn't been to Wally's before. Wally had always been a very humble guy — especially for someone who had clearly done some remarkable and diverse things in his life. I expected his house to be visibly affluent, yet as humble as he was.

Instead, I discovered that the gates at the entrance to his yard, if laid flat, could have served as an adequate roof to my home. The house was a luxurious, formal mission-style house with generous swaths of dark wooden casework. Wally's gracious wife greeted us and guided us through the house to the back yard. My wandering gaze pulled my focus away from the path in front of me, so I tripped and stumbled at each threshold as we navigated the house. This is where Wally lived. I had never seen this side of him. My perspective of him widened. My admiration and appreciation—of the courtesy, warmth and respect he had always shown to Jeff and me—grew.

The back yard was immaculate, with carefully maintained gardens, tennis court, swimming pool, gazebo and lawns. Our boys were introduced to Joe's son. Typical boys, they grunted awkward greetings and avoided eye contact. Wally's poised and friendly teenage daughters then discreetly shuttled the kids away, showing them the various amenities.

Even though we had arrived fashionably late, Anni and I were among the first to arrive. Joe greeted us warmly. Unlike the previous evening, we were able to exchange small talk with Joe and his girlfriend. Joe almost immediately gushed to Anni about what an amazing company Jeff and I had built. He was very upbeat, charming and talkative. We learned all about the challenges he and his girlfriend would have to face, if they were to relocate to the area.

Others arrived and Joe's attention was diverted for the rest of the evening. Anni and I watched the kids swim and chatted with some of the other couples until dinner was served.

As the formal, catered meal was served, everyone's eyes were discreetly on Joe. He openly discussed the pros and cons of the two other opportunities, compared to the Neoforma opportunity. He seemed to be very positive about Neoforma. He even seemed to be mischievously thrilled by the thought of how the other companies would react if he took the Neoforma position instead of theirs. The smile on Bret's face was radiant. I was so used to his more common, less respectful smile, that I found this genuine smile quite disconcerting.

Bret's smile momentarily faded when Joe suddenly interrupted the wine-enhanced conversation and toasted Jeff and me. This sort of attention to Jeff and me was not what Bret wanted to see. The time when a new CEO comes into a company, just before an IPO, is the best time for early investors to gain control. Bret wanted to ensure that he was in a good position to switch the balance of control from the founders to the investors—well, really, to himself.

Although the atmosphere was generally jovial and upbeat, I noticed that Jeff's mood was uncharacteristically dark. While his preference for CEO candidates had always been clearly in favor of Bob, Joe's intelligence and energy impressed Jeff. As time went on, Jeff became increasingly adamant that Bob was the only good choice. I agreed that Bob was better, but believed that Joe could be good too. Sure, he'd stir up a lot of the employees and boot us out as soon as possible, but he just might be strong enough to pull off something good for Neoforma.

This evening Jeff was feeling particularly concerned. He had been getting a nagging feeling that Joe might not actually have what it took to meet the challenges of our young company. Joe had a cocky confidence in himself. He had accomplished a lot. He had a well-deserved reputation as someone who could fix a big, complex company. But, Neoforma didn't need fixing. It needed building, and that was something else entirely. It took a different kind of confidence.

After dinner, we broke up into groups. Some of us checked on the kids, who were happily watching a movie on a theatre-sized screen in a darkened room with tiered seating. Out of the corner of my eye, I saw Jeff chatting with Joe alone in a hallway.

By the time everyone gathered for dessert, Joe was a different man. He was serious and distracted. I leaned over to Anni and said, "I don't know what happened, but we just lost him." He seemed anxious to finish-up the evening. He said his son needed sleep.

After Joe had departed, Bret and JP were still very upbeat. They thought he was definitely leaning our way. I thought not.

The next day, I asked Jeff what he had said to Joe.

Jeff's doubts about Joe's willingness to take risks had prompted him to settle the issue once and for all. He took Joe aside after dinner and asked him what he thought of the Neoforma opportunity. Joe was very positive, even excited. "So, this company you've built has real potential?" he'd asked. "It's going to be very big, right?"

"Yes, Neoforma has real potential," Jeff had answered. "But, frankly, there is real risk here. I mean, healthcare is a very entrenched industry. It will take a long time to make a real difference. Years, maybe decades."

Jeff was absolutely right. But, apparently, Joe didn't like hearing it. Everyone had been so upbeat about the market opportunities and IPO returns, due consideration had not been given to the nature of this challenge versus the other opportunities Joe had. Jeff, knowing how important this evaluation was, had forced Joe to confront the true nature of the risk. Better to find out now than later.

We didn't hear from Joe during the next week. It had Bret and JP on edge. Joe wasn't returning phone calls. Then we heard the news: Joe had accepted the job at the food company. Then, a week or so later, we heard more news. Joe hadn't formally accepted the job with the food company, after all. They just thought he had. It had been a simple misunderstanding. What he had actually accepted was the number-two job at Amazon.com.

Later I heard that, once Joe met the Board of the food company, he had become disillusioned. He thought he was going into some vibrant environment, to be the hero and save the day. What he met there was a very conservative and restrained audience. As he was mourning his fate, he received a call from none other than the legendary John Doerr of KP.

Doerr had a reputation for brilliantly exploiting the buyer's remorse that individuals often feel after being aggressively recruited in a competitive business environment. KP had invested heavily in Amazon.com. Doerr made one last run for Joe. He flew Joe out to meet with him and the famous CEO of the retailer. They convinced Joe that a guy as innovative as Joe belonged in the world of the Internet, not some stodgy food conglomerate.

Joe's defection became a scandal. Not only was the food company furious, investors at Amazon.com were angry at the generosity of Joe's compensation. In addition to substantial stock options, Joe would be paid more than three million dollars in cash if he stayed there for only one year, regardless of how well the company did.

Ultimately, Joe didn't stay long at Amazon.com. The company's stock took a dive. He stayed there one year and a couple of days. He accepted his money and moved on to the number-one spot in a then-buzzing Internet business-to-business company, VerticalNet. He didn't stay there long either—about six months. That company's stock took a dive. He resigned, pocketed a couple of million dollars and moved to a large manufacturer of household items.

Bret would later say of Galli, "We sure dodged a bullet there!"

In spite of my worries, Bob was still interested in the Neoforma position. Interested enough to begin negotiations. The recruiter had a good idea what it would take to get Bob—a very large compensation package and a bit more equity than either Jeff or I had. I was okay with the stock, but a bit chagrined by the salary expectation. I thought, *After all, this is a start-up. We all make short-term sacrifices.*

But it didn't take long for me to realize I was wrong. This wasn't a start-up anymore. We didn't want someone to come in with the idea of short-term sacrifices for short-term gains. We wanted someone looking for long-term gains. I believed that's what Bob was looking for. At least, I sure hoped so.

In spite of a few rough spots during the negotiations, Bob eventually decided to join Neoforma. Jeff and I were thrilled, to say the least.

At Neoforma's peak, John Thompson's stock compensation for recruiting Bob would be was worth thirty-one million dollars. Such were the times.

By coincidence, there was a major healthcare trade show scheduled during the week that Bob was completing the final paperwork. Bob attended the trade show as a representative of his other company. During a break between conferences, the CEO of Medibuy, our not-very-serious competitor, came up to Bob and excitedly told him, "I want you to be among the first to know. We've just been funded by Kleiner Perkins. I am sure you know that this means we'll be the leader in the healthcare supply chain space."

Bob complimented him on that admirable accomplishment, thinking, *I don't think so!*

When Bob told us about Medibuy's news, Jeff and I freaked, fearing that Bob might change his mind. We knew how tough Bob's decision had been. Now he had been informed that a competitor was being funded by the most fearsome VC in the Valley.

KP had been flirting with Neoforma during our previous funding round. They had expressed serious interest in investing in us, even though they usually preferred to invest in earlier funding rounds. They had implied that we were the only company they were considering in the healthcare supply chain. Now we had confirmation of what we had suspected at the time—they had only been trying to slow us down, to postpone our funding, while lining up a younger company to get a large piece of and then set up as a competitor to us.

To Bob's credit, he wasn't threatened by the news at all. He wasn't from the Valley. He was from a world where VCs were investors. Nothing more, nothing less. And he didn't think he'd have any trouble finding people to invest in him.

Bob's resignation from his other company and acceptance of the post at Neoforma was big news in the industry. On the day before the announcement was to be made, Bob visited Neoforma with his wife, Patsy, and their children. When I heard that he had arrived, I scurried into the office we had set up for Bob. It was a large office, by Neoforma standards, located in the corner of the building. Jeff and I had moved into regular offices nearby.

I was feeling very proud of the company and its quarters, and I was very excited to welcome Bob. Bob was already in his office with his family when I arrived.

My excitement plunged to despair as I saw the expression in Patsy's eyes. I could hear her thinking, *YOU IDIOT! You gave up everything you had for THIS?!*

As I looked around, I could see her point. The furniture was mismatched. Through the narrow windows of the ground floor office, the view consisted of an assortment of car grills, parked almost against the tilt-up concrete building.

I walked up to Patsy, looked her in the eye, and said, "I'm sorry, but we needed him . . ." She might have tried to smile. I couldn't tell.

Next, we called a company meeting. By now, almost everyone knew that we had hired a new CEO, but they didn't know who. When the sixty or so employees based in the home office had gathered in our lunchroom, Jeff and I walked into the room, followed by Bob.

Jeff made the announcement. He gave a glowing summary of Bob's career and made some comical remark about how relieved he would be to hand over the CEO job. He wanted to make sure that everybody understood he had no reservation at all about handing over the reins to Bob. He then handed the microphone to Bob.

Without thinking, Jeff and I both stepped back toward opposite corners of the room, further exaggerating Bob's larger stature. Bob, with eyes wide and intense, said a few words to the gathered strangers. The strangers stared back at him with equally wide, uncertain eyes.

Jeff and I finally got what we asked for and we hoped that we had asked for the right thing.

July 1999

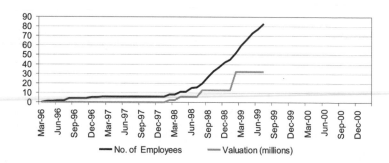

| | No. of Employees | Valuation (millions) |

Chemdex Shines on Market Debut

Chemdex, an online seller of laboratory chemicals and equipment with sales of $29,000 last year, rose almost 60 percent in its first day of public trading . . . The Palo Alto, California–based company rose 8.87 to 23.87 . . . The company closed with a market value of $758.65 million.

    Chemdex's investors include Silicon Valley venture capital firm Kleiner Perkins Caufield & Byers . . . The company will use $30 million of the net proceeds to fund anticipated operating losses . . . It will use the rest of the proceeds . . . possibly to acquire complementary businesses, it said.

CNET News.com
July 28, 1999

The Cast

Doing what's good is not always what's best.

At first, I didn't see much of Bob. After a few weeks of familiarizing himself with the company by interviewing the managers in charge of each department, Bob came into my office and said, "Wayne, it seems that whenever I ask employees why something is the way it is or who they take their direction from, your name comes up. I guess I should be turning to you for more information on what's going on around here."

I was surprised and somewhat flattered to hear this, which, I suppose, was the idea.

I told Bob that I had not wanted to prejudice his own evaluation of the company and its employees. I did not want to dilute the value of Jeff's unbiased appraisal of the company. "Also, I wanted you to know that I do not see you as a threat in any way and that I have no desire to manipulate you. We hired you because we sincerely believe that you will make the best decisions for Neoforma."

Bob asked me many questions about the organization — how it had evolved and why, what I thought its strengths and weaknesses were, what I thought of the senior managers—that kind of stuff. It was our first real conversation. When the meeting was over, I felt more confident about the future of Neoforma than I had in a long time.

From that day on, Bob consulted with me on many organizational issues. However, there were many issues he did not discuss with me. He knew the risk of getting too close to me, or anyone else. He endeavored to make everybody feel important and nobody feel indispensable. That was his job.

And his job was a tough one. Bob had been hired to star in and direct the company. Our investors were in heat. Their scent was followed right to Neoforma's doors by reporters, bankers, lawyers and accountants. His first major challenge would be to prepare the company for its public premiere. And he wasn't given a long production schedule.

Our investors wanted an IPO before the end of the year. Since IPOs don't tend to do as well in the last couple of months of the year, the IPO would need to occur in September — or October at the latest. Extensive IPO documents needed to be filed with the SEC at least a month before that. That meant that Bob had two months to figure out the company, get it under his control and fill in his executive team.

The quality of a company's management team is a major factor in how well a company will be received by Wall Street. Bob had a good reputation there. And the Street already knew a little about Frank, our CFO. We had located him through some investors many months before, but we had just hired him. Beyond Bob, Frank, and Sonic, we didn't have any well-known or proven executives on board.

Bob knew that he was an outside guy. He was good at managing outside relationships with key customers, partners and investors. His most critical need was to hire someone to manage the company's operations, someone he could trust to run the inside of the company. Someone capable of taking over the company in the event that he wasn't available. With a confidence in his own skills that only the best leaders have, he strove to make himself dispensable.

Bob knew who he wanted for this role. He wanted Dan.

Dan had been a fierce competitor of Bob's for many years. Dan was president of the healthcare division of a large distributor. His mid-thirties youthfulness, calm demeanor and reputation as a strong, ethical competitor had made him very popular in a tough industry. I would later interview a number of individuals who had worked for him who told me, "I would walk off the edge of the world for Dan."

Dan was a forward-thinking guy. Bob had little difficulty coaxing Dan to join Neoforma. Dan saw it as an opportunity to fundamentally improve healthcare. However, as it turned out, convincing Dan was the easy part.

When Jeff and I left Varian, the few *Good luck!* comments were cursory. Afterward, we were generally despised as traitors. When Bob resigned from his job, he had been very excited about the possibility of collaborating with his old company. He'd even thought that they would embrace the idea of investing in Neoforma. Instead, he faced rejection, indignation and anger to a degree he could not have imagined.

When Dan resigned from his job—well, let's just say that Jeff, Bob and I had been warmly nudged from the nest compared to the ordeal Dan went through.

His former bosses were incensed. Dan's company, like most of the large distributors, had been having casual discussions with Neoforma about ways we could improve their business. The managers of Dan's company were known for their warrior's sense of loyalty. You were either for them or against them. They felt betrayed that the young executive they had groomed so affectionately would jump to a little start-up company. And they were not inclined to forgive such treachery.

So, they did what any self-respecting company does when it craves revenge: they sued Dan. But that wasn't all. They garnered from a friendly Texas court a restraining order, forbidding Dan to work at Neoforma, any similar company, or any distributor until the lawsuit was settled. Such lawsuits can take years. They knew they were starving him of his livelihood. But their anger was still not satisfied. Private detectives were hired to follow Dan and pry into his personal life, trying to dig up dirt on him.

I met Dan only briefly in the week between his being hired, then legally banished. He seemed nice enough, but I was amazed by how unabashedly committed Bob was to helping Dan through his legal mess. In no uncertain terms, Bob told us that Dan's position would be open for as long as it took for the lawsuits to settle in Dan's favor.

There were suits and countersuits. There were motions and appeals. And, there was absolutely no progress toward resolution. If anything, everyone's position became more hardened.

As I've said, when Jeff gets his mind set on something, he won't let go. After about three months of wrangling, Jeff got fed up with the whole legal battle for Dan. It was distracting and destructive.

He told me, "You know, I'm just going to visit Dan's ex-bosses and get this thing behind us. The lawyers won't like it, but tough shit."

Now, the last thing that lawyers *ever* want to see is their clients talking directly with the other side. So, it was over their objections, then only with careful coaching, that Jeff visited Dan's previous employer.

Jeff's meeting started with great hostility. Then Jeff turned on his intellect and charm. I don't know how, but by the end of the meeting Jeff had essentially settled the issue. There were still a lot of details and gripes to work out, but he had, in less than two hours, miraculously turned these angry bulldogs from arch-enemies into friendly partners. The lawyers lost *big* that day.

Dan rejoined Neoforma and lived up to his reputation. That Dan had managed to remain level-headed throughout that nightmare presaged his ability to cope with the challenges he would meet in the years to come.

While recruiting Dan had turned into a mess, Bob had no such trouble recruiting the best sales team in the business. He knew nearly everyone who was anyone in the healthcare supply chain. He built an enviable sales organization almost overnight.

After operations and sales, we had a few more executive roles to fill. Both the marketing and engineering groups were floundering under a lack of leadership. Most of us on the Board believed that these roles would likely be filled by people outside the healthcare field. Bob asked me to take the lead on filling these last two positions. JP agreed to help with the marketing position. Alexander agreed to help with the engineering position.

I knew these would probably be the last key positions I would fill, so I took this task very seriously. After reaching consensus with Bob and others about the type of leaders we were seeking, I began working with a top recruitment agency to locate candidates.

As I have said, we had been looking for our marketing VP almost continuously for more than a year. The fact that we had not been able to fill this gap successfully did not look good. Our earlier candidates had, for the most part, come from technology industries. We still considered technology experience to be acceptable, but had begun to believe that someone with more consumer branding experience might be preferable.

Branding, the creation of very broad name recognition associated with positive emotional responses, was then very popular in the Internet press and very important to JP, Alexander and Bret. If Neoforma was going to be the First Mover in Internet healthcare B2B then we needed a BIG brand.

Though our selection of candidates was severely limited, one seemed to fit the bill quite well. Tim was a marketing executive at a major television network. The network was undergoing a management shake-up that had just placed Tim on the job market. Jeff and I first met Tim over dinner at a local restaurant. Gregarious, selfish and insensitive, Tim was the opposite of the type of person we had tried to recruit into Neoforma. But he did seem to know a lot about branding and he was clearly strong enough to lead people. He reminded me of a great cat—his large frame always relaxed, yet ready to pounce at any moment without the slightest hesitation or self-doubt.

With one eye on the disastrous hiring and departure of Mara, our last marketing recruit and cultural reject, and the other on our history of problems created by periods of uncertain leadership, I reviewed the feedback from our team. We all saw the risk inherent in Tim's coarse style and obvious financial motive, but we all agreed that stirring the company up a bit before the IPO probably wouldn't be such a bad thing. So we hired him.

Tim swept into Neoforma with a level of vigor and recklessness that dwarfed Mara's earlier invasion. He pissed people off. At the same time, he garnered and elevated a crew of loyalists. But, unlike Mara, he was good at choosing very smart loyalists. And, he spent money as if money were an obstacle to be obliterated. He shoveled a path through it, scattering bits here, there and everywhere.

He did know how to build a brand that Wall Street could appreciate. And, he did know who he shouldn't piss off. So, I was willing to put up with the stream of angry, long-time employees into my office, at least until we made it through the IPO process.

The last big position we had to fill was someone to lead our engineering organization. Through trial and error, we had been able to bring in good engineering management, but had been unable to locate someone with the combination of engineering expertise, technological vision and strong leadership that Neoforma would need in its next phase.

We all felt that this was the most important position of all. Because of Bob's extensive experience in the healthcare supplies and pharmaceutical markets, the company's trend toward enabling high-volume, mission-critical supplies purchasing would continue. This would require some very big decisions and heavy investment in hardware and software. Bad decisions could severely damage the company. We needed not only a celebrity, but also someone with extensive experience and credibility. Our list of candidates for this role was even shorter than the marketing list had been. Venture capital investment was at an all-time high. The type of person we were looking for usually founded companies rather than worked for them.

Nobody we interviewed even came close to satisfying our need, until we met Ajit. Like Bob, Ajit had started out as a long shot. He was up for the prestigious lead position in a lucrative Internet portal being created by a merger between one of the largest Internet search engine companies and the Internet division of one of the largest entertainment companies. The CEO of the entertainment company was courting him personally.

But, for some reason, Ajit was willing to spend some time with us. Small in stature and awkward, with his difficult, East-Indian accent, Ajit did not make a strong first impression. Bob sent me an email that captured the experience well . . .

> *I spent three hours tonight with Ajit. The first hour . . . he was non-specific . . . a little arrogant . . . poor eye contact . . . etc. I didn't like him . . . at all. Then something just clicked and he began to get very focused . . . specific in his experiences and how he'd apply them at Neoforma.*
>
> *He's obviously very intelligent . . . technically savvy . . . can cover high-level tech issues as well as drill down to specifics . . . knows how to make money . . . is ambitious . . . knows Silicon Valley and is well-connected . . . has a great brand name with his experience . . . can interface with exec level, works hard . . . wants to get into healthcare . . . all brothers and sister in healthcare. Clearly . . . he can cover more than just chief technology officer.*

We all felt the same way. He was very bright and would be very challenging to get along with. He could communicate brilliantly one minute and drift into inarticulate arrogance the next. I was very concerned about how Ajit would be received by our perpetually fussy and critical engineering team. I asked several of the engineers I most trusted to interview Ajit. I wanted them to be very frank with me about how they would feel reporting to him.

Their reviews were all similar: "Ajit would be difficult to work with . . . but he is one of those rare people that I could learn a lot from. I would be willing to report to him."

This was the most positive assessment of a candidate for engineering management I had heard. So, we hired him. I figured that the worst that could happen was that our many very good engineers might finally unify, if only around some kind of cultural rejection of Ajit.

That's pretty much what happened.

Ajit joined the engineering group with the sensitivity of a building inspector with a grudge. He made sure that everyone knew that he was not pleased with what he found. He concluded that some engineers were not up to par and that most of the team's previous decisions had been short-sighted and ill-informed. He made it clear to the Board that he had not been hired to win a popularity contest; he had been hired to bring the company to the next level. Since he shared their lust for large financial returns, he was given substantial latitude.

In addition to increasing the line of angry employees at my office door, Ajit did accomplish quite a lot. He expanded the mind of every member of the engineering group. Most of them improved—sometimes through education, but more often out of spite for Ajit. He unified the engineers around the idea that they really could do more and better than they had—preferably without Ajit.

Ajit did what he was hired to do. Under his leadership, Neoforma developed a world-class engineering organization. He made very few friends and he made many mistakes, but it is hard to fault him. We knew that he had not joined Neoforma because he particularly cared about its mission. He was primarily at Neoforma for fast money and résumé enhancement. Tim had joined Neoforma for much the same reasons.

We had hired both of them for their assertiveness and celebrity. I didn't have to like them to know that they were playing an important role in the company. I just had to do my best to minimize their short-term damage to the positive elements of the culture Jeff and I had so carefully nurtured. I spent a great deal of time espousing patience to those employees who turned to me in frustration and confusion.

It wasn't until I was confronted by many loyal Neoforma employees that I fully acknowledged why I had accepted, and even promoted, two such abrasive personalities into the company. Despite an abundance of talent in each group, marketing and engineering had become so political and inwardly focused that I felt the need to treat the situation aggressively.

There wasn't much time before the IPO. In a manner similar to the radiotherapy machines at Varian that delivered large doses of dangerous radiation to destroy tumors that were even more dangerous, I had hoped that a few toxic individuals could remove the dangerous pockets of inertia in those two departments.

I had faith in the company's ability to heal. All I had to do was cope with my own moral anxiety about how willing I had been to create such discomfort for employees I respected and cared for. It seemed that ambivalence about my decisions was always an inevitable part of leadership.

Ajit and Tim displayed no such ambivalence. In spite of their rejection by the Neoforma culture, it appeared that they would be quite comfortable at Neoforma for as long as it remained in the spotlight.

August 1999

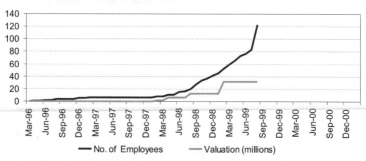

—— No. of Employees	—— Valuation (millions)

Neoforma.com, Inc. Acquires General Asset Recovery, LLC

B-2-B Services to Include Live Auction, Internet Auction, Classifieds and More. Neoforma.com, Inc., the global healthcare marketplace, announced today that it has acquired Arlington Heights, Illinois–based healthcare auction company General Asset Recovery, LLC (GAR) . . .

Neoforma Press Release
August 17, 1999

eBusiness and the Supply Chain

Are you at risk of being "Amazoned?" Depending on who you talk to, it's more a probability than a possibility . . . Can a fledgling dotcom company really swoop into health care and "re-intermediate," as Amazon.com has done in the publishing industry? . . . "Any GPO or distributor that signs a contract with an e-commerce company will have just signed its own death warrant," says one GPO executive . . .

The Health Strategist
August, 1999

Land Grab

It's funny to think of eBay and Amazon.com as the dinosaurs of the Internet. But it's becoming clearer that the Web's real promise lies not so much in auctions and consumer sales, but in the exploding business-to-business market . . .

Forbes
August 23, 1999

Pick-ups

A company's ultimate product is its culture.

Whenever we saw a gap in our organization, Bob, Jeff, some other manager or I would meet with others to discuss the need. If possible, we would fill that need by utilizing an internal resource. Usually, this meant rewarding someone with a longer title. Sometimes they'd get a bit more money too.

If the need was short-term or temporary, we would try to outsource it. A consultant could easily be dismissed when the job was done or if they didn't work out. If a need was critical, long-term and could not be met by existing employees, we would be forced to seek new talent.

In any company, a new hire is a risk. It's never certain how a new hire will perform with existing employees. Even if a new person is very good at what they are hired to do, that doesn't ensure that he or she will be effective.

The challenge is amplified by magnitudes when a big project needs to be staffed—right now. It means one person can't be hired at a time. The company has to hire a bunch of individuals at once, throw them together and hope for the best.

It was always a precarious situation. But, in the beginning, it had been our only option for big projects. Later, we had other choices.

When Neoforma was a couple of months away from filing an IPO, our cash reserves were high and our stock had become very valuable currency. The risk-to-reward profile of pre-IPO stock made it a tantalizing treat to dangle in front of outside talent.

The more that notable talent was brought into the company, the more valuable the stock became. So, in certain cases, it made a lot of sense to look at the possibility of acquiring *companies* instead of individuals.

Companies that have managed to produce something have been "cycled." They have worked out at least some of the interpersonal kinks.

When we observed that a large portion of our website visitors were seeking used medical equipment, we researched the market for second-hand equipment. It was a large and fractionalized market—two essential criteria for us to consider getting into a market.

Our first step was to leverage our substantial website traffic and Internet software expertise. We used a combination of internal developers and external software to quickly build a very functional auction site. We partnered with many existing used equipment dealers to quickly add equipment listings.

We had some success, but the many cultural, logistical and regulatory challenges inherent in the used medical equipment market seemed to be keeping us from being anything more than a peripheral player. That wasn't enough for us. There was too much about the process that didn't make sense.

Take your most negative stereotypical image of a used car salesperson—with slick hair and cheap suit—standing outside, among rows of evenly spaced cars and surrounded by colorful banners, waving eagerly in the breeze. He smiles very broadly, as he points to the large numbers taped to the windshield of a shiny, high-mileage coupe. Now, add some gaudy jewelry to the suit and grease to the hair.

Replace the image of the orderly car lot with that of a cluttered warehouse. Replace the shiny vehicle with a pile of dusty IV poles and bedpans. Add to the background a few shadowy pairs of foreign nationals, whispering in assorted languages, as they inspect the merchandise. That is the market our group of Silicon Valley techies was trying to enter.

Unlike the new equipment market, we didn't have much first-hand experience with the used market. It did not take us long to realize that the gritty nature of the used market required us to build a solid bridge between our computers and the warehouses that housed the equipment.

John, one of our salesmen, was the one guy in our organization with a strong connection to the used equipment market. From the beginning of our auction program, he had been a key facilitator in establishing relationships with existing dealers. One day, a couple of months before Bob joined Neoforma, John suggested to Jeff that if we really wanted to establish a foothold in the used market then Neoforma should buy GAR.

GAR was the leading used equipment auctioneer to the healthcare industry. John thought that GAR might consider selling their business to Neoforma. There was precedent for us to consider acquiring a land-based auction house. A few months earlier, the leading consumer Internet auctioneer, eBay, had acquired Butterfield & Butterfield, the fourth-largest auction house in the U.S.

Jeff was not particularly thrilled with the idea of buying a "bricks-and-mortar" company, as non-Internet companies are called, until John convinced him to observe a large auction by GAR of used equipment.

Jeff came back to the office very excited. "We have to buy this company. It makes so much sense. It's what our strategy has been missing." His excitement was contagious. I wanted to see one of these auctions too.

A couple of weeks later, I stopped by General Electric's medical equipment division headquarters in Milwaukee on the way to another East Coast meeting. GAR was facilitating an auction for GE. GE had a substantial business in the refurbishment of used medical equipment. I was particularly intrigued by this auction because I was already leading a number of discussions between GE and Neoforma. If GAR could make a very fussy company like GE happy, then they had certainly earned my respect.

I was met at the airport by Gino, the CEO of GAR. Gino was young, tall, dark and handsome, with expensive clothes and gilding—in the form of large gold bracelets and neck chains. To ensure that he would be noticed and appreciated from a distance as well, he showed up in a very posh, new Mercedes. He was so polished that I half-expected him to squeak as he moved against the leather seats in his car.

Gino greeted me warmly, immediately commenting on how much younger I was than he had expected. I told him the truth: I only looked young.

Feeling old, short, light and cute, I found it difficult to focus on Gino's words as we drove to the GE warehouses. I was entranced by the shiny wood surfaces and digital displays. I couldn't get my mind around the idea that my company was planning to buy his company.

His was a small company, made up of about twenty employees. His company was still young and struggling to get out of the red. Yet here he was, clearly living a life of luxury. As he described his large home near Chicago, I thought about my battered family wagon with missing hubcaps and my small house on a busy street. I couldn't imagine how someone could start a company and yet meet his own needs for a glamorous lifestyle so early on. I thought back to Jeff's comments during our last funding round about how he and I had always put ourselves on the bottom — low salaries, no bonuses, no company cars or other perks, and the lowest stock preferences. I felt a sense of indignation about how Gino had unapologetically put himself first. Warning bells started to go off in my head.

But all of that faded when I saw Gino in action. He was a classically trained auctioneer — all fast talk and innuendoes. Watching him was a thing of beauty. In a matter of minutes, he sold more used equipment than Neoforma had sold in six months.

Neoforma ended up in a bidding war for GAR against our main competitor, Medibuy. We were already in the middle of negotiations when Bob joined Neoforma so he had a limited role in the acquisition process. Medibuy was offering substantially more to Gino than the already astronomical amount we were willing to pay. Although I hadn't been involved in the negotiations, it started to look, at one point, like the deal was going the other way. Everyone was so frustrated with each other that the dialog had almost ceased. So I called Gino.

I talked with him, founder to founder. Then I put on my recruiting hat. I explained why short-term valuations would be irrelevant in the long run. In other words, our lower price was worth more than the other company's higher price. After all, we were mostly talking about non-liquid stock anyway. Gino expressed his appreciation for my directness and agreed to try not to sweat the small stuff.

Ultimately, we did acquire GAR. Some good things resulted from the deal. We quickly expanded our product offering. We significantly boosted our revenue during a critical period. And we were able to establish some good relationships with large hospitals. But some bad things happened too. The gold could only gild the blemishes for so long.

Despite our two completely different cultures, GAR and Neoforma managed to get along pretty well. Neither pretended to be like the other, but, for awhile, that was okay. We only had to interact at a few key points.

Eventually, the carefully staged bluster that supported Gino's charm began to fade. His credibility and effectiveness began to erode. He had been very aggressive in a small business but did not have the discipline to thrive in a large one. He couldn't meet his numbers.

Under pressure to narrow its focus, Neoforma eventually sold off GAR. Nobody from GAR remained with Neoforma. Not surprisingly, Gino's negotiations had yielded him far more money from Neoforma than any other individual made on the deal. And he eventually went right back to the same small business again.

All things considered, the acquisition hadn't been a bad one. Had the economy not gone into a tailspin, we might have been able to make things work out. But we should have given more credence to our warning bells. And I learned another important lesson as well. When they were made of a different moral fabric, companies—just like individuals—did not have the strength to bond with Neoforma under stress.

When it came time to buy the next company, we kept these lessons in mind.

I had long believed that, prior to an IPO, we needed to address content management once and for all. As Neoforma had grown, so had the quantity of assorted valuable data we needed to manage. Most of our development resources were dedicated to developing e-commerce functionality. We wanted to capture maximum revenue from our site visitors.

In the meantime, our electronic catalogs were not being given the same attention. Our administrative interfaces made product information difficult to add, edit and categorize, and even more difficult for our visitors to find. I considered our shortcomings in this area to be our greatest company risk, by far. Without a good catalog, who would want to shop at Neoforma?

Our needs were far from unique. So, rather than try to build advanced content-management tools from scratch, I asked two of our most demanding, creative and technically astute employees, Roy and Dave, to try to find existing tools that we could plug into our solutions. After extensive research, they identified a software company that seemed to have just the kind of tools we needed.

While Pharos clearly had a great product, there was some risk in working with them. They were a small, young start-up company, based in San Francisco. Knowing that I had placed this assignment in the best of hands, I did not meet with Pharos during our evaluation phase, but I was intrigued by one thing that I heard in Roy's reports to me: Our team and their team were getting along extremely well. I could see fondness and respect in the faces of both Roy and Dave when they spoke of the Pharos team. I knew Roy and Dave very well. Both were notoriously fussy. They could sniff out technological bluster before anyone else had even noticed. If they were this fond of the Pharos team, it was a very good sign.

Without the slightest doubt in my mind, I decided that we should pursue an acquisition of Pharos. My hunch that their team of fifteen or so was a perfect match to our development group was quickly confirmed when I met their founding team. They had a good product, but it was not their product I was after. I wanted a team of very good engineers who worked well together and understood how to organize and manage large quantities of information.

Most of the Neoforma executive team, including Bob, disagreed that acquiring Pharos was mission-critical. But unlike other times, when I had been willing to back down from my opinion for the sake of consensus, this time I would not let go.

I knew it wouldn't be easy to get Pharos. They were a hot company in a hot space. Companies like theirs were being purchased for a hundred million dollars or more by some of the biggest Internet companies.

I had been willing to let go of much at Neoforma, but I refused to allow this hole to be unfilled. I put everything I had into convincing Pharos and Neoforma that marriage was a good thing. It was touch-and-go for awhile, but Neoforma did eventually purchase Pharos.

The members of the Pharos team were great contributors to Neoforma. A few of them became key executives in the company. Several others became crucial leaders. Others just did their jobs, but did them well.

Months later Bob would say to me, "Man, thank goodness for that Pharos team. I don't even want to *think about* how things might have been without them!"

I felt very good about that. Acquiring Pharos was the most intuitive decision I had ever made at Neoforma. I had pursued them because the people *felt* right, not only because it seemed like a smart business decision. Too many times, I had ignored my feelings for the sake of a "smart decision," when someone or something just didn't *feel* right. And I'd almost always regretted it.

In those early years, Neoforma made a number of other acquisitions— some large, some small. In all cases, if the cultures were disparate, the results were somewhere between poor and disastrous. Matched cultures did not ensure success, but they greatly increased the odds that the people involved would be able to act naturally and cohesively when improvisation was required.

September 1999

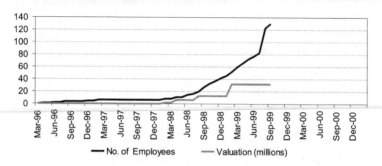

	No. of Employees	Valuation (millions)

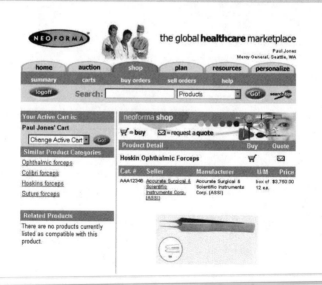

The Ramp

Money brought everything to the surface.

Everything had been set up. The pieces were falling into place. The press was talking about us. Investors were buzzing about us. Wall Street was in a frenzy of excitement. Money was breeding money, and its offspring were fertile at birth. As Neoforma prepared for its public debut, the legal and accounting bills were becoming astronomical. I watched in wonder as flocks of unfamiliar suits moved in and out of our offices each day.

To ensure that nobody doubted that Bob was in firm control of the company, I stayed very much in the background. Jeff was equally deferential toward Bob. He was very pleased to be out of the spotlight. Our burdens lightened, Jeff and I were actually starting to speak to each other again. We made it clear to Bob that we were happy to help out wherever we could.

In order to create the biggest buzz, the IPO production consisted of three primary parts. First, the company needed to get bigger, stronger and better. We were building the strongest team possible to accomplish this task. Second, we needed to build an even stronger financial foundation. If we brought in more money prior to a public offering, we would be much less vulnerable to an unpredictable future. We figured that—*oh, about $70 million*—would do the trick. And, if that money came from strong corporate partners, we would create a security buffer around our relatively new enterprise. Third, we had to select a strong banker to usher us through the IPO process.

For the most part, Jeff and I were helping Bob along the lines we had established early on: Jeff assisted Bob with tasks involving investors and I helped with tasks involving personnel and operations. However, these areas began to overlap heavily as we lined up our strategic funding round.

Neoforma's place in the limelight gave us the previously unimaginable power to focus more on who we would *allow to invest* rather than who we *could convince to invest*. In July, Chemdex, the Kleiner Perkins (KP) –backed B2B company, had made a very successful IPO debut. Chemdex became the overnight benchmark for valuing new B2B companies. Their company had a huge valuation and their market in laboratory products was very small, compared to the healthcare market that Neoforma dominated. With Neoforma's IPO imminent, just about any corporate investor would jump at the nearly certain chance to double or quadruple their money in six months or so.

We created a dream list of the types of strategic investors we wanted to have in our final pre-IPO investment round. First, we wanted at least one solid, household-name company to invest in us. Gaining the confidence of well-known companies would help us project a very good image.

Second, we wanted to get support from an established software technology company. There had been much speculation in the press that the big software companies were aggressively targeting the markets of some of the new B2B companies. We wanted to distance ourselves from the new software technology companies that might easily be made obsolete by established players.

Finally, we wanted some of the big suppliers in healthcare to invest in us. By now, everyone knew that one of the biggest uncertainties in the business models of B2B companies was what the established suppliers might do to resist the newcomers. It makes it very difficult to sell stuff when the seller refuses to sell.

The generic identities of the companies on our list were gradually replaced with actual names. Assorted relationships that Neoforma had already established quickly yielded leads on interested corporate investors.

Dell Computer Corporation had a strategic investment fund that was interested in leading the round. With Dell's reputation for innovative business management at its peak, adding them to our list would certainly achieve our goal of being associated with a household name.

SAP America, the U.S. branch of the huge enterprise software company, seemed to be a perfect choice as a software technology investor.

Their software had a substantial presence in the offices of healthcare suppliers, as well as at large hospital systems. We had been partnering successfully with SAP for several months. While they didn't have a fund dedicated to the pursuit of strategic investments, they were very interested in pursuing an investment in us.

We hoped to get an investor in each of three supplier categories: medical equipment, medical supplies and medical distribution. Other than pharmaceuticals, which was an area we weren't interested in pursuing in the near future, these were the three big areas in healthcare.

In our early days, we had found General Electric to be one of the most stubborn medical equipment manufacturers for us to deal with. Their aggressive pursuit of dominance of each of their markets created such a strong outward force that their corporate policies were nearly impenetrable. They did not like the idea of allowing upstart companies to get so much as a foothold in their domain.

Though we had been cautiously probed by some of their largest competitors, GE had shut its doors tightly on us. They made it clear to us that they believed there was nothing we could do that they couldn't do better on their own.

Then, as we were building up to the IPO, GE called us. They wanted to talk. One of the lead managers in their strategic investment fund had seen Bob speak at an investor conference and reported that Neoforma held far and away the most exciting potential of any company he'd heard about at the show. That got the attention of GE management.

Healthcare was a large part of GE's business and yielded among the most consistent and lucrative profits. The margin — the amount of money made on each sale—was very high in healthcare equipment. If there were a company out there that might threaten those margins, and if that company were to acquire enough assets, well—that would be very bad for executive bonuses.

So, GE had done some very serious investigation of the increasing numbers of B2B healthcare companies and had come to the conclusion that Neoforma was simultaneously the strongest and least threatening of the bunch. At least that's what they told us.

We certainly couldn't argue with their conclusion. We *were* the strongest and we had always held a participatory, rather than confrontational, position with suppliers. Our main competitor, Medibuy, was openly and foolishly promoting a *let's band together and screw the manufacturers* message to potential hospital customers.

We had no doubt that GE considered us the lesser of evils, rather than the greater of opportunities — but, hey, they *were* GE, and GE was the undisputed U.S. leader in healthcare equipment.

In an initial meeting with us, the GE representatives had come in with a very condescending attitude. When we made it apparent that we didn't consider them much more important than the other ten thousand medical manufacturers, they were visibly startled. The tone of the conversation changed quickly. After a few meetings, they informed us that they would be happy to extend to us the privilege of consideration for investment. And we told them that we'd be happy to listen to what they had to say.

GE was to healthcare equipment what Johnson & Johnson was to healthcare supplies. And it just so happened that J&J was interested in us too — though for a very different reason. Whereas GE saw us as a threat, J&J saw us as an opportunity. They did not like what the group purchasing organizations had done to their margins in the supplies markets. They wanted to crush the GPOs. They saw Neoforma as a chance to do just that. But that meant, they'd need some control over us. When they expressed their interest in investing, we said okay.

The largest distributor of healthcare supplies was Cardinal. When Bob accepted the top job at Neoforma, he had been certain that Cardinal would be enthusiastic about investing in our strategic round. But when Bob's former boss at Cardinal decided that Bob had betrayed the company by leaving, that was no longer a possibility. Fortunately, there were several other large distributors with which we were on friendly terms, so we discussed strategic investment possibilities with them. Two of them thought this was a good idea.

Several of our previous venture firms and many new ones wanted to play too. Jeff and I were both receiving calls from venture firms all over the country, espousing their connections and expertise, asking to be considered for participation in the funding round. They were offering to put millions in, *no questions asked.*

One of the calls was from Jack, our mentor and first attorney. He told me that a partner from one of the first venture firms we had made a presentation to, two years earlier, had called him to ask "a big favor."

He wanted Jack to convince Jeff and me to include his firm in the round.

I could tell that Jack was perversely thrilled to deliver this message. I remembered our presentation to this guy very well. He had been among the most dismissive and condescending VCs we had met. And that was saying a lot.

Jack knew our answer, but wanted to hear us say it. He had been so enthusiastic about us at the time and had been very upset that the VCs didn't see why. He had taken it personally. It was a pleasure for him to deliver our answer personally.

Everything seemed to be lining up nicely. This list of investors was more than we could have hoped for. I was very excited by the knowledge that our team of partners could not possibly be topped by Medibuy, however powerful their *keiretsu* was.

Keiretsu is a term borrowed from the Japanese. It refers to a conglomerate of businesses linked together by a common financial interest. The term had become associated with KP because of the way they were leveraging the power of companies they'd previously invested in to support their newer investments. We knew they were trying very hard to gain ground on us. KP was not used to settling for second place.

With such a powerful list of investors lining up behind Neoforma, all we had to do was to work out the details. In a few short months, we needed to get them all to agree to a set of financial terms that were favorable to us. The higher our valuation, the lower our dilution would be and the more money our investors could recover after the IPO.

Bob was swamped. His time was consumed with learning about and building his organization, while simultaneously preparing the company for an IPO. He did not have the time to coordinate the negotiations between the disparate investors. So, Bret, who was still on our Board, volunteered to lead the investor negotiations.

While I did not care much for Bret, I didn't mind the idea of him leading this effort. In the previous funding round, he had been a champion of getting the highest valuation for Neoforma. His confidence that he could get Neoforma a valuation greater than $250 million in this round was appealing. Most of us thought that anything above $150 million would be stretching it. But, if Bret could get a higher valuation, more power to him.

Which is what we gave him—more power. Previously, Bret had been a bit player. Even though he was well-positioned, he didn't know much about our business or the people in it. He had invested some money and was only interested in seeing that money grow.

The first time we saw Bret around our offices—following his investment in our first venture round—was just prior to our most recent funding round. That was when he fought with Jeff over Bret's insistence on securing a participating preferred clause favoring his investment in the funding documents. His bullying had been brief, but effective. When it came to handling the company's valuation, thanks largely to my own naïveté he had pretty much gotten his own way. His investment money had nicely multiplied due to the new high valuation, which he could show on his reports to Venrock.

Then he had become active in recruiting a CEO. His unbridled enthusiasm for Joe had almost put Neoforma on the track to self-destruction. But in the end, he had been influential in helping convince Bob of the potential financial value of Neoforma. Bret took full credit for hiring Bob, in spite of Jeff's leading role in getting Bob. He had also assured Bob that he would be there to help him through the next funding round.

For the most part, Bret's contributions had been good for the company. Luck had been on his side so far. I could tolerate another period of personal awkwardness while Bret fought for our team.

So Bret informed all of the potential investors that he was the man in charge.

Shortly thereafter, Bret walked into my office, sat down and smiled so widely that my defenses sprang instantly into action. He had never been that familiar before. Just the fact that he'd come in and taken a seat was unnerving.

"Wayne, I want to talk to you about something. Now that I have looked into this next funding round . . . well, I just have to tell you, there is a heck of a lot of work to do."

"I thought that was part of your job, as a representative of Venrock," I said, "to help the company recruit senior people and help get funding when needed."

"No, no, my job was to invest the money. That is what I do. A phone call or interview here and there, that's about it. I went way beyond the call of duty in hiring Bob. This funding . . . well, this is a big project."

"But . . . you're going to be helping increase the value of Venrock's . . . and your *own* . . . investment by *double* what we think we can get. Isn't that what you do too? Isn't that enough reason to do this?" I said.

"No, that's where you have things mixed up. It's Bob's job now to get funding and so on."

"But," I said, "Bob's too busy with the IPO process to get involved in every detail here."

"Oh, I agree," Bret said, "And I am happy to help out. It's just that . . . well, I would expect the company to compensate me for my extra effort."

"You mean, you want us to pay you to help us increase your investment? I'm . . . well, this just doesn't sound right at all. What are we talking about here? Venrock gets paid in stock for your time?"

"Oh, no, this activity goes well beyond my role with Venrock. The stock would go to me."

"Can you do that?" I couldn't quite believe what I was hearing. "I mean, isn't there something in your agreement with Venrock that keeps you from personally benefiting from your role representing other investors?"

"No," Bret said with an expression of indignation. "I can still represent Venrock just fine. My role in evaluating the initial investment is over. There is nothing unusual about someone like me getting compensated for extra work. Venrock knows all about my outside projects. It's all out in the open."

"Well, obviously I need to speak with Bob and Jeff about this. How much stock are you asking for?"

"Oh, no. It's not for me to put a number on that," Bret said, with sudden modesty. "I'm on the Board. The other Board members need to decide what a fair amount would be. Talk with JP about this. I've already discussed it with him and he agrees completely." He assumed a hurt, indignant tone. "If you don't want me to help out . . . hey, that's fine with me. Neoforma is only one of my investments. If I'm not appreciated here, my time can certainly be spent more productively elsewhere. I'm okay with that . . . though I do need to remind you that several of the investors have indicated that their confidence in Neoforma is greatly enhanced by my participation. Several of them . . . including Dell . . . might pass on the opportunity, if I dropped out. They'd wonder why." He smiled again. "Anyway, let me know your decision."

He stood and abruptly left my office.

I was fuming. I just didn't get it. How could he be so selfish when we were all working so hard? What made him think that he was so special?

When my breathing returned to normal, I picked up the phone and called Jeff. He was traveling. I got him on his cell phone and explained the situation. I became seriously worried about the safety of those around him as he yelled some very creative profanities into the phone. I could feel his clenched anger struggling to squeeze through the holes in my earpiece.

We agreed that I should approach JP before bringing this issue to Bob. It was the last thing we wanted to add to Bob's plate right now. Certainly JP would squelch the idea that Bret deserved more than he was already getting. After all, JP and Alexander had put an enormous amount of time and energy into Neoforma.

JP joined me in my office later that day. He looked very nervous. I had the feeling that he already knew why I had wanted to speak with him so urgently.

I wasted no time. "Bret came into my office today and asked for additional stock as compensation for his involvement in the funding. Did you know anything about that?"

"Yes, we did talk about that . . . in very general terms. He has been putting a lot of time into Neoforma. He got us the high valuation last time and he hired Bob."

"But *everybody* has been working hard and everybody benefits from their own work. It wouldn't be fair if we just gave a bunch of stock to Bret and left out the other investors."

"Well, actually, not all investors have been putting in the same amount of work. Bret had been very active and . . . Alexander and I have been too. We still are." He paused for me to let that sink in, then went on. "I think it's only fair that the extra effort be compensated."

I tried to stifle my shock. "So . . . let me get this straight. YOU are asking for more stock too?"

He shifted in his chair and avoided eye contact. "Not a lot. But it's only fair that we are rewarded for our ongoing efforts."

"But you have already been paid in stock for helping the company."

"Yes, but that was only for our time getting you and Jeff through a venture round. Who knew that we'd still be helping out for this long?"

"You're helping out for this long because you are increasingly likely to get a very large return on your investment. Isn't that what it's about?"

"We've already made our investment. There's no reason for us to be here . . . *if we're not appreciated* . . ." He put on the same air of indignation that Bret had used. I had the feeling that this had all been rehearsed, just as the first presentation by JP and Alexander to the Venrock partners had been.

"Just how much stock were you thinking about?"

"Oh, not much. I figure . . . about four hundred or so for Bret. Less for me and Alexander. You know . . . maybe a hundred."

"A hundred what?"

"A hundred thousand shares for Alexander and me."

"Divided between you?" I said.

"No . . . each," he said.

"And four hundred thousand shares of stock for Bret!? That's what we give to our executives for four years of sixty-hour weeks."

"You can't compare what we get with what the employees get. We're the ones with the connections. Without us, there wouldn't be a Neoforma. If you don't want us around, just let me know. I have plenty of other things to do . . . you know, things that get me a better return on my time."

I couldn't discuss this with him any further. I could tell that Jeff, Bob and I were being set up. Now that the IPO was getting close enough to taste, these guys were done pretending to be nice. It was all about the money. "Have you discussed this with Alexander?"

"Yes, of course."

I couldn't believe that Alexander would have a role in this obscenity. I called Alexander and insisted on meeting with him. The only time and place that worked for us was his house, early the next morning.

When Alexander greeted me, he could tell immediately that he didn't want me within shouting distance of his family, so he guided me to some chairs in his back yard. This was my first time at his house. Through my fury, I noted that, while his house and property was large, it did not display the same level of opulence as the houses of other investors I had seen.

The sun was shining, but a morning chill was still in the air.

Alexander shook his head and smiled, "Oh, the things I find myself in the middle of! Okay, Wayne, what's on your mind?"

I told him. Then I said, "Is this your idea? Did you all talk this over? Do you think you all deserve this extra stock?"

"I don't think it's inappropriate to compensate Bret for his efforts. I'm not sure what the amount should be though."

"Don't you agree that four hundred is too much? This will not look good to any of the future investors and it sets a bad precedent. Who proposed this amount?"

"Hey, this wasn't my idea. Bret proposed the idea that our extra involvement should be compensated. Someone came up with that number. I don't know the exact sequence. If Bret can get a high valuation, then four hundred thousand shares is nothing in the big picture, right?"

"True, but it's still not right. And it's not right that you're going along with this."

"Wayne, I'm fine, with or without extra stock. Right now, you need to keep the momentum going forward. Just go along with this and Bret will be gone from your life after the close of the round. Think about that."

"What do Wally and David think about this idea?" I asked him. Wally was still on our Board and so was David. David was the VC on our Board who had officially represented the previous round of investors.

"As far as I know, they don't know anything about it."

Later that day, I reluctantly brought the whole unruly mess to Bob's attention.

After listening to my summary, he said, "I've got to tell you, Wayne, I hate that he is doing this to us. But I can't do this on my own at this time. I know you guys would help out . . . but if Bret stepped out of the scene right now, it would spook our investors—unless they thought I was simply asserting my new authority."

"We have to give him what he asks for," Bob said. "Why not try to negotiate him down from four hundred? That's just so excessive . . . I worry that future investors won't look fondly on the fact that we compensated a Board member so disproportionately. Make sure to let the other Board members know about this too. I'm sorry to ask you to do this on your own, Wayne, but Jeff is out of town and I am booked solid."

If I had not had Anni to vent my frustrations to that night, I would have burst. Why, after this long, was there always some new catastrophe threatening the company?

I called Wally and let him know what was going on. His reaction was only slightly less spicy than Jeff's had been, but he entered a state of resignation more quickly. "You know, Wayne, sometimes that's the way it is. You have to deal with the worst side of people, when big money is involved. I'm not happy about this low blow, but I'll go along with whatever decision you and Jeff think is right." Loyal to the end, that was Wally.

"So you don't have to worry about me," Wally continued, "but David has never expressed confidence in Bret and will be very incensed by the whole thing. I've known David for a long time. You better let me give him this news."

A few hours later Wally called me. He said, "I underestimated David's reaction. He is threatening to demand all of his firm's money back if we give *any* stock to Bret. He's going to make a very big fuss that would certainly chase away all but the most steadfast investors."

I asked Wally to set up a meeting with David. At first, David refused to meet, saying there was nothing to discuss. Finally, David did agree to meet with me, as long as Wally was there too. Or maybe Wally insisted on being there—to reduce the risk of violence.

David and I had not interacted much, but he had always treated me with respect. I knew that he had a reputation for being as fair as he was aggressive. I was hoping that this would help me.

David wasn't just angry, he was livid. His moral indignation at Bret's behavior overshadowed everything else. He had a great deal of pride in the value of what he did and he could not stand the idea that someone who represented a top-tier VC would act the way Bret was acting. And he strongly disagreed with Bret's suggestion that extra compensation for funding assistance was common practice. "Everyone knows that creates a conflict of interest. My apologies to you, but I'll take this company down before I'll let him benefit from this disgusting behavior."

I was not happy to be there. I wanted to be anywhere but there. What I wanted to do most was hold onto my own sense of outrage at Bret's behavior. My instincts, too, were to stop him at any cost. But my investment in Neoforma was deeper and more personal.

So I sat there, arguing against my own position — telling David that the best thing to do was reach a compromise with Bret. It wasn't easy, but by the end of a long meeting, we had come up with a plan that might work. All I had to do was work out a few details and figure out how to lower Bret's expectations.

When I phoned Bret to discuss the issue, he was not in the mood for compromise. After I explained the other investors' concerns about his conflict of interest, he said, "If David thinks he can do a better job with the round than I can, let him lead the effort!! The four hundred is not negotiable!!" Having nowhere else to go with his argument, Bret resorted to attitude alone. "In fact, that's it. I can see I am not appreciated here. I am done. I don't want to be a part of the funding any more . . . regardless of how much you pay me." He hung up.

Several calls and meetings later, everyone was calmer and more willing to talk things through. But the illusory smiles were gone.

Bret had agreed to come to our offices to meet with Bob. Jeff had returned from his trip and Bret made the mistake of entering his office. Jeff and Bret exchanged a few words. Their brief encounter can best be characterized by the fact that Bret used his foot to launch Jeff's wastebasket against several walls.

After that colorful encounter, Bret met with Bob. Bob graciously expressed his need for assistance and told Bret how much we wanted his help. He talked persuasively about how little the additional stock compensation really mattered in the overall picture.

Feeling properly appreciated, Bret agreed to help out—but only as a personal favor to Bob (a marker that will, no doubt, be called in one day). Bob put some conditions on what Bret would have to accomplish to earn various levels of stock compensation. Something like an agreement was formed. Nobody was happy with it, except Bret, who made a point to say that the last thing he had ever meant to do was upset anybody.

Dealing with unpleasant internal conflicts and working through the financial terms with the strategic investors were only a few of the challenges in getting this round closed.

Since we had selected prominent companies to gain their endorsement of our business model, we had to negotiate operating agreements with several of them as a condition of their investment.

Avoiding conflicts between our new corporate investors and our customers, who were in many cases competitors with our investors, presented a substantial challenge. But we faced a unique and even greater problem.

The representatives of many companies with which we were trying to negotiate were quietly slipping their résumés to us under the table. The closer to the IPO we got, the more résumés we received.

Everyone wanted to work at Neoforma. Everyone was fed up with the inefficiencies inherent to the healthcare establishment and nobody could deny the financial appeal of a pre-IPO company. While dishing out the usual cautions, threats and deal points, these business development representatives tried to make sure to negotiate with us very aggressively—so we would be impressed enough to hire them!

The trouble was, if we accepted their résumés, we would create an unacceptable rift between objectivity and familiarity. If we rejected their résumés, we risked the wrath of an indignant contract negotiator. It made for many awkward scenes.

To ensure that we had maximum focus and decision-making power on each deal, Bob assigned an executive to each strategic investor to work on these complex operating agreements. Jeff got J&J. I guess I drew the short straw. I got GE.

GE had a reputation for ruthlessness. Its contract negotiators were well trained in their aggressive tactics. They were not allowed to accept the weaker side of any deal.

My natural tendency is to go for the fair deal and waste no time with posturing. Posturing was everything to them. They asked for absurd levels of control over Neoforma. They pounded me with demands. They asked for all kinds of sensitive information. The process was very unpleasant, but we seemed to be moving toward a generally acceptable conclusion.

Every time I held firm to a position, Chris, who was my primary contact there, would sigh and say that he'd have to run something this significant by Jack. He was referring—with practiced informality —to the legendary head of GE, Jack Welch. I strongly doubted that Mr. Welch knew any part of Chris's name—first or last—but I played along, trying to look suitably impressed.

The other deals seemed to be moving along in a similar pattern. Some bumps here and there, but it looked like we might just be able to pull this off . . .

However well things seemed to be going with our primary group of investors, it was prudent for us to pursue alternative investment options. Bret was far less interested in working with strategic health-care partners than Jeff, Bob and I. As far as he was concerned, big money was better than good money. So he lined up visits to a number of prominent venture capital firms.

One firm with deep pockets and a great name was Vulcan Ventures. It was run by Paul Allen, co-founder of Microsoft Corporation. Bret set up a visit for Bret and Bob to meet with one of the partners at Vulcan.

On the way into the meeting, Bob asked Bret, "How much do you think we should tell them we want them to invest?"

"When they ask," Bret said, "we'll say that we were telling them about the round so that they would have a good idea what was going on in the healthcare space. Then we'll tell them that, we're sorry, but the round is already fully subscribed."

Bob looked surprised.

"Look, that's the way these things work," Bret told him. "Everybody wants what they can't have."

The presentation went very well. The partner asked about the details of the funding round. Bret played his card. The partner acted suitably startled that Bret would have had the nerve to waste his time, then excused himself for a few moments.

A more senior partner returned with him. The senior partner was quite persistent in his declaration of the great value that Vulcan brought with its investments. Perhaps Bret and Bob would reconsider their position on the funding round if Vulcan took a *large* part of the round.

Bret didn't think so, but he vacillated. It was possible that we might be able to consider alternatives, under the right terms. In the end, they didn't offer as much value as the strategic healthcare investors, but it was great to have a back-up plan.

Another investment firm with even deeper pockets approached us at about the same time. Softbank, the Japanese multinational conglomerate was at its peak in late 1999. Having made a fortune from its investments in such companies as Yahoo! and E*Trade, Softbank was aggressively trying to gain control of huge portions of the Internet. Its president and CEO, Masayoshi Son, was one of the foremost darlings of the business press. Through a series of intermediaries, we had been told that he wanted to meet with Bob and Bret at a very high-end business hotel.

They were met at the door by a somber security guard, wearing a communications earpiece. He guided them to the penthouse suite. Bob and Bret entered the huge suite at one end. Seated at the other end was Masayoshi Son.

Bob and Bret approached and greeted him. Bob then gave an hour-long summary about Neoforma. Masayoshi Son listened politely, but gave no indication of his thoughts, until Bob finished speaking.

Masayoshi Son presented a brief summary of Softbank.

Then he asked about the details of the funding round. Satisfied that he had the information he needed, he made a proposal. Softbank was only interested in investing if they could take the entire round.

In exchange for that exclusivity, Softbank would invest a greater sum of money at a greater valuation—say, $100 million, invested at a $400 million valuation. Simple as that.

Bob thought this sounded pretty good. So did Bret. They said they would review this offer with the other investors and get back to Masayoshi Son.

When I heard about this offer, I thought it sounded pretty good too—maybe even good enough to risk the ire of the strategic health-care investors we had lined up. Maybe.

However, when we followed up with Softbank, something had happened. At first, we were simply told that Masayoshi Son was not available. Then we were told that he had changed his mind.

After persistent inquiries, we were told that someone from KP had heard about the Softbank proposal and contacted Masayoshi Son. They had informed him that an investment in Neoforma would be a bad idea. It would adversely affect all of the other deals that KP was bringing to Softbank. Anyway, Softbank was informed that they could get a much better deal if they invested in Medibuy instead.

This was very frustrating, but we felt confident that our strategic healthcare round was still a very likely and powerful alternative. That is, until J&J started to get cold feet . . .

Well into the final stages of the deal, an internal struggle within J&J surfaced with unpleasant suddenness. They told us that they weren't so sure that this was such a good idea anymore. We found out later that they had been approached by several GPOs that had heard a rumor of J&J's investment in us. The GPOs had suggested that perhaps J&J was being a bit rash in their decision, perhaps they should consider how such an investment might affect which products the GPO member hospitals purchase.

I am sure that nobody said anything about an actual outcome, but the threat of losing market share was present any time a GPO chatted with a manufacturer.

J&J and GE had formed a disconcerting bond during the term-sheet negotiations. They had been working in concert to bring an uncomfortable number of new terms to the table at the last minute. Now that J&J was reconsidering their position, the GE commitment seemed in jeopardy. And, if GE dropped out, Dell was likely to get skittish.

Once again, all of the progress we had made seemed to be slipping from our grasp. *Why did everything have to be so damned hard in this industry?*

While some of us were struggling to coordinate the perfect funding round, others were busy trying to line up the perfect IPO. And then there was the perfect banker to consider . . .

The biggest decision that a company has to make, when organizing an IPO, is who to hire as the banker.

There are usually several banks involved in an IPO, but the lead position is the most important. In 1999, there were many banks competing to take companies public, but there were two banks most associated with Internet IPO blockbusters: Goldman Sachs and Morgan Stanley. A third firm, that had an equally prestigious reputation, but less experience with Internet IPOs, was Merrill Lynch. We wanted one of these three banks to take top billing on our IPO filing.

In order to avoid any perception of conflict of interest, the major banks will not usually work with companies that compete with each other. Since we were the first IPO in the healthcare supply chain, we didn't think it would be difficult to recruit one of the top banks.

We queried Morgan first. They had been the bank to take Chemdex public, so they were the logical one to work with us. We were immediately told by Morgan that they had a conflict of interest. KP, the investor in both Chemdex and Medibuy, had already requested that Morgan prepare for a future IPO by Medibuy. Since KP was the source of so many hot IPO prospects, who could turn them down?

Goldman was the obvious next choice for us then. At first, Goldman seemed like a go. They liked our story. They liked our press coverage. Everything seemed to be going well, until they started to shrink back from us. It was as though something had bitten them.

Then we heard, through the rumor mill, that Goldman had been hired by KP to *explore strategic options* for Medibuy. *Exploring strategic options* means looking for companies to buy or be bought by. The rumor was that, in classic *keiretsu* style, KP wanted Medibuy to get ahead of Neoforma on the way to public company status by having Chemdex purchase them. Since Morgan was already the bank and, by default, the lead mergers and acquisitions (M&A) representative for Chemdex, KP had to use a different banker to pursue this deal. It seemed far more than coincidence that this arrangement inhibited Neoforma's ability to work with the two hottest Internet banks.

Goldman had been comfortable with the idea that M&A activity for Medibuy could be run by a separate team, isolated from their IPO team. They had been so comfortable, in fact, that they had failed to mention this potential conflict to us. Unlike what we observed in their recent IPO activity, they had been coaching us to wait six months for an IPO. Their attitude did not make sense to us, until we discovered their relationship with our primary competitor through KP.

Bob was angered, but not overwhelmed, by the knowledge that the mighty *keiretsu* was fighting us with such fury. Business was business, but he didn't like being messed with. He immediately dumped Goldman and pursued Merrill. Bob was actually quite content with the idea of working with Merrill. His background in a more conservative industry gave him confidence in the more conservative Merrill.

Many weeks had been wasted on Goldman. To enter the IPO window before the end of the IPO season, Bob had be very aggressive and work very fast. And, Merrill wasn't sure yet how far they wanted to go into the wild world of Internet stock. They wanted time to think about it.

If Merrill didn't lead the IPO, then Neoforma would have to select a less prestigious lead banker. That would affect everything. Our perceived value upon an IPO would be smaller. Our appeal to the current group of strategic corporate investors would be reduced. Our IPO would be delayed by months. Our competitor might beat us to an IPO, and they would be led there by a more prestigious bank. Regardless of anything they or we did, they would then be perceived as the market leader, which would reduce our ability to work with the larger industry partners and customers.

So, our minds became quite free from idle moments of pleasant thoughts. Each day brought new and increased tension.

Jeff and I had expected a reprieve from such pressure when Bob joined us, but we hadn't let ourselves relax so much that this new volley attack could do much damage. We just resigned ourselves to perpetually living life on the edge.

I wondered what Bob, so new to this bizarre world, must be thinking about this seemingly endless, upstream struggle. In each email or call from Bob, I expected to hear him say he was leaving immediately.

Finally, we were able to negotiate an acceptable deal with Merrill. They would lead our IPO.

When it became clear that our IPO could not be stopped by limiting the choice of banks, KP thought they might be able to slow us down by entertaining the idea of a merger between Neoforma and Medibuy.

They were quite willing to consider a fifty-fifty merger. In spite of their gains in the press, we knew very well how little Medibuy really had. A marriage of equals was absurd, but discussing a merger between the two companies could not be summarily dismissed. The combined companies could add even greater distance to the growing pack of pursuers. But it soon became clear to us that their exploration of a merger was little more than another delaying tactic.

J&J eventually confirmed our fear. They were not going to invest in our funding round. GE got very shaky. As their primary contact, I spent an extraordinary amount of time severing the bond that Neoforma had formed between J&J and GE. Some conversations went well. Others were very tense.

As the completion of our IPO paperwork approached, I couldn't get GE to firmly commit one way or the other to our funding round. This was making several other of our investors *very* edgy. A certain investor was particularly edgy, though in an opposite way from the rest.

Flip had made a fortune selling his company to Computer Associates. He had used his money and experience to create his own investment fund. A big, self-made man, with long hair braided into a ponytail, Flip was not one to follow the flock. But his faith in Bob was without bounds.

When Flip heard about GE's waffling, he told Bob not to worry. He would encourage the group of investors to make their final decisions.

Bob scheduled a conference call with all of the investor representatives. By this time, we had only a week before we were scheduled to file our IPO paperwork. We needed to include all the details of the funding round. Bob was firm. Everyone had had enough time to make the decision. The round was closing today. He wanted to know who was in and who wasn't.

When some of them started to waffle, Flip interrupted and said,

"We could go on about this forever, but I know enough about this company and have complete confidence in Bob and his team. If anybody wants to drop out at this time, I'll be very happy to take over their investment, up to fifty million. I'll sign the paperwork today."

There wasn't much to discuss after that. GE and the others stayed in the round.

The lawyers and accountants and investment bankers and strategic investors were properly groomed and lined up with the company. It was time to get on with the show.

November 1999

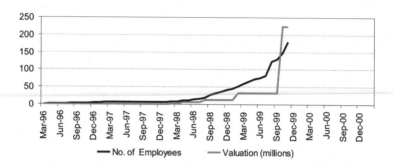

No. of Employees — Valuation (millions)

Compatriots

I hadn't exactly expected to metaphorically run toward each other in slow motion, arms outstretched, through a field of flowers on a sunny day. I just thought that we had been watching each other fondly from afar for so long that something slightly magical might happen between us when we first met.

VerticalNet had been founded in 1995, just a few months before Neoforma. We were both old-timers in Internet B2B. Neoforma had been founded on the idea of using technology to improve the unique problems inherent in the healthcare supply chain. VerticalNet had been founded on the idea of using technology to improve the common problems inherent in the supply chain of many industries.

In our early days, Jeff and I had been approached by all sorts of people who liked what we were doing for healthcare and wanted us to do the same sort of thing for their industry. This was very tempting. Creating fundamental change in healthcare was huge. The idea of replicating that change in multiple large industries was mesmerizing. We could be the Microsoft of business processes.

However, each time we looked at the specifics of another industry, we came to the reluctant conclusion that, while there were certainly many similarities between each industry's inefficiencies, the differences were too large to ignore and too massive to address.

That didn't keep us from watching VerticalNet try though. Our own insecurity over our decision to limit Neoforma's scope had fueled our criticism of VerticalNet over the years. VerticalNet had made a different choice. They'd gone a mile wide and an inch deep, but that just didn't seem to cut it. Their most innovative feature, a fairly recent function that broadcast email from a single visitor to multiple manufacturers, seemed to be a nearly exact copy of the system we had deployed years earlier.

We watched them add one vertical industry after another, knowing that someday they would add healthcare to their portfolio. We hadn't been particularly nervous about this, since we knew how difficult it would be for anyone to quickly develop the kind of depth that we had achieved in healthcare.

Their successful IPO in early 1999 had set the stage for B2B companies like Neoforma. By September, VerticalNet had become a nearly $5 billion company. They had recently received a $100 million cash infusion from Microsoft, as part of a strategic partnership. And one of their most recent acquisitions had been of a direct competitor to our medical auction business. We were now officially competitors.

While we knew that VerticalNet could not develop a marketplace to compete with us, they now had deep enough pockets to buy our most significant competitor.

We knew that Medibuy was four to six months behind us on the IPO track and at least a year behind us in technology, so an acquisition by a cash-rich, equity-rich company would be very appealing to them.

I didn't want to see that happen. Not only because it could change some people's view of Neoforma as the clear B2B leader in healthcare, but because—well, because it would be wrong.

Medibuy was an also-ran, a copycat—the product of financial opportunism. Whatever I thought about the flaws in their business model, VerticalNet was the real thing. The founders had started the company with the sincere and primary objective of making a difference. They had started early, personally gone deeply into debt and struggled against the odds to their lofty perch.

So I tried to contact one of the founders of VerticalNet. Like me, Mike was still an executive in, but not the leader of, the company he had founded. The founders of VerticalNet had recruited a well-known CEO too. I knew that Mike had already been able to sell enough stock to pay off his debts and ensure his future comfort. In a few months, I would be there. At least, I thought I might be.

Mike didn't respond to my first query. Or my second. I was quite frustrated. I knew how busy he was. I was too, but I always responded to everyone—if not on the first day, then at least within a couple of days.

After my third message I received a call from a business development guy. "I understand that you want to talk to us about possibly working together. What did you have in mind?"

I told him that I had some ideas to discuss with Mike. He tried to dissuade me from pursuing direct communication with Mike: "He's a very busy man. I'm sure that I can help you with whatever you need to discuss."

I was upset. "Look, I'm very busy too and I don't want to waste my time or yours. The things I need to discuss will eventually end up on Mike's desk. When can I speak with Mike?"

We scheduled a phone appointment in late September. During our call, Mike was polite and attentive. After a brief conversation, Mike agreed that it might make sense for us to talk in person. I already had a trip to the East Coast planned, so I suggested that I stop by his office. Besides, I was curious.

VerticalNet was in the process of consolidating its operations at a huge new headquarters. There were no signs up yet. I had to wander around the building until I found some construction personnel who could tell me where to get in. From there, I wandered through dusty corridors lined with taped drywall. Eventually I arrived at an empty counter in what looked like would eventually become a reception area. I peaked into nearby cubicles, trying to get someone's attention.

When the receptionist was found, she told me that Mike was tied up on an important phone call. After I'd waited long enough to contemplate leaving, I was shown into Mike's office.

A few minutes later he finished his call and greeted me formally. He was a tall man with simultaneously intense and vacant eyes. I could tell that he was trying to "be here and now," but that his mind was somewhere else entirely. I knew the feeling and didn't like being on the receiving end of it.

He immediately notified me that he had to cover a press interview for the CEO who had been called into a crucial meeting at the last minute. We only had about fifteen minutes to talk.

He got right to the point. "So what are you guys up to? Are you filing for the IPO soon?"

I told him that I couldn't discuss specifics, but that a filing seemed likely. I did tell him that we were finalizing a large strategic funding round. I dropped a few names of the companies participating, then I went into my spiel about how we had been watching VerticalNet for some time now, knowing that we would eventually bump into each other.

He told me that he had been watching us too. "You have a nice website. Whenever I get fed up with our user interface group I tell them to visit Neoforma for ideas."

I told him that I had noticed some similarities. We shared a millisecond of mutual appreciation, then I went on, "As I see it, we have a mutual enemy in Chemdex. While they started out in laboratory products, they are now trying to expand into other verticals . . . including medical. They seem to be using their Kleiner Perkins connections to compete against you."

Mike's negative reaction to the mention of Chemdex told me all that I had come here to find out. VerticalNet was not likely to buy our Kleiner-funded competitor, Medibuy. Mike hinted that Chemdex and VerticalNet had spoken often in the past, but that something had happened that left a very bad taste in his mouth.

Mike said, "David Perry wasn't satisfied to stick with what he knew. Now he's going after us. Believe me, we don't ever see ourselves competing with a Neoforma. We wouldn't likely be able to . . . we can't go that deeply into healthcare. We want to leverage our ability to deliver common solutions to multiple industries, not solve unique problems in each one."

Mike dropped the Microsoft name many times during our conversation. We spoke exclusively about healthcare's unique problems and didn't expand our conversation to other industries. We both knew that we weren't being entirely truthful.

VerticalNet would be very happy if they could be very deep into every industry they targeted. Neoforma would be very happy if we could gradually expand into adjacent vertical industries. But, for the moment, we had a mutual enemy: Chemdex — or, for us, the KP *keiretsu* that supported Chemdex and Medibuy.

I proposed that we take advantage of each other's strengths and try to create a powerful node at the intersection of their horizontal and our vertical strategies. He agreed. Simple as that.

This entire conversation had lasted about ten minutes. He said,

"Hey, I am confident that our two business development groups can work out the details. And to make sure that they do, why don't we put a couple million dollars into your current funding round?"

I told him that I would certainly take that idea to our Board, but I thought it made a lot of sense.

And, on that note, our meeting was over. We shook hands, and never met again. In spite of what had been accomplished, I left the meeting feeling very empty. There had been no personal spark between us. We hadn't reminisced about the tough old days. None of the isolation that I felt within Neoforma was going to be abated by this man with whom I thought I had so much in common.

VerticalNet did invest in Neoforma's October funding round and the two companies did enter into a very friendly business partnership in November. However their miniscule website traffic and shallow supplier relationships proved unable to add quality—with the exception of the PR value of working with the current dotcom darling.

December 1999

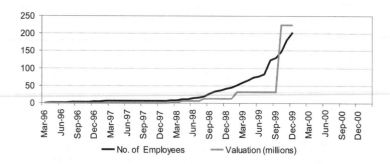

Legend: No. of Employees — Valuation (millions)

Starving Artist

Reality was increasingly out of sync.

In spite of many setbacks in getting the IPO documents filed, our advisors still felt that there was a chance we could host our public offering sometime in early December. However, the stock market was cooling down after its year-long adrenaline rush. The bankers believed that creating demand for our stock in a cooling market would be risky. The IPO was postponed until January.

This was hard on the morale of a company nearly paralyzed by the suspense of a pending IPO. There were many restrictions on our business due to the "quiet period"—the period after filing for IPO, during which the company must be very cautious about everything it says.

A company is strictly watched during the period between the filing and the IPO to ensure that it does not behave in any way that appears as if it is trying to influence individual investors. No big deals can be discussed without immediate public disclosure. No information can be shared with anyone outside the company, unless it is shared with absolutely everybody outside the company. No advertising can be done that might appear as if the company, rather than a particular product, is being promoted.

We were so used to the buzz that this silence was suffocating. So, we each tried to make the best of the extra time.

One of the most bizarre issues I had to deal with was preparing to be rich.

Upon filing the IPO, hundreds of investment managers from big investment companies began calling me. I was easy prey because I had made it my policy not to have my calls screened. These cocky guys— and they were all men—almost always made a point to say, "I don't usually call potential clients directly, but you are so *special* . . . I wanted to call you personally." Of course, a month ago they would not have acknowledged my presence at a party.

They each gave me their pitch about how they could help wealthy individuals like me quickly diversify my assets — meaning, sell my stock. They talked about all sorts of schemes that would let me sell my stock without really selling it. These schemes would also allow me to use my company stock as collateral for short-term cash.

This perplexed me, because I knew that I had signed an agreement with the company that I would not sell or leverage my stock for at least six months after the IPO. This is called the lockout period. "Well . . . ahem . . . if you feel that these plans wouldn't honor your agreement with the company, you could wait until after the six months, but there *are* ways to do it before. They just involve a little risk. We'll be happy to lend you money to invest or buy a house . . . without officially using the stock as collateral . . . just because we want your business. It will be easy for you to pay it back when your lockout ends."

While I had every confidence in Neoforma, borrowing money against something I couldn't control didn't seem right, nor did the schemes that would have enabled me to disguise the fact that I was leveraging stock. I had had my fill of risk for the time being. And I knew that Anni was even more conservative on this issue than I.

The managers also espoused their clever tax avoidance schemes. "After all, half of everything you make will go to Uncle Sam, if you don't manage your tax strategies properly."

I understood very little of their spiels, but one thing that I knew was that the IRS looked very carefully at people whose income changed drastically. And I knew that our accountant had been less than competent in handling our taxes to date. I had found some ridiculous errors he had made in the past. And if *I* could find an accountant's errors, they had to be blatant ones.

One reason we had been able to fund Neoforma in the early days was that we could benefit from the deductions associated with a high-risk investment. I figured that this made sense. It encouraged people like me to take risk. Our accountant wrote off all of the loans. That had been a great relief.

I asked an associate who had been through the IPO process for recommendations on an accounting firm. He gave me the name of a small accounting firm that specialized in *high-net-worth* clients. (Apparently, it is not proper to use the word *rich*.)

I felt strange setting up an appointment with such a firm, but I figured that this was the right thing to do. Before long, Anni and I met with Mike, the accountant, and Paul, his right-hand man. They were kind. They were respectful of the fact that we were broke and yet were asking them how to manage the millions of dollars we might have soon. They had seen others like us many times.

Paul would be our primary contact at the firm. He was a young guy and very passionate about his business. He *almost* made accounting seem interesting. He clearly knew what he was doing and he was so patient that I almost understood a few of the tax-management issues he discussed. "Of course, the first thing we need to do is have a look at all of your tax filings since you started Neoforma . . . just to make sure that everything is okay."

A couple of weeks later, he called us to review his findings. He explained about something called the at-risk rule and said that our earlier filings had been inaccurate. "We will need to restate your last three-years' tax filings." It wasn't all bad though, since in one of the years, we actually hadn't gotten enough money back from the government. The other two years weren't quite as good.

"You owe about thirty thousand dollars," he said. "And you really need to pay it quickly. The penalties are already costing you a bundle." To help out, he offered to defer his accounting fees.

Now, *this* was ironic. Here we were, thinking we were being conscientious in finding out how to manage our ensuing fortune, and instead, we owed thirty thousand dollars we couldn't afford.

Even in the time before Neoforma, Anni and I had fallen victim to that number-one cause of marital strife — *money*. We had run very lean each time Anni had switched to part-time work to take care of our infant sons. We had been able to catch up each time, but never get much ahead. Since that first check went to Neoforma in 1996, our money shortage had been constant. We had managed our credit, but we had been unable to save or splurge. This, combined with my general mental absence, had stressed us to the point that any new financial issue sent us immediately into despair.

Rationally, we knew that—however well the IPO went—we would

soon be very wealthy on paper. And, in seven months or so, after the lockout period, we would be able to get out of debt for good. But right now, during another depressing holiday season, we were once again going to have to put every penny we had into Neoforma.

When Neoforma had paid us back the previous June for our loans to the company, we had been able to pay off the father-in-law loans. We were still about a hundred thousand dollars in debt, but we had been able to build up a small emergency cash reserve. Now that would be gone.

The old panic set in again. I stopped answering my work phone. I wasn't interested in how brokers could help me manage all of my money. The money I didn't have now was more pressing than the money I might have later.

January 2000

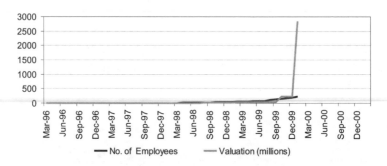

| Mar-96 | Jun-96 | Sep-96 | Dec-96 | Mar-97 | Jun-97 | Sep-97 | Dec-97 | Mar-98 | Jun-98 | Sep-98 | Dec-98 | Mar-99 | Jun-99 | Sep-99 | Dec-99 | Mar-00 | Jun-00 | Sep-00 | Dec-00 |

—— No. of Employees —— Valuation (millions)

Neoforma.com IPO Takes Off

While many stocks were sold off on Monday, the initial public offering of Neoforma.com (NASDAQ: NEOF) performed like a typical high-flying, shot-from-a-cannon, business-to-business IPO . . .

E-Commerce Times
January 25, 2000

Market close on day of Neoforma IPO at NASDAQ headquarters on New York's Times Square. From left: Chris Bing, Wayne McVicker, Fred Ruegsegger, Bob Zollars, Jeff Kleck, Kali Coffman and Amanda Mogin.

Photo: Alan Perlman

The Premiere

I was sitting in my office, futilely trying to focus on the business unit plan I was editing, when Stephen—who had a tendency to boast about the important, successful people he knew—walked into my office, sat down in a chair, leaned forward and said, "Hey! I just realized that, in a few weeks, you'll be the richest person I have ever known!"

What an odd thing to hear someone say!

Bob and Frank, meanwhile, were out on the Road Show.

This rite of passage is among the most revered of experiences in the start-up world. It is a kind of fraternity initiation ceremony. Just before a company goes public, the management team ventures out on a grueling two-week trek to the financial centers across the U.S. and Europe.

The purpose of this trip is to drum up interest in a company's upcoming initial stock offering and to create buzz. At the same time, the team tries to get an idea of how many shares of the company's stock are going to trade hands on the first day of sales. This assessment of the level of interest helps determine what the offering price should be on the day of the IPO.

An investment bank's reputation rests on its ability to realize high returns to its clients. The bank's objective, during an IPO, is to ensure that their clients benefit from as large a portion of a stock's first-day gain as possible. So, the initial offering price is often set at a level lower than they think the stock will bring on the market. That way, the investors who get to buy the first shares of the company stock can benefit from large gains with little risk. The banker gets a substantial amount of control in allocating who gets to buy those shares. This is how friends are made in the IPO game.

Actually, there are several investment bankers on a typical deal.

Once a lead banker, who gets control over the largest percentage of shares, is selected, several other bankers line up to scrabble over the remaining shares.

Who gets to play depends on who convinces the company and the lead banker that they will be able to sell the most company shares for the highest price.

The fighting between the bankers can get very nasty. Each one is fighting for their reputation on every deal. The order in which they are listed on the official offering document updates their relative status in the industry. Being at or near the top of a single deal that produces huge returns can upset the status quo, leading to defections of current star employees or buzzy companies in the pipeline.

Of course, buying stocks is nothing more, or less, than gambling. Bankers are bookies. Their objective is to beat the odds in any, mostly legal, way they can. Their clients are paying them to do that. And everyone knows that the house always slants the rules to come out ahead. There would be no house otherwise.

By definition, stock purchasers are betting that someone else will lose. There can be no gain without loss. All financial advisors are trying to beat the odds with their own system.

A stock's actual value is only a small percent of a fraction of a fraction of the company's physical assets — minus its outstanding debts and obligations. In other words, pretty near zero, in most cases.

The rest of a stock's value is speculation about whether this horse is going to come out ahead of that one. They are betting that a particular company will do its very best to get ahead of the other companies on the track. And everyone buying stock should know this, and most do.

So, it was Bob and Frank's responsibility to get the interest so high that Neoforma's share of the kitty was worth the hassle.

Everyone in the company was getting daily email updates from Bob and Frank. They humorously summed up the multitude of presentations they gave each day. Here are a couple of Bob's observations:

> *On a side note, when checking into the hotel late tonight, Frank and I checked in together. He got his room and then I got mine.*

As we were walking away, the receptionist said, "Mr. Zollars, I upgraded you to a suite." Frank's response was, "Okay, I know where I stand." As he tried to get into his room, the key didn't work and he had to go all the way back to the lobby! The good news is when he got there, after significant groveling, the receptionist upgraded him too!

And . . .

First, the surfboard saga. As many of you know, it is customary for a company going public to provide a banner which is hung in the lead underwriter's trading area. Never a company to do the usual, average thing, we thought providing a surfboard with the Neoforma and Merrill Lynch logos would be a memorable "banner." Our Executive Vice President of Surfboards, Dave Juszczyk, arranged for a 12' 8" tandem surfboard to be prepared with the appropriate artwork. Through an incredible effort, which we will let Dave tell us about at an upcoming NeoLunch, the surfboard was shipped to New York last week. Tuesday morning the Merrill folks were beginning to worry that the board would not arrive in time. After tracking down the Emery air bill, the board was located in New Jersey.

Problem 1: No truck large enough to hold the surfboard was scheduled to get to Manhattan in time. The Merrill folks begged and pleaded and finally Emery was able to arrange delivery to the Merrill loading dock mid-Tuesday.

Problem 2: The board was packed so well, the receiving people couldn't open it using conventional means. One of our bankers, let's call him Andrew, made the trek to the sixth sub-basement of Merrill's Manhattan headquarters to personally supervise the efforts of a handyman to open the crate. Under the watchful eyes of many curious onlookers, the board was unpacked, safe and sound.

Problem 3: How do you get a 12' 8" surfboard from the sixth sub-basement to the fifth floor of an office building? The ever-intrepid Andrew, continuing to uncover parts of the Merrill facility he never knew existed, was able to see the board safely transported to the appropriate location using a marvelous technology he referred to as a "freight elevator." You will all be proud to know that the Neoforma/Merrill Lynch surfboard is now hanging prominently in the Merrill capital markets area and has been the subject of much attention.

And . . .

One of the things Frank and I discovered is that we are at polar opposites with our hair. Frank went through an 18-hour day and his hair never moved (aka The Helmet/Helmut). My hair (or what's left of it) was never in the same position over each of these eight presentations. Not sure what this means, other than when you're really tired, you notice weird things.

And . . .

We did four presentations in Philadelphia and surrounding suburbs. The presentation is starting to settle into a groove and by the end of the day on Friday we have now given it about sixteen times — only sixty or so left to go. One of the things that happens after hearing the same thing so many times is that you begin to pick up funny little nuances in the presentation. The problem with this of course is that the "funny little thing" starts to sound hilarious when you have to suppress your laughter. Andrew and I had a brief episode during the last presentation and almost took Bob down with us. Fortunately, we managed to control ourselves sufficiently so that I don't believe the potential investors to whom we were presenting realized that anything was going on.

And . . .

As Frank mentioned yesterday, you can tell we're getting a little tired; i.e., I tried to leave the plane without unbuckling my seatbelt, and today Frank had a heck of a time pronouncing "sophisticated" . . . it came out kind of like sssssssssssssppppppppppppppp-ttttttttttttttttt . . . a little Daffy Duck–like . . . a couple of times.

*The investors didn't seem to notice, but because he did it twice,
the Merrill guys and I were really just trying like heck not to
break into laughter.*

Seven days a week, they began presenting as early as 6:00 in the
morning and went well into the evening. Presentations and travels
were orchestrated to the minute. They would arrive, give a quick presentation, answer questions and rush to the next meeting. They made
sixty-five presentations in twenty cities. On one day, they presented
in five cities.

They were getting a strong reception. Many conservative investors
were telling them that this was the best story they had ever heard.
Large pre-orders for the stock were already coming in. That was good
to hear, because there were many articles in the press expressing
doubt that the IPO boom was going to continue into the new millen-
nium. We were the first scheduled IPO of 2000. We were the infantry,
sent into the field to test the firepower ahead.

Until I began researching our own IPO, I had not known much about
the stock market. I didn't know that a market cap was the product of
the share price and the total number of shares. I didn't even know
how stocks were bought and sold. I still don't understand how it all
holds together every day, but human vices do have a way of getting
otherwise incompatible people together.

So, when the time approached for the IPO, I had no idea what to
expect. Bob and Frank ended the Road Trip where they had begun—
in New York. Anni and I, along with Jeff and his wife, Julie, were
planning to meet them there.

The IPO was scheduled for Thursday, January 20. We were flying
to New York on Wednesday. Since this was our first trip to New York
together, Anni and I were planning to do two days of exploration after
the IPO.

I called each of Neoforma's angel investors the day before our flight to
New York and said, "Whatever happens Thursday, I want to thank
you for believing in us so early in the game. We would not have made
it this far if not for your faith in us."

I meant it. And I took some satisfaction in the fact that not one of them said they were surprised we had made it this far.

I did not call the VCs. Their investment in Neoforma had not, for the most part, been a personal matter. It had been all business. They could have called me to say thank you, but none of them did. They were busy calculating how to use their contribution to the Neoforma IPO for leverage in their next deal.

I spoke only briefly with Alexander and JP. They were cursorily congratulatory, but, somehow, in a self-congratulatory way. They really seemed to believe that *they* were responsible for the IPO, as if Jeff and I had simply been good actors for their show. This was especially hard to swallow. After all, we had started this business, had risked everything to be here and worked the 20-hour days and . . .

Well, come to think of it, the IPO was simply the opening day, not a proof that the show will become a classic. Alexander and JP had been the producers, whose job was to ensure that the show was a commercial success. And the truth was that Jeff and I certainly had not once thought of going for an IPO before they'd mentioned it. They made it clear right away that the IPO was their ideal goal.

JP was still focused on this goal. The VCs were absolutely focused on the IPO.

Denis, Wally and Jack, on the other hand, were certainly happy about the IPO and took pride in it. But it meant much more to them than that.

Neoforma had become personal to them. Alexander had wanted to be a dispassionate investor, but couldn't. He cared too much to be completely detached. His great passion had forced him to care about the results of his efforts to help the company. It drove him—and us—nuts sometimes. It was bad enough to have two overly passionate control freaks—Jeff and me. But Alexander's personal interest meant a lot to us.

I had to admit that they really were the ones who had gotten us *here*—to this IPO. We had been going over *there*. But they had convinced us that the way to make the most impact on humanity was over *here*, where we could control the eventual large-scale implementation of our vision. It was as if we'd been making a cool little indie flick and they'd teased us, supported us and helped us get the funding to make *Star Wars*.

OK, so they *did* have reason to think that this was their show.

Later that day, the day before we would be flying into the unknown, I received an email containing the next bombshell.

A company with "forma" in their name had filed a lawsuit against us. They had just filed it—no calls, no questions, no discussions. They sent us a letter—two days before our IPO—saying that they were suing Neoforma for name infringement. They asserted that their reputation and brand recognition had been irreparably harmed by the fact that we had "forma" in our name. They claimed that a customer had called them once to ask if they were related to Neoforma.

And then, just before our IPO, this company appears out of relative obscurity, the day before we are flying to New York, and claims we've stolen their name—so that we could leverage their brand identity!

The inconvenient timing of the lawsuit and the lack of preceding dialog instantly triggered suspicion in me and Jeff. By this time, we had been fighting against powerful, unseen forces for long enough to learn that not all paranoia is delusional.

Our first results when searching the Web for information about this company was a page hailing its partnership with Ventro, a Kleiner Perkins (KP) company, and *this company that was suing us*. This smelled like more than coincidence, but it seemed silly to imagine some great conspiracy. And the company firmly denied any knowledge of our IPO timing or outside influence. They claimed this was a simple matter of clearing up customer confusion, even though there were dozens of other medical companies with "neo" or "forma" in their names. But when Jeff confronted their president on the suspicious timing of the lawsuit, they immediately scrambled to give us written assurance that the issue should be able to be resolved without us having to change the company name.

In any case, our entire team of consultants was thrown into an intense debate. *Was this an event that had a material impact on our IPO?* However indignant we were at the impersonal, but seemingly malicious, nature of this attack, we had to acknowledge that the outcome of the issue was unpredictable. The ultimate question was: *Would it have a significant effect on the company . . . if we had to change our name?*

Our conclusion was *no*. Ventro, a public company, had recently renamed itself. The public impact was mostly positive. We did not consider our company name to be inseparable from the company and we had the other company's assurance that minor logo adjustments should be able to address their concerns, so we simply added the disclosure to our final documents. However, adding doubt over this issue to a load of other concerns did not enrich my wait for the IPO.

Neoforma splurged on first-class seats for us. That was good, because our nerves were so taut that the flight would have been far less bearable without the wine they served us.

We were taken from the airport to the Palace Hotel in a limousine— always an awkward experience for me, since I like to open my own doors. The surreal opulence of the old establishment hotel added to my feeling of detachment. Marble floors, classical details—the place was drenched in tradition and formality. Contrary to my usual behavior, I allowed the bellman to carry my luggage up to the room, but only because Anni had all of her stuff too.

The bellman told us that Prince, a musician we enjoyed and for whom we had great respect, was staying there too. We whimsically wondered if, since we were all guests of the same establishment, we could just knock on his door and introduce ourselves. I thought not.

This must be happening to someone else. There is no connection here . . . between my past and my future . . .

The four of us—Bob, Frank, Jeff and I—along with our four wives, met in the lobby before dinner. As we were gathering, Bob told Jeff and me about a call he had received from the CEO of our major competitor, Medibuy, informing him that WebMD was not going to renew their agreement with us when it expired later in the year. Instead, WebMD was going to partner in a very visible way with Medibuy.

WebMD was the physician portal that had acquired Healtheon in its acquisition frenzy. Healtheon had been started by Jim Clarke at about the same time we started Neoforma. By acquiring Healtheon, WebMD had acquired a partnership with Neoforma. They had even tried to acquire us, but our price was too high.

The fact that WebMD was not going to renew our agreement was no surprise to us. KP had a substantial investment in Healtheon. Once KP invested in Medibuy, it was only a matter of time before Healtheon would be pressured to terminate a previously upbeat partnership with

Neoforma. WebMD had been telling us that it would cost us tens of millions of dollars to renew the previously cashless agreement. In addition to the fact that our links to the WebMD site had been nearly worthless, we had calculated that all physicians whom WebMD was planning to aggregate would have to buy all of their supplies through Neoforma for more than ten years for us to break even. The economics didn't make sense.

So it was no big deal. The WebMD partnership had not been included in any of our financial projections. It was a non-event. But, on the night before our scheduled IPO, this guy called Bob out of "courtesy" to tell him that he was going to take over the WebMD partnership?

The deal wasn't even due to expire for six months. Clearly, they had rushed into an agreement in order to take some wind out of our sails. It didn't succeed, but it was just enough to raise goosebumps at the thought of the degree to which some people would go to try to knock us down. We vaguely wondered what Medibuy had paid to rush this deal through. We found out later that it had been an astronomical amount.

We were laughing at the transparency and pettiness of this ploy when the rest of our group joined us in the lobby. Everyone was introduced. We were four couples, brought together under this most bizarre of circumstances.

Anni and I did not sleep that night. The adrenaline coursed though us at unprecedented levels. We lay next to each other, tossing and turning all night, our minds grasping at shadows for something solid to anchor to.

Assuming we received the official SEC blessing Thursday morning, which was just a formality at this point, the IPO would begin at 10:00. Bob and Frank left for the Merrill offices before dawn. Jeff and I were in no hurry to get there before the NASDAQ market opened. There wasn't anything official for us to do, except wait. And waiting was not appealing.

Jeff and I took a limo to the Merrill offices at about 7:30. Our wives were to join us just before the IPO. By his uncharacteristic silence, I could tell that Jeff had not slept well either. We spoke very little. We simply stared, unseen, out of that black box of a limo into the morning.

It was very cold outside. Steam was rising out of the streets in front of the buildings. I stared out the window at the assortment of characters on their way to work, their typically fast paces quickened further by their rush to get out of the cold. I tried to relate to them in my mind, grasping for some point of reference.

I knew that whatever happened today represented only one step in a long and unpredictable process, that any financial gains today would be gains on paper only. But I also knew that this was opening day— the day on which our once tame idea would be officially released into the wild. Anything could happen. I had done my best to ensure it had the traits it needed to survive. *Hadn't I . . . ?*

The driver opened our door in front of a tall building. We entered the maze of stone and glass and gave our names to the security people in the lobby.

When we arrived in the conference room, the atmosphere was tense. Bob and Frank were there, speaking quietly into their cell phones. Amanda, Kali and Chris, our PR team, were there. We were introduced to a couple of other people who worked for Merrill. They would be responsible for choreographing our day.

The first thing we were told was that someone had cut the power to the Neoforma servers during the night. Somehow, in this very secure data center, the emergency power shutdown switches on our circuits had been activated. It was probably an accident, but we couldn't help wondering at the timing. The switches were designed to be very difficult to accidentally shut off. And the procedure required two people. Nobody should have been messing around near our cages in the middle of the night.

For the first time, I truly realized how much money was at stake. I thought of all the movies I had seen, where all sorts of nasty deeds were done over a million dollars. Yet, here there were tens—or even hundreds—of millions of dollars at stake. I couldn't help but shiver. *Would someone really go this far to slow us down? Surely not . . . This was only business.*

But the short-term power outage was not the primary reason for the nervous tension in the room. One of the Merrill reps quietly updated us: "The SEC has asked a few last-minute questions this morning . . . purely routine. Apparently, they have reversed themselves on how you should report one of your acquisitions. They will have to get new information before they will clear you for the IPO." When he saw our apprehension, he reassured us, "We should still be able to have the offering today though . . . it just might be delayed a couple of hours." That didn't sound good, but it didn't sound that bad either.

When it became clear that it would be awhile before our team at the home office could settle the issue with the SEC, Jeff and I were given a tour of the Merrill offices.

We visited all the major showpieces. There was the huge bull statue in one of the lobbies, looking strong and proud. And there was the trading floor, which we viewed from a second-floor overlook: a bright, high-ceilinged room, lined with TV monitors and stock tickers, buzzing with activity. Our guide pointed to a section of the room: "Casual visitors are not allowed on the trading floor, but that's where you will be standing when your stock begins trading."

We watched the action through a large glass window. A few of the brokers watched us, too, as they spoke into their headsets. I supposed that we were no less abstract to them than they were to us.

The markets had just opened. Row upon row of men and women were positioned in front of two, three or four computer screens each. Periodically, they would gesticulate wildly, calling out the bets, I supposed. Serious-looking pit bosses were posted here and there. I had no idea what anyone was actually doing, but they reminded me of the crowds of enthusiastic people that gather around a craps table — another wild game controlled by rules I am unfamiliar with.

When we returned to the conference room, the atmosphere was even more somber. It was a half-hour before the scheduled time for our IPO and now there was doubt that we'd be able to have the offering at all that day.

Apparently, there was a huge snowstorm heading into Washington DC, where the SEC offices were located. Many SEC employees, including those handling our IPO review, were leaving the office early to beat the storm home.

The main concern that Merrill had was not that the offering would slide a day, but that the investors might read something negative into the delay. A rumor might start circulating that the SEC had found some major problem with Neoforma. The investors might not purchase the stock after all. If a few key investors backed out, others might follow . . .

A tall, serious and self-important man came into the room around noon to speak with Bob and Frank. He was David Risinger, one of Merrill's analysts. He said the SEC would not be getting back to us today. But the good news was that the major investors were not going to back out, even though the offering would be moved to a Friday.

Friday, I learned, was generally a bad day to have an IPO, since there is often a lower stock sales volume and not as much press coverage. "Too bad," someone said. "Today was a good day in the market. You could have done very well."

We were all exhausted from lack of sleep and the emotional letdown of the day. I wanted to go back to the hotel and collapse, but Merrill had already arranged our celebration party for that evening and had reserved a private room at a very prestigious restaurant. Since the reservation couldn't be changed, we had to show up.

I am sure we ate good food and drank good drinks that night, but I mostly remember the atmosphere of desperate obligation. The bankers were disappointed. They had missed out on a huge opportunity today. They knew that the risks of diminished returns increased with every delay. And now they were forking out a small fortune for this cheerless gathering.

Our Neoforma team was feeling tired and defeated. We had already heard about the rumors of our demise spreading on the assorted online IPO message boards. Our PR team was frantically trying to reschedule the crop of media interviews they had set up with Bob. It wasn't looking good. A company that sold hospital supplies wasn't a very sexy story to begin with, so getting last-minute interviews slotted into a Friday was not going to be easy.

Bob gave some kind of speech, trying to sound upbeat. I may have too. I don't remember.

By the next morning, when Jeff and I arrived at the Merrill offices, the situation had gone from bad to worse. Our team in the home office had worked through the night to revise and resubmit the documents to the SEC specifications, but nobody at the SEC was answering their phones. The storm there was so intense that most people weren't going into the office.

Various, increasingly senior, people at Merrill visited our conference room throughout the morning. They were using all of their connections to find out what the heck to do about our IPO. Somebody finally got through to someone senior at the SEC. The good news was that the SEC was very apologetic. The bad news was that there was no chance of getting a response today. Almost everyone was snowed in. The IPO would have to be postponed to Monday, at the earliest.

The only day worse for an IPO than Friday is Monday. Because there is so much staging that must be done the day before an IPO, the bankers weren't even sure that it was possible to have an IPO on Monday. After doing some research, they found that there had been a handful of successful IPOs on Mondays and agreed that maybe we could pull it off.

Key investors were polled again. This time, they expressed a bit more concern, but the coalition seemed to be holding together—for now. Everyone still thought there was money to be made here.

After hastily arranging plans for someone to watch the kids an extra two days, we made the best of our weekend. We hustled through the bitter cold, seeing some museums and catching a jazz show. But, try as we might to keep our minds on the present, the future kept pulling us forward. Time seemed as frozen as the air.

On Monday morning, we glanced hesitantly through the doorway, expecting the worst. But this time everything was different. It was as if the ground had slipped out from under me, propelling me at full speed into the room. Things were moving with purposeful frenzy. We had received our clearance from the SEC. (A few weeks after the IPO they would take the unprecedented step of sending us a letter, apologizing for delaying the IPO in the first place.) But in this moment, everyone was focused entirely on the near future.

This time, we called our wives and asked them to join us soon.

A young, stark woman I had seen only once on Thursday and once on Friday, entered the room with intense focus and seriousness. She was in charge of choreographing the first few minutes of our IPO. She said various things to the Merrill folks in the room. Her words seemed to indicate that everything was coming together. I found myself thinking, *She is so efficient at this that I bet she makes a fortune.* Some signals were exchanged and she sailed back to the floor.

Anni and the others, including Jeff's two daughters, arrived soon thereafter. We were escorted through some doors and walked out onto the trading room floor. To our immediate left, high up on the wall, was the Neoforma surfboard. We were told that the surfboard was very popular.

A few of the brokers cheered. Most interrupted their business only long enough for quick glances our way. I knew that they had witnessed this scene many times—founders and executives walking onto the floor for the IPO ceremony. But I knew that their interest was about more than us. Our offering would be the first test of the IPO market since the Y2K jitters had evaporated. Our success would help predict their success.

After a brief photo session under the surfboard, we were hurried around the corner to an intersection of aisles. To the right of us was the computer that would officially start the sale of our stock. To the left of us were the rows of brokers who would handle the individual sales of our stock. A bullish, well-dressed man, the pit boss, described what would happen. I heard his words, but was too hypnotized by the rows of letters and numbers cascading down the screens and across the tickers to understand what he was saying.

David Risinger joined us. I knew that the time had come. I held Anni's hand. The man at the starting computer pointed out the numbers for us to watch. One number represented the current asking price and the other represented the current offering price. When the two numbers intersected, a sale would be made, representing the current value of the stock. With a simple nod of David's head, the selling began.

The group of previously calm brokers suddenly began gesturing wildly—talking into phones, shouting numbers back and forth. To give my paralyzed body something useful to do, I focused on the numbers on the screen.

The first number I saw was $39. The brokers had settled on a starting price of $13. How had the number jumped to 39?

That's what my brain was busy working on. My body, however, was working on holding Anni up, when my own legs were hardly working. I felt her slump against me. She was having a hard time standing too.

We listened to the brokers yelling out this or that about so many shares of Neoforma. We watched the numbers change . . . $40 . . . $41 . . . $42. It seemed to slow down there. Someone, probably one of the brokers, commented that there was not much else to see here, and herded us off the floor.

We gathered in a larger, more luxurious room with an amazing view of a bright New York skyline. Champagne was poured. We shared smiles, handshakes and hugs, but neither Anni nor I were much in the mood for conversation.

We had put a lot on hold for Neoforma. Whatever the future held for Neoforma, it didn't need us anymore. We'd still be there for it, but it had its own life now.

Before dinner, Jeff and I were going to ride along with Bob, Frank and our PR people for the press interview tour. Bob would be the only one speaking, but we all wanted to be there, watching. We said reluctant goodbyes to our wives and hit the road.

Because it was a Monday, our PR group had had difficulty setting up the kind of high-profile interview that they had arranged for the previous Thursday. However, once the news spread about the scale of the stock's success, new interviews were being requested by the moment.

We rushed in and out of limousines, reaching some television interviews minutes before the scheduled airtime. Bob would quickly be wired up for each interview, shake hands with the host, get asked general questions, respond with well-rehearsed answers, and move on. In the limo, between TV interviews, Bob was on the phone giving interviews to other members of the press.

As we watched Bob live on the studio monitors, we saw the price of the stock at the bottom of the screen. It was still going up.

We met up with our wives at the last stop on the press tour, the NASDAQ building. Here, the official welcoming ceremony would be conducted and broadcast immediately after the market closed.

At market close, a NASDAQ executive formally welcomed Neoforma. Bob gave his usual speech, then gestured to Jeff and me. He wanted us to speak too.

Acckk! I can be a good, calm speaker with a little preparation. But I am usually ludicrous without preparation. I tried to control my panic, as I walked toward the podium. Our stock ticker was prominently displayed on the room-high screens behind the podium. We were the top gainer of the day. The stock had closed above $52 per share. Jeff said something first, then I said some awkward, overzealous words.

Our next stop was at the offices of Neoforma's PR agency, where we would officially speak to the company employees who were gathered in the lunchroom back home. Jeff, Bob and I ended up alone in a small elevator, riding up to the PR office. We hadn't had a chance to speak with each other since the IPO.

Bob towered above us in the small dark space, grinning. "So, do you realize that . . . between the three of us . . . we represent almost a billion dollars on paper?"

We nodded, and shared disbelieving smiles moments before the elevator door opened.

We crowded around a speakerphone in a small conference room. There was a great deal of raucous cheering on the other end of the line.

Bob and Frank spoke first. Jeff and I spoke too. This time, I could speak from my heart. I said that the real heroes behind this day were our partners, spouses and children, whose patience and support had made this all possible.

The restaurant that night was very hip and very loud. An array of exotic drinks tempted us. We obliged them. Long before appetizers were served on the long, up-lighted, curving marble table, I was thoroughly soused. I remember exotic, artistically presented food. I remember a wall of chatter around me.

I also remember Risinger walking up to me, shaking my hand, and saying "Congratulations!"—the first and last word he ever spoke to me.

Anni and I caught the last flight out of New York the following morning, just before the airport was shut down. A heavy snowstorm had hit the region hard during the night.

Ours was one of the last flights out before the local airports were closed. Bob and his wife Patsy didn't beat the storm to the airport. Bob had been on the road for three weeks. He and Patsy were determined to get home, any way they could. So, they rented a car, braved the storms and headed home to Ohio. I can only imagine the surreal scene during the five hundred mile trip — whiteness everywhere — small portals on the front window of the car, displaying little more than a moving stillness.

Inside, there must have been a restless stillness too, on that journey from an excess of everything through an excess of nothing.

Throughout our harried ride to the airport Anni and I had believed that we wouldn't make it out. But we were so anxious to get home and back to our children that we wanted to try our best.

When we picked up our kids at school that afternoon, we were greeted enthusiastically by one of my older son's best friends. Miles ran up to us and yelled, "Congratulations! You're rich now!!"

Our boys were six and nine. We had tried to explain to them what we were doing in New York, without referring to the financial aspects of the IPO. And only a few people at our kids' school knew that I had started a company, let alone that it had posted the sixteenth largest IPO gain in history the day before.

Glancing around as discreetly as I could to see if anyone had overheard, I said "Thank you," hoping nobody had heard this exchange— or that, if they did, they had dismissed it as childish exuberance.

That evening, I reviewed the *Wall Street Journal*. There was an article about the success of our IPO. They said it seemed the market was still alive after all—a company called Neoforma had proven it!

At the end of the article, a mention was made about the fact that Jeff and I were now worth more than $204 million each.

Everything felt the same. Nothing felt the same.

February 2000

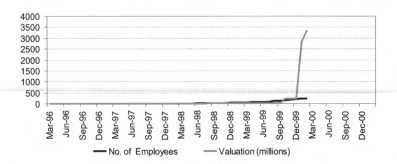

- No. of Employees   Valuation (millions)

What the Heck is Healtheon?

Jim Clark set out to build an Internet start-up that would revolutionize healthcare . . . Clark, never one to admit mistakes easily, concedes his vision was perhaps "a bit" too big and the industry more resistant to change than he had imagined . . .

Fortune
February 21, 2000

Fame

I was lost in the place between external validation and internal detachment. Between elation and dread.

In the jubilant days after the IPO, we quickly realized that our stock, which eventually moved into the seventies, was so valuable that we could accelerate our business in ways we hadn't imagined—through acquisitions and partnerships. Everyone wanted to be bought by us.

Our sudden prominence meant that everyone in any business that, however remotely, overlapped with ours was calling to propose that we *work together*. They saw our $4 billion market cap as a gold mine.

The opportunities that flooded our doors required thorough analysis before reaching any kind of negotiation phase. So, I had the bright idea that the company's five primary iconoclasts—Jeff, the wanderer; Anil, the missionary; Dave, the inventor; Stephen, the salesman; and me, the architect—band together and tackle the task of researching opportunities.

Short, intense, intelligent analysis combined with a shrewd knowledge of the complex healthcare and Internet markets—that sounded like something this bunch of misfits could handle. The company liked the idea too. They weren't quite sure what to do with us anyway. We were good start-up types, but no one wanted us to disrupt the execution phase.

So, I assembled the crew together and we began to analyze the opportunities. As I should have foreseen, asking this group of people to narrow the list of prospects was an exercise in futility. We were too used to seeing every obstacle as an opportunity.

The group only met for a couple of months before we scattered back into various folds of the company, trying to recover the sense of importance and belonging we had once felt there.

With Neoforma entering adulthood, the boundaries and main ideas had been set. It was mostly about execution from here, at least for the next couple of years.

The idea of helping hospitals and suppliers connect more efficiently *was* being implemented. The ethical and caring culture *was* there. But the basic idea of helping healthcare providers and their architects build better hospitals and efficiently equip them was gone. It was not about equipment anymore, it was about supplies. A subtle shift from what Jeff and I knew—to what we didn't.

I was struggling to get the company to hold onto the architectural part of the business. After the R&D group disintegrated, I became the official manager of the business we called Plan.

There were about twenty of us, swimming upstream in a company that had diverted its attention elsewhere. We were very close to break-even, bringing in a substantial portion of the company's revenue. However, the development effort to build our business was so out of sync with the rest of the company that it didn't make sense to divert much attention to it. I knew that, but I couldn't let go.

The reality was—Neoforma didn't need me anymore. And I didn't need Neoforma. But that didn't mean that a separation would be easy. I had experienced my last attempts to find a long-term role in the company, though it would take a full year after that for me to come to terms with the inevitable separation.

March 2000

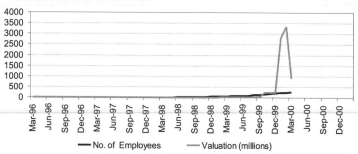

No. of Employees — **Valuation (millions)**

Burning Up: Warning: Internet Companies Are Running Out of Cash—Fast

When will the Internet Bubble burst? For scores of Net upstarts, that unpleasant popping sound is likely to be heard before the end of this year. Starved for cash, many of these companies will try to raise fresh funds by issuing more stock or bonds. But a lot of them won't succeed. As a result, they will be forced to sell out to stronger rivals or go out of business altogether . . .

Barron's
March 20, 2000

Neoforma.com Chief Bridges Old and New Economies

Robert Zollars is not your stereotypical Silicon Valley chief executive. Before taking over the top three posts at Neoforma.com . . . he spent nearly 20 years working his way up the corporate ladder of the healthcare products industry . . . After less than a year at the helm of Neoforma.com, he took the company public. It now boasts a hefty $3.3 billion market capitalization . . .

Forbes Magazine
March 28, 2000

Neoforma.com to Acquire Eclipsys

Neoforma.com Inc., operator of an online medical marketplace, agreed to acquire Eclipsys Corp., a healthcare software and services provider, and a related company for stock totaling $2.72 billion.

Associated Press
March 30, 2000

Fortune

Over dinner one evening, I glanced up from my plate, assumed an air of casualness, and said to Anni, "We made twenty million dollars today."

I just had to say it, once. Anni frowned at me, scolding, "It's *not* real, you know. It's only on paper. Anything could happen." I knew it was only paper, but even a fraction of that paper would get us out of debt. Anni would finally be able to quit the graphics job she dreaded more each day. She could finally catch up on a hundred unfinished projects. She could finally get back to fine art. I felt good about that.

But Anni had been well trained by her father, whose family had lived during the Depression . . . *Nothing is real until it is real.* I begged to differ. *Nothing is real until someone imagines it to be real.*

I did not want to act on an uncertain future, but neither did I want to deny it. While I have never been one to lean toward extravagance, I couldn't help having some small fantasies about what I could do with some of this unexpected money.

I imagined creating and funding a guild of talented architects and craftspeople, dedicated to building the beautiful and experimental buildings I had visualized in my design school days. My new business skills could be creatively applied to a profession that I believed was sorely lacking in innovation. I just had to figure out a way to do it without becoming obsessed with or consumed by it.

This seemingly small rift between Anni's caution and my optimism amplified all the other rifts that had developed over the past decade. I was trying to allow myself some hope that all of the sacrifices we had made would finally be, somehow, justified. She had seen enough hopes suffocated by my pursuit of this venture to be less optimistic.

Neoforma had been working for almost a year to come up with a way to work with Novation, the largest group purchasing organization, the big daddy of GPOs. Their mission was to save hospitals huge amounts of money by aggregating their spending, thereby getting a negotiating edge on the manufacturers.

On the other hand, the manufacturer's job was to carve out for themselves as much of the healthcare bill as possible. To stay alive, the GPOs needed to carve out a significant part of the savings for themselves too. We walked into one big angry community of sharing with the naïve idea of saving everyone time and money by making the process more efficient.

Of the GPOs, Novation was not only the largest by a hair, but it had a reputation of being one of the most ethical—or maybe just the least belligerent. That kind of fit with Neoforma's personality. If we could work out a deal with two thousand hospitals at once, our need to waste resources fighting inertia, one hospital at a time, would be nearly eliminated. Our ability to focus would be luxurious.

It was a simple matter of economics. Why should we have a large sales force to sell our services a couple of hospitals at a time, when Novation has already done that job? And why should Novation create an entire technology organization to improve their communication between their suppliers and their member hospitals when technology was not their business?

The GPOs had taken different approaches to fight the broad category they labeled "the dotcoms." The second largest GPO had decided to aggressively build its own dotcom, investing $50 million to fight us. The third largest GPO had partnered with our second largest competitor, Ventro, which had been a company like us in the laboratory supply space.

Ventro, funded by Kleiner Perkins (KP), had come up with the ultimate way to turn their substantial equity value into astronomical equity value. Their idea was to take a successful public niche company, like one serving the laboratory market, and clone it to serve another niche, like healthcare. The plan was to spin out each company as a new public offering, and so on.

So they reached out and acquired a small, niche medical Internet supply-chain company, Promedix, for $20 million, and became our competitor overnight. At their request, we had spoken with Ventro several times in the past about partnership opportunities. But we were told by their representatives that their investors didn't like the idea of sharing a large industry that they believed they could dominate. And then there was the ego of their CEO and co-founder, David Perry. Mr. Perry had painted quite a picture of himself in the media. Thanks to the KP machine, his had been the first B2B supply-chain company to go public. And the company stock had done very, very well. Mr. Perry had taken the bulk of the public credit, becoming something of a rags-to-riches darling in the business press.

Ventro wasn't satisfied with owning only one company in competion with Neoforma. Our position in the market was too strong. So they orchestrated a major play in the medical supply-chain space. They partnered with the third largest GPO, Broadlane, to create another business chasing Neoforma. With KP's substantial interest in Medibuy and Ventro, they controlled our three largest competitors.

Novation made their decision in early 1999. They were going to partner with someone, rather than build their own marketplace. They had evaluated more than one hundred candidates for that partnership, but in the end, we like to think it was a cultural issue that swayed their final decision.

Neoforma's culture, for better and worse, was driven by a standard of cooperation rather than of confrontation. This was ironic, because we had always been seen by the industry players as "an upstart interloper in a system that was already balanced quite well, thank you."

Novation was a company with a culture similar in many ways to Neoforma, though different in one key way—they moved very, *very* slowly, by the standards of Neoforma.

It was clear from our first meetings in early 1999 that our companies were a good fit for each other. We shared common goals, from a cultural standpoint.

But they needed time—to think about the implications and objectives of a partnership, to discuss it with all of their key members, then make a decision based on the overwhelming consensus of hundreds of hospitals, then send that decision back around for review and consensus.

After all, this is how they made all of their decisions. Making those decisions, carefully and deliberately, was what Novation was all about. Their service was literally about making the decisions on which products to use for a large group of healthcare providers who use those products to save lives every day.

Their decision process dragged on and on. We had meeting after meeting, followed by weeks or months of silence, followed by more meetings. They were in no hurry. They knew that most new health-care products or services took a decade or so to get into practice.

We weren't on that kind of schedule. When we became a public company, many analysts had pointed out how beneficial, even critical, it was for Neoforma to partner closely with one or more GPOs. Leveraging their power was central to maintaining our first mover status.

Novation wasn't particularly impressed with our IPO success.

They kept saying they were close to making a final decision and they indicated that we were on the short list to be the beneficiary of that decision. But nothing really changed, except our market cap . . .

Which wasn't really *nothing* anymore.

Although there had been no public disclosures, we had heard the gossip rampant throughout the healthcare industry that we were close to a deal to partner with Novation, and that Medibuy (or, The Bug, as we called them) was close to a deal to partner with Novation's primary competitor, Premier, the second largest GPO.

The Bug was still struggling to pull together their IPO. We had been working with Novation in the background for so long that we had taken this pretty much for granted. When Novation continued to drag its feet after our IPO, Bob stepped up as CEO and kicked things into high gear. While Novation was far and away our first choice, due to its great cultural fit and dominant size, we couldn't afford to just sit back and wait for something to happen.

In February, Bob boldly called the head of Premier and offered $1 billion for Premier's electronic commerce business. Even for a business that managed about $30 billion worth of spending each year for its members, this was a hard number to ignore.

In contrast to Novation's reputation as a company driven by process and consensus, Premier had a reputation for forcefulness. Bob, who understood every fiber of this industry, was betting that a decision by Premier would drive the other GPOs into action. This would quickly drive Premier to either us or The Bug.

His gamble was that, if Premier went to The Bug, Novation would accelerate their move to us. Either we would acquire a large number of

Premier's hospital customers or we would weaken KP's hold on The Bug by substantially increasing Premier's equity expectations.

Bob's initiative did instigate a series of hastily assembled meetings between Premier and Neoforma. Premier seemed to take our offer very seriously. While the cultural match between the two companies was far from strong, our common drive toward quick decision was a welcome relief. A deal structure was quickly sent to the lawyers. It looked like Bob's ploy had worked.

When we thought the deal had been all but formally signed, our execs investigated the housing availability in La Jolla, California, where Premier was headquartered. In addition to beaches and great weather, housing was available for a fraction of the astronomical Bay Area housing costs. They liked that.

Then we heard some disturbing rumors from friends in the industry. Premier's negotiations with us were a guise.

Premier figured they could trump The Bug by saying that if they didn't receive a *much* larger piece of Medibuy than they were going to get from Neoforma, they were going to do a deal with Neoforma. That would practically squash The Bug's hopes of going public.

And until The Bug caved in, Premier could keep Neoforma from proceeding with Novation, by pretending that they were still proceeding with us as planned. That way, they could announce the merger with The Bug as part of an IPO filing, garnering maximum buzz. Premier and The Bug were convinced that their public valuation would far exceed ours because of the aggressive nature of their mutual businesses.

Hey, it was *business*. Nasty stuff, but you had to play tough to get on top.

Once we validated these rumors, only a week before the deal was to be publicly announced, we feigned ignorance of the Medibuy deal, calmly stalled all dialog with Premier and notified Novation that we had heard that Premier was going to announce a deal with Medibuy very soon.

Novation may have been the quiet force among these fiercely competitive GPOs, but they *were* the largest. And their lead against number-two Premier was not very great. They knew a threat when they saw one.

By the time the hastily assembled Premier/Medibuy deal was announced in early March, Novation was wide awake. They were intensifying their talks with us. The preferred outcome to Bob's plan was working out as planned. However, Novation, in negotiating the best possible deal they could, had made it clear that we had only made it to the short list. We had not yet been selected as the finalist.

As the press speculated about who Neoforma and Novation would partner with, we couldn't help but look at our future without Novation. If Medibuy were to go public with a huge GPO partner and we did not partner with the only other one that mattered, we could be propelled from the clear market leader to a bit player, overnight.

The tension at Neoforma was very high. We all tried to pursue our assorted tasks with typical enthusiasm, but we knew that our fate was about to change dramatically, one way or the other.

Most of the time though, we assumed that an agreement with Novation was inevitable. That is, until our stock value began to decline. While our stock had climbed as high as $78, it had seemed to settle in the low fifties in early March. However, speculation about how critical a Novation deal was to Neoforma, combined with assorted jitters in the press about how new companies could suffer if the economy slowed down, began to nibble, day by day, at our stock value. By mid-March, our stock had drifted down into the thirties.

Bob had always made sure to emphasize that, as a newly public company, our stock price would be volatile. So we should not be concerned if it went down. We had a lot of work to do before our company grew to fill our market cap.

During our IPO party, Bob did allow a rare moment of indulgence, when he announced: "As of last week, Neoforma now has over a hundred millionaires!" Needless to say, those hundred millionaires cheered heartily at this boast.

Bob didn't express concern to me about the stock price decline until it dropped into the twenties in late March—the week before our deal with Novation was due to be announced.

"It's easy to give away a large, but minority, piece of Neoforma to get a deal for a third of the U.S. healthcare market, when our stock is in the fifties or even the forties," Bob told me. "When it's in the thirties, our negotiating position becomes much weaker. And in the twenties, it's nearly impossible."

For the first and only time, I saw panic in his eyes. For a moment, his innate certainty that his abilities could get him through anything seemed to be faltering. He saw the possibility that we might lose the deal and did not like it.

Once Novation decided to move forward with an Internet initiative, they decided that the best way to ensure quick adoption by hospitals was to incentivize the hospitals that signed up early. The best incentive for the nation's struggling hospitals was money. And the best way to get that money to the hospitals would be to distribute Neoforma stock to them.

One of Novation's key missions was to increase the quality of products purchased while saving money for their hospital members. Any money Novation made beyond what was required to support them went back to their members. The only way for all members to fully benefit from an automated commerce system would be to ensure wide adoption of a single solution. Returning money to their membership hospitals was consistent with their way of doing business.

The only problem was that, once they had set their expectation of how much money that would be, it would be hard to adjust to an increasingly lower number.

But the *bigger* problem was that Novation and their owners felt the need to combine their other software partnerships into one big new solution. They were insistent about it.

Novation had partnered extensively with a healthcare information technology firm called Eclipsys. They had even created a joint venture, HEALTHvision, targeted at helping hospitals set up their own websites. Novation wanted to trump the Medibuy/Premier deal by uniting these companies together into a single initiative. They wanted to add one plus one plus one to make ten.

This arrangement was not popular at Neoforma, to say the least.

First of all, Eclipsys was a large legacy. In other words, it was a maker of cumbersome, difficult-to-update software with well over a thousand employees. They were far from the largest player in healthcare information technology (IT), but far from the smallest too.

Most of the software they developed wasn't Internet software. And its applications served needs across the entire hospital, not just the supply-chain.

But Novation insisted that any solution they embraced needed to accommodate a transition from their older IT initiatives to their new ones. Novation wanted to include them in the deal—or else there would be no deal at all.

I had an aesthetic aversion to the idea of diluting the purity of our Internet model with an older technology solution. On the other hand, I had been in the healthcare market long enough to recognize that the newest solution is not always the one that will be adopted by this sluggish industry. But I knew this would be a pretty gutsy move, putting us in competition with some of the largest IT companies serving healthcare. And that might be fun.

Eclipsys had the challenge of moving from a legacy software provider into an Internet solution provider. Neoforma had the challenge of nudging the Industry's inertia in our direction. *It just might work.*

Then I received a call from Debbie, an associate of one of our investors, who had heard that we might be partnering with Eclipsys. Her usually cheerful voice edged with panic, she said, "There's someone you *must* speak with before you let this happen!" She asked if we could get together on the East Coast next week.

Jeff and I had a customer visit to New York already scheduled. We agreed to meet her mysterious person there.

When Jeff and I arrived at the trendy New York restaurant, Debbie and Dale were already seated at an appropriately private table. Dale was a friendly man, a decade or two our senior. He seemed like a man who had seen just about everything. He was a senior executive at one of the largest healthcare IT companies and had worked closely with the CEO of Eclipsys many times over the last several decades.

Dale spun a yarn about a man who was simultaneously despised, feared and respected throughout the healthcare industry; a man known—among his employees as well as his competitors—for his viciousness; a man appreciated on Wall Street for his singular focus on the stock value.

"This man will take Neoforma, strip it, and sell it for parts," Dale said, with conviction. "He lives on the edge. His current company is struggling with its old, underperforming software. He has been having greater difficulty each quarter meeting his numbers. He is just looking for some fresh meat to chew. And believe me, he's done this many times before. He is a fierce survivor."

My heart sunk as I listened to this summary of the man who would become the number-two guy at Neoforma. *What would this do to the culture I had so carefully constructed? How could I let this happen?*

On the other hand, the way the stock had been sinking, maybe we needed an experienced survivor on our team. Neoforma was going to be the acquirer. Maybe the Neoforma culture was strong enough to survive the influx of an extra thousand or so people. Ultimately, we had little choice in the matter. Our new knowledge would only make my suffering that much more exquisite.

After weeks of intense negotiation, from which I was completely isolated, the day for the public announcement was finally selected.

The press and analysts expressed increasing concern over our lack of a GPO partner. Our stock continued its slide into the low twenties. But we knew that the stock would soar again on the news that we had partnered with the huge GPO. How else could investors react to the announcement of two thousand new hospital customers?

The announcement was scheduled for a Tuesday. The release was being carefully orchestrated. Neoforma, Eclipsys and Novation execs were going to carefully present the new company to key investors, analysts and press contacts. Each company would enthusiastically present a unified vision to its employees.

Then, on the Tuesday a week before the big day, Jeff received a call from a reporter he had spoken with in the past. "I'm doing a story tomorrow on your upcoming merger with Eclipsys," the reporter said. "I was wondering if you'd like to comment?" He disclosed enough details on the deal structure to verify that someone had leaked every detail of the merger.

In addition to being very angry that someone had leaked the story, we were panicked about the implications of an early release of the deal. We knew that there would be some initial confusion about why Eclipsys was part of a Novation deal and were not confident that we could convey the benefit convincingly.

But there was no time to control that message. The story was going out almost a week early. Investor confusion could unravel the entire deal before it was even signed.

Hundreds of frenzied calls were exchanged between all parties. A new consensus was quickly reached. In spite of horrendous logistical problems, we would somehow get the final details complete in time for a Thursday morning announcement—just after the leak was to be published.

On Thursday morning, the Neoforma lunch room was decorated profusely with balloons and banners for a big celebration of the formal internal announcement of the merger.

The press announcement had been released prior to the market opening that morning. Anticipation of a huge stock surge, driven by a Novation deal, was trampled soundly by a huge backlash against the Eclipsys announcement.

Everyone hated it.

The investors hated the idea that they had invested in a B2B Internet company that was merging with an old-economy software company. They felt their shot at the astronomical B2B stock returns that other companies had seen was diminished by the merger.

The analysts hated the fact that the merger turned Neoforma into an impure entity. They had made their reputations espousing the wonders of pure Internet e-commerce. This did not fit their vision of a new economy.

The press hated it because it made a better story to hate it.

By the time our company celebration was about to start, Neoforma's stock had dropped nearly $10 per share. Employees dejectedly trickled into the decorated room. Many didn't even come. Everyone was angry about everything.

Our execs tried to paint a pretty face onto the ugly reality. I gave a spontaneous speech about the fickle nature of investors and how little they reflected the strength and value of a company. As the crowd filed out of the room, it was clear by the expressions of despair that everyone was getting very tired of fighting . . . for . . . every . . . little . . . bit . . . of . . . ground.

Within a month of the announcement, our stock was down below $7 and still falling.

A year or so later, an analyst told us, "You know, based on what has happened to the pure-play companies versus what has happened to those companies that blended the new and old, I can see now what you were trying to do. It was absolutely the right thing to do. But it was too far ahead of its time."

I never indulged in fantasies of great wealth again.

April 2000

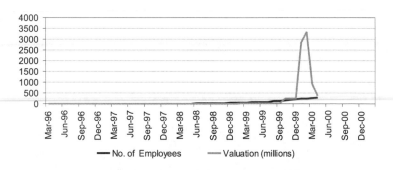

4000
3500
3000
2500
2000
1500
1000
500
0

Mar-96 Jun-96 Sep-96 Dec-96 Mar-97 Jun-97 Sep-97 Dec-97 Mar-98 Jun-98 Sep-98 Dec-98 Mar-99 Jun-99 Sep-99 Dec-99 Mar-00 Jun-00 Sep-00 Dec-00

— No. of Employees   ▬▬ Valuation (millions)

Major Medical Products and Services Companies Establish Global Healthcare Exchange

Johnson & Johnson, GE Medical Systems, Baxter International Inc., Abbott Laboratories and Medtronic, Inc. announced today that they are creating a global healthcare exchange that will be an independent Internet-based company . . .

Business Wire
March 29, 2000

Five of the Major Healthcare Products Distributors Are the Latest Members of the Healthcare Industry Creating Their Own Web Sites to Challenge Online Companies.

Facing competition from companies such as Healtheon/ WebMD Corp. and Neoforma.com Inc., as well as a similar company being formed by a handful of medical device manufacturers, the drug and medical product distributors, such as Cardinal Health Inc. (CAH), are turning to the Internet to preserve and perhaps enhance their traditional role in the supply chain for healthcare products, an analyst said . . .

Dow Jones News Service
April 18, 2000

The Majors — Part Two

It was nothing personal. Business is business.

Okay, so we had a bit of a setback with the Eclipsys merger. So what. We had fought back many times before. This would be no different, right?

We were still fairly confident that we would come out of the merger mess with a strong relationship with Novation. Their membership included more than a third of the hospitals in the country. That was no small thing.

However, the gap between confidence and certainty was spanned by a precarious tapestry of hope and despair. The stock market was looking more dreadful each day.

Everything that had made sense yesterday was foolish today. Nearly everyone seemed to be cowering under the weight of uncertainty. Dreamers were redefined as fools. Investors were redefined as dreamers. Gamblers were redefined as investors.

Deflated hopes turned into over inflated anger. We had no way to be certain that our strong partnership with Novation could weather such a powerful tempest of emotions. But there was one good thing about the market downturn. There was no way that any new competitors would be able to host an IPO. We hoped that this would solidify our position as the best choice in the industry. In fact, we thought we might become the only choice.

It turned out that we weren't the only ones who saw the new market condition as an opportunity.

The huge manufacturers of healthcare equipment and supplies had been very nervous about the possibility that their dominance might be unsettled by the wealth of well-funded dotcoms. They had been so concerned about the scope of our potential financial capitalization that they had gone through the motions of trying to work with us prior to the IPO. True, GE had even invested in us, but they had turned their back on us immediately thereafter.

Now that we were weakened by a controversial merger and deflated stock value, they saw an opportunity to crush us.

We had known that J&J and GE had formed an uncomfortably tight camaraderie while they were both planning to invest in Neoforma. What we hadn't realized was that they had maintained their communication at the highest levels long after J&J had backed out on the investment. They were discussing ways to keep Neoforma and its competitors from gaining a foothold in the industry they controlled.

Several coalitions of industry players had been formed in the last year or so to fight off the wave of upstart intermediaries. In many instances, they had been able to stop the new players in their tracks. We knew that this threat existed in healthcare too, but we believed that several factors made this unlikely.

First, the healthcare industry is riddled with very complex processes that control the pricing and distribution of medical products to an extraordinary degree. It would be difficult for manufacturers to band together on anything without triggering the wrath of insurers and government regulators.

Second, the competition between the big manufacturers is fierce. Jeff and I had seen first-hand how difficult it could be to manage the interests of a few competing manufacturers, let alone a coalition of them. We had originally formed Neoforma with the idea that manufacturers should band together to eliminate redundant processes and improve customer support. For the most part, they had reacted with extreme resistance to the idea that they should share *anything* with each other.

And third, the GPOs represented a powerful force in the industry. If suppliers were to band together, they would risk raising the ire of a majority of their customers.

So we had been a bit skeptical when we first heard rumors that the manufacturers were about to announce their own Internet coalition. As these rumors came to us with increasing clarity, we became very concerned.

We knew that anything they might announce would only be smoke and mirrors for years to come, no matter how much money they threw at it. But, in this shaky environment, that would be enough to do substantial damage. Bloodlust was driving investors and the press to turn against us with the same frenzy that had initially driven them toward us.

By the time the manufacturers announced their coalition, we had already prepared our official comments: "It is a good thing for the industry that the manufacturers can establish standard practices. That will make it much easier for us to do business with them."

The manufacturers, led by J&J and GE, were equally and ludicrously dismissive of the idea that they were competing with us. "We will be happy to work with all manufacturers, distributors, healthcare providers, GPOs and Internet companies."

Regardless of the friendly rhetoric, most observers saw right through this veil. The manufacturers were making a run not only at us, but at the GPOs. The big GPOs had all formed some kind of partnership with Internet companies. Now that the Novation/Neoforma partnership was vulnerable and none of the other GPO/Internet partners would be able to go public, the manufacturers were struggling to loosen the binds that the GPOs had on them.

Feeling left out of this huge power play, the major distributors scrambled to form their own coalition. They made no clear statements about what they were going to build, but, within ten days, they had assembled a hundred million dollars and a press release.

Articles appeared in industry media, eagerly reporting the demise of Neoforma and the rest of the dotcom upstarts. Some analysts pointed out that these coalitions themselves were little more than press releases and that the GPOs might have some substantial influence on the success or failure of these ventures. After all, competing against one's customers is not usually in one's own interest. And that is exactly what these coalitions were doing, however much they tried to position themselves differently.

So there we were. The market was crashing. Our merger was threatening to fall apart. Company morale was low. The major industry players— with a combined market valuation of nearly a trillion dollars—had created two coalitions with the sole purpose of defeating us. The press was happily writing our epitaph.

All Jeff and I had wanted to do was fix a few things.

Really. I still remembered those early days, when a growing number of visitors thanked us, desperately grateful for the information we were providing them. I remembered the time that a doctor in a Third World country, after exhausting all conventional means, had found and purchased a previously inaccessible device on the Neoforma website. We had worked with the manufacturer to rush the device to the doctor, who had immediately implanted it in a patient. Had the patient received the treatment a day later, the patient would have *died*.

That's the kind of thing we thought we had started a company to do. But we had started something else.

May 2000

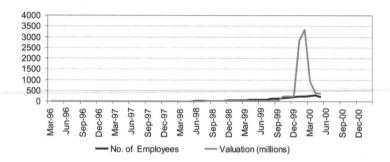

— No. of Employees	— Valuation (millions)

Neoforma Lays Off 80 People

Just days after announcing the abandonment of previously announced merger agreements that would have added Eclipsys and its healthcare Internet affiliate HEALTHvision to its holdings, Neoforma.com has announced that it is laying off approximately 80 employees . . .

AuctionWatch
May 26, 2000

Cliffhanger

Thalia was one of those rare women who seemed completely oblivious to her extraordinary attractiveness. Her face seamlessly blended innocence, youth, intelligence and beauty, yet her manner was awkward and self-conscious. She walked as if the act of wearing shoes was foreign to her.

Each time I gave one of my heartfelt, but often rambling, talks to the employees about the bizarre state of our company and the world crushing it from the outside, most of the employees seemed oblivious to, or cynical of, my words. I was as perplexed as anyone by what was happening around us, but I felt obligated to share my core of rebellion and optimism.

Each time I gave such a speech, a few employees would send me a message expressing their appreciation for my talk. This was the extent of my personal connection to the majority of the staff. But that was all I needed to get up the nerve once again to speak, unrehearsed, in front of the increasingly large and unfamiliar group of employees. If my own limited experience was helping a few, that was enough.

Thalia didn't write me messages. Instead, she would nervously approach my office, peek in, and say, "Thank you for your talk today. It meant so much to me. You're so . . . humble."

Well, gosh. What could I say to that? "Oh . . . um . . . thank you. I'm glad that my perspective on things helps someone." And that's about how our conversations went, the times we spoke. Not much else could be said without us both going out of bounds. Thalia was an administrator who worked on the other side of the building. I didn't interact with her at all during the normal course of work.

I was not flirting with her and she was not flirting with me. At a very guarded, yet deep level we were fulfilling a need in each other. I felt increasingly isolated from the company I had formed. And she felt increasingly overwhelmed by the company I had formed. Her brief comments after my talks helped make my segregation bearable.

I was giving a lot of talks these days. Many of the employees were freaking out. They had almost no information on what was happening with the merger or the Novation agreement. Bob tried to communicate often, but he could only say so much about nothing. And nothing was certain.

Neoforma stock continued to fall. In fact, just about every company's stock continued to fall. And, entire companies were beginning to fall. Especially Internet companies.

After an excruciatingly long time (two months), Neoforma was able to announce the break-up of the merger plans and reaffirm a ten-year partnership with Novation.

At long last, we had the deal we had wanted in the beginning, but under much less favorable terms. As part of the deal, Neoforma was giving up more than half of its stock to Novation and its owners. The stock would be used to help member hospitals cover the expense of converting from their inefficient paper processes to Internet-enhanced processes.

We expected an enthusiastic public reaction to our announcement. In one deal, we had secured business with *more than a third* of the country's hospitals. After our IPO, the analysts covering Neoforma had been adamant that Neoforma must do a deal with one of the two lead GPOs to continue to justify the current company valuation.

Now that we had achieved that huge landmark, these same analysts were complaining that Neoforma would get too much of its business through one partnership.

Regardless of what the analysts or press thought, it *was* a huge deal. We needed to convert a company focused on developing, marketing and selling stuff to a few hospitals into a company focused on implementing, installing and supporting stuff for *thousands* of hospitals.

Now that there was no longer the possibility of selling additional stock to the public markets, we needed to do this with fewer resources than we currently had.

Our accounting team had run the numbers many times. The good news was that we would be able to survive the gap between when we implemented connections to hospitals and when we derived revenue from them.

The bad news was that we would only survive if we immediately cut our staff by more than twenty-five percent.

Long before most other young, previously popular companies began to trim their own expenses, Bob refused to delay the inevitable. There could be no reduction in the amount to be trimmed. Now that we had a single focus, it should not be very difficult to figure out who should stay and who should go. He instructed every senior manager to make a list of which employees in their area would go.

Tim and Ajit put their own names on the list. They both knew that their high salaries and aggressive, outwardly focused styles were unnecessary for the company in the next phase. They knew that they were not popular with most employees. They also knew that they were not going to make the fortune that they had expected.

Once the lists were made, we got together in an off-site conference room and laid it all out on whiteboards and large sketchpads. We drew up a new organization chart and moved the names of employees around. If someone did not fit anywhere, their name was set aside.

Nobody liked what we were doing. Nobody joked around. But neither did anybody shirk their responsibility. New leaders began to emerge from the flattened organization. Some previous leaders moved themselves down the ladder—just because they knew it was the right thing to do.

When it was done, many great employees were left without a place in the new company. I was able to feel okay about that. My years in an architecture office had shown me that not only did most people survive layoffs well, but many thrived in their new jobs.

Once everything had been laid out, there was one more set of employees to allocate. The pool of administrators needed to be trimmed and reassigned to newly formed departments. None of these choices was going to be easy.

The administrators formed the social core of Neoforma. They were the ones with flowers and photos and homemade snacks at their desks. It was around their desks that the business of Neoforma most often joined the people of Neoforma.

Several of the choices were obvious. In the end, though, we were left with two administrators and only one position.

One of the two was Sheila, my team's administrator. Sheila's efficiency, support and loyalty had been unflinching for the year that she had worked for me. I liked her and respected her. She had made me feel special and she had taught me that it was okay to depend on someone else to get things done.

The other administrator was Thalia.

One of them had to go. And since Sheila had been my administrator, Bob and the others agreed that it was my choice.

They were both very good at their jobs. Sheila had worked at Neoforma for much longer than Thalia, so it was logical that Sheila should stay.

Nobody knew about my special bond with Thalia. I knew that I could ask to swap Thalia with someone else, but there was no rational reason to do that. The very trait that Thalia had complimented me on was the trait that kept me from using my influence to change the course of this decision. I was unwilling to use my position in the company to unfairly or inappropriately influence a decision.

Bob was never one to shrink from taking responsibility for his decisions. It was very important to him that he be upfront with the people who relied on him.

The day before the layoffs, Bob gathered the company together and announced that a large number of employees would be laid off the next day. He wanted everyone to be together when they heard this sad news.

The next day's activities were very orderly. But it was dreadful—a factory of pain.

Sheila eyed me nervously that morning. I knew she thought that she was going to lose her job. I pulled her aside and told her that she was not losing her job, but that she would not be working for me anymore. She was both terribly relieved and saddened by this news.

Thalia hadn't reported to me, so I wouldn't be the one giving her the bad news. I kept glancing out my office window that day, expecting to see her on her way out with short, awkward steps and hunched shoulders, crying at my cruelty.

But I didn't see her that day. Or ever again.

June 2000

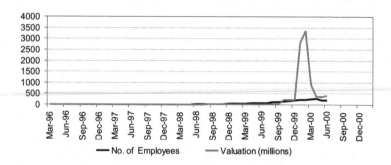

No. of Employees   Valuation (millions)

Hospital Purchasing Co-Ops Link Up to Make Buying On the Web Easier

Buying co-ops representing more than two-thirds of the nation's hospitals are banding together with three fledgling electronic-commerce companies to demand that manufacturers and distributors of medical supplies adopt standard product codes to ease the buying of supplies over the Internet, Wednesday's *Wall Street Journal* reported . . .

Dow Jones Business News
June 14, 2000

Posing

Properly decorated and fluffed, the lightest of feathers can display a magnificent confidence.

I was still focused on the remnants of the capital-planning group in the company. We were bringing in just enough money to justify our presence in the new, lean and mean Neoforma. I still believed that Neoforma would eventually need to focus on capital equipment again, but I was also increasingly resigned to the fact that Neoforma might not have the luxury of keeping us around that long.

Jeff's role in the new organization was much less defined than mine. And he was definitely happier with his unconfined position. He had been assigned a small number of limited-duration projects by Bob. In his free time, Jeff assigned himself some additional tasks.

One day, my phone rang. "Wayne, how are you doing . . . Hey! I have a brilliant idea!" It was like old times.

Jeff's voice had that old, familiar fighting edge. His brilliant idea this time was to lead the formation of an industry standards group. The group would create standard ways of classifying and identifying health-care products and initially consist of GPOs and Internet e-commerce companies.

"The manufacturers and distributors have come together around some fuzzy idea of fostering efficiency through cooperation," Jeff said. "If we combine the major e-commerce players with the major GPOs, then we'll have nearly all of the hospitals banding together to *reject* the idea that the suppliers could or should control how they get their supplies. All of their expensive new offices and empty press releases would be useless!"

"Well," I said, "it seems to me that the suppliers should actually be the ones to drive standards, don't you think?"

"Yes, of course, but once the GPOs band together, the suppliers will have to capitulate and lobby to join the new standards group. After all, they can only go so far to alienate their customers. Plus, if the GPOs band together with the e-commerce companies . . . that will raise our position and reinforce our permanence in the eyes of the entire industry."

I wasn't sure that Jeff would be able to convince the very competitive GPOs to band together with Neoforma and its customers. And I wasn't sure that this level of posturing was necessary.

But I had always been so frustrated every time I thought about transparent promises by the suppliers, that I thought Jeff's cynical approach might be worth the effort.

Over obstacles that only Jeff could hurdle at his best, a new standards organization was formed. Jeff brought together the necessary parties without anyone quite knowing who had even started the idea for the group!

With substance equal to the two supplier coalitions, the new standards group was announced.

The press wrote about what great potential such an organization had to improve the healthcare supply chain. They wrote about how much doubt this new group shed upon the purpose of the supplier coalitions.

The industry heaved a collective sigh. Balance between buyer and supplier had been achieved again.

The standards group was eventually joined by the manufacturers and distributors. They did implement some major improvements to the way things were done. Their open standards would fundamentally shake loose some of the mechanisms manufacturers used to control the flow of information to hospitals. Jeff had created a very useful organization.

On one hand, Jeff and I were disappointed that we had lowered ourselves to playing the game on the same field as these opponents. On the other hand, we took some satisfaction from the fact that we did know how to play that game when necessary.

It reaffirmed our conviction that Neoforma was going to survive in spite of them.

July 2000

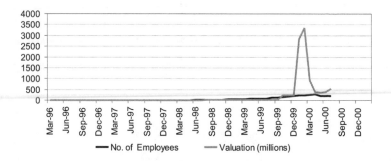

— No. of Employees	— Valuation (millions)	

A Virtual Turf War . . .

. . . is breaking out in the healthcare industry as emerging dot-com companies, established manufacturers, distributors, and traditional brokers scramble to establish competing Internet marketplaces for buying and selling everything from Band-Aids to JPI machines. At stake are potentially billions of dollars in revenue, savings for hospitals and their IT departments, and a controlling interest in the way health care goods are bought and sold in the future . . .

InfoWorld
July 3, 2000

Royalties

The entrepreneurial pot of gold shone like a lump of clay.

The Internet can be an amazing thing. Nearly every obscure fact (and fiction) is available at the touch of a few keys. And for those who hate to shop (or only like to shop for obscure things), the Internet can be like magic.

Only a few years ago, the idea that we would be able to shop for just about anything and at the same time find reviews of that thing by actual customers would have been unimaginable. That a large percentage of these reviews are articulate and useful is absolutely amazing.

Of course, not all of these reviews are quite so useful. Some reviewers are clearly biased or ignorant, or both. They've got a gripe with someone or something and they have found a place to vent, if only for a few seconds. With the good, we have to accept some bad.

When I was studying the stock market in preparation for our IPO, I had been surprised to see how many investors had shared their own reviews of public companies, via the broad assortment of Internet message boards tied to stock information.

A single company might have hundreds or thousands of people submitting their two cents' worth of information. And that is about what the information was generally worth.

Only about two out of a hundred messages had any real value to an investor. The rest seemed to be written by individuals who had lost their debate team finals and were out to angrily prove themselves in front of the broadest possible audience—but had instead demonstrated why they had failed.

The first time I saw Neoforma mentioned in these message boards was just after we filed for the IPO.

At the very moment Neoforma became NEOF, message boards

sprung up everywhere. At first, I was fascinated by these dens of ignorance and anger. Whether for or against Neoforma, the participants on the boards laced their mostly mundane comments with spite and insults. Once in a great while someone would post something accurate and informative, but the vast majority of comments were false and empty of anything but venom. I couldn't imagine why people were expending so much energy to say so little.

Despite myself, I often became angry as I read some of the ridiculous comments. I didn't like getting angry, so I had stopped reading the message boards long before the IPO. But many of Neoforma's employees had continued to read the message boards. They'd come into my office and ask me if I knew anything about the latest rumor someone was posting. I'd tell them to stop reading the boards. "Nothing good can come of it. Nothing."

But sometimes, they couldn't help themselves. And, as a result, they inadvertently empowered a few anonymous idiots with control over their own emotional well-being.

Bob knew what I thought of the message boards, so he could not resist forwarding a summary of one of the current message threads: "Quite a dialogue on one of the boards today about an $800,000 house you're buying with the proceeds of your sale!"

Now that the six-month lockout period (the period after the IPO during which company employees and private investors cannot sell any of their stock) was over, I was anxious to pay off the debt that had weighed my family down for so long. Several Neoforma execs and Board members urged Jeff and me to sell as little of our stock as possible. Many of Neoforma's early investors were already selling their stock. They did not want us to increase the amount of Neoforma stock available to an already unstable market.

At the same time, every financial and business advisor we had was telling us to sell most of our stock immediately — arguing that our sales would have no impact on the stock whatsoever.

Jeff and I had argued with each other about this issue. Jeff was adamant that we would be foolish to ignore our own interest by continuing to keep our entire assets in one volatile stock. "We aren't controlling the company anymore. Why would we put ourselves at risk when we have no ability to affect that risk?" He pointed out that we had put our assets into the company years before the other investors who were now selling stock at a substantial gain.

I saw the logic of his arguments, but I couldn't quite get myself into that frame of mind. It didn't seem right for us to reap large financial returns when the dreams of so many others had been shattered.

Jeff reluctantly deferred to my optimism that the stock would eventually recover and we both agreed to set up plans whereby we would sell a small amount of stock over a long period time. Based on the stock price at that time, my family could still be out of debt by the end of the year.

While I was no longer an officer of the company, I had been one less than ninety days earlier. That meant that each time I intended to sell stock, I had to file a document with the SEC stating the maximum number of shares I might sell in a particular period.

But one of my brokers made an administrative mistake. Instead of filing a series of these documents over time, he filed a single document. That made it look to the outside world as if I were going to sell a large number of shares all at once.

Jeff hadn't been an officer of the company as recently as I had been, so he wouldn't need to disclose his activity.

Through Bob and others, I heard that the message boards had a field day. But they weren't the only ones snarling at my perceived greed.

I noticed it on the morning that the SEC filing was made. Before I'd even heard about the erroneous public disclosure, I observed that many Neoforma employees were avoiding eye contact with me as we passed in the aisles. Finally, one employee I considered to be a friend came into my office and said, bluntly, "You're the talk of the morning. Nobody can believe that you are dumping that much stock at so low a price. They're very upset. They think you're selling out."

The power of the Internet thrives under two primary motivations — the delivery of pleasure and the alleviation of pain. On multiple levels, Neoforma had been formed to alleviate pain. We had sought to ease the distraction and burden that hospital personnel faced when they tried to locate and buy the tools of their trade. And their trade was focused on the alleviation of pain.

So, in the early days, most of our employees had *believed in* what we were doing with an uncommon passion. When their belief was assaulted by the realities of business in a hostile climate, their pleasure at relieving pain was harshly obscured by unimagined forces. We had shared so much enjoyment together in the early years that we could not help but feel our dissociation from our ideals and from each other very intensely.

But I had great difficulty believing that their morale was still linked to *me*. Jeff had long ago been the designated leader. I had assumed that most employees had transferred their devotion to him long ago and were now well along the way to transferring it to Bob. I had seen very few signs to the contrary.

My first reaction to my workmates' indignation was anger. I could ignore the idiocy of the message boards, but I couldn't accept the ire of so many Neoforma employees.

I thought surely they knew how bad my financial situation was! But, then I remembered how careful I had been to avoid sharing that with anyone, except Jeff. They didn't know that we had taken low salaries and few benefits. How could they?

My anger gave way to resignation. Much as I wanted to hold onto the idea that I had some ongoing role in directing the story called Neoforma, everything was easier when I didn't. I considered the employees' rejection of me to be a natural element of their acceptance of new order.

In the end, Jeff and our financial advisors had been correct. Had we sold more stock, there would have been absolutely no negative impact on the company stock. The financial price Jeff and I paid for what we believed was the morally correct — though rationally incorrect — decision was high, but we did okay. Our goal had been to make enough money to buy a house and we did. We received a good return on our high-risk investment. We just didn't get the emotional residuals we had hoped for.

August 2000

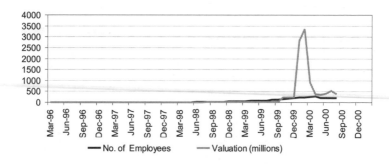

| 4000 |
| 3500 |
| 3000 |
| 2500 |
| 2000 |
| 1500 |
| 1000 |
| 500 |
| 0 |

Mar-96 Jun-96 Sep-96 Dec-96 Mar-97 Jun-97 Sep-97 Dec-97 Mar-98 Jun-98 Sep-98 Dec-98 Mar-99 Jun-99 Sep-99 Dec-99 Mar-00 Jun-00 Sep-00 Dec-00

— No. of Employees   — Valuation (millions)

**40 Healthcare Facilities Now Signed Up for marketplace@novation.
Signed Healthcare Organizations Represent More Than $1.2 Billion In
Annual Supply Purchases**

Neoforma.com, Inc. and Novation today announced that an
additional 21 healthcare facilities have signed contracts to
use marketplace@novation, powered by Neoforma, as their
Internet purchasing solution. A total of 40 healthcare facilities
are now signed up . . .

August 3, 2000
Neoforma Press Release

Continuity

Even as the physical residue of our influence upon Neoforma continued to dissipate, I saw great evidence that something solid was still firmly planted underneath.

Jeff and I were seeing less and less of Bob. Onsite, we communicated with him formally a few times a month, but that was about it. We both felt it was important that neither of us seemed to be struggling with or exercising any control over Bob.

The company needed clear leadership, as it struggled against the fierce storms outside. So Jeff, Bob and I agreed to meet informally offsite every couple of months or so. We called it a Founders Dinner. While Bob was always very careful to avoid any disclosure of Neoforma's business, these dinners became an opportunity for the three of us to openly discuss our cultural observations about the company and its industry.

At one dinner, Bob brought up how, in his long and aggressive business career, he had never experienced so much lack of integrity. I panicked for a moment, thinking he was talking about me or Neoforma. But then he explained how perplexed and chagrined he had been by the high level of deceit, greed and malice he had witnessed each day in his normal business dealings.

He was frustrated by how effective some our competitors' and enemies' blatant media manipulations were. Each new feature, obscure award, new customer or supplier seemed to warrant the publication of a press release.

But Bob refused to yield to the idea that more information was better information. When the company had something truly significant to brag about, that is when he would approve a press release.

And, he refused to work with any person or company that displayed unscrupulous behavior. Based on the abundance of shady characters prowling around at the time, Bob found himself refusing many deals that would have made great press releases.

There were those within the company who were saying that Neoforma had lost its vision. They complained that we were missing opportunities to do this deal or that deal. They thought that we were losing the PR wars.

Bob held firm to his position that long-term integrity must not be sacrificed to short-term overstatement. He knew a lot about healthcare. He knew how long it would take to change it. He was running a marathon, not a sprint.

Neoforma was only four years old. In its fourth year, Microsoft had revenues totaling $2.4 million — close to Neoforma's fourth year revenue. Six years later, Microsoft had announced its first version of Windows. Seven years after that, it had released its first moderately successful version of Windows.

Neoforma was still very young. And its long-term potential was still intact.

Bob had preserved the core culture of integrity that we had carved so quickly but carefully. Then he had shaped it, smoothing some of the rough edges. Though our tethers to Neoforma were becoming increasingly long and narrow, some part of Jeff and me would remain there forever.

September 2000

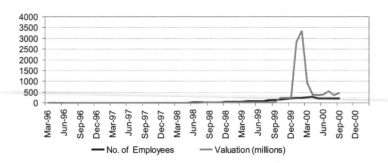

| | No. of Employees | Valuation (millions) |

Neoforma.com and Novation Reach Target Ahead of Schedule.
79 Hospitals Representing $2 Billion in Purchases Sign Up

Neoforma.com, Inc. and Novation today announced the addition of 39 new healthcare facilities, bringing to 79 the number of hospitals signed to purchase supplies through Marketplace@Novation, the online purchasing solution powered by Neoforma. This figure exceeds Neoforma's goal to have 56 hospitals signed onto Marketplace@Novation before year end . . .

September 7, 2000
Neoforma Press Release

E-Biz

. . . PricewaterhouseCoopers, which has launched the *Healthcast 2010: E-Health Quarterly* [says]: "A shakeout is in store for some 50 companies that now market e-procurement services in the U.S." . . .

Materials Management in Healthcare
September 2000

Editing

It had started so simply. Or rather, in the beginning, it had appeared to be so much simpler than it was.

There was Neoforma. That was about all that could be said about it. Nobody knew what a Neoforma was. Neoforma was not *like* anything else in particular.

One step at a time, we struggled to define Neoforma. For nearly three years, there was nothing much *like* Neoforma. Then there was one other company like Neoforma—then another—and another.

Our competitors had begun to define themselves by how they were like Neoforma, and how they were unlike Neoforma. Each new company had spliced themselves into the increasingly complex landscape, until there were more than a hundred of them, fighting for attention.

Then a few ran out of money. And a few merged together. Some lost interest when the rewards were less grand than they had anticipated. A few simply disappeared, as soon as the light stopped shining on them.

Many tried to merge with us. As we evaluated each one, layer upon layer flaked off at our touch. We poked and probed each insubstantial mass, but seldom found anything solid inside.

When it became clear to these companies that we weren't willing to pay a premium for bluster, they flocked to our less-discriminating competitors. Sometimes that worked. The distributors' dotcom merged with the manufacturers' dotcom. Other mergers made for some great press releases.

When there were only a few survivors left, everything became much clearer. We all knew who and what was real again. It was almost like starting over, only not nearly as fun.

January 2001

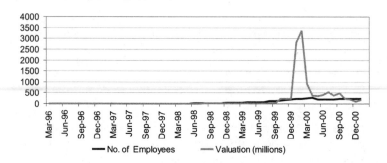

4000		
3500		
3000		
2500		
2000		
1500		
1000		
500		
0		

Mar-96 Jun-96 Sep-96 Dec-96 Mar-97 Jun-97 Sep-97 Dec-97 Mar-98 Jun-98 Sep-98 Dec-98 Mar-99 Jun-99 Sep-99 Dec-99 Mar-00 Jun-00 Sep-00 Dec-00

— No. of Employees   — Valuation (millions)

Neoforma Sharpens Focus on Core Strategy, Will Divest Two Business Units

Neoforma.com, Inc. announced plans to divest certain business units that are not aligned with its core strategy of building and operating Internet marketplaces that empower healthcare trading partners to optimize supply chain performance . . .

January 25, 2001
Neoforma Press Release

The Sequel

The seed of Neoforma was contained in the remnants of the capital equipment planning division, a group of mostly early employees — who either did not fit or did not want to fit into the new core of the company.

In a last ditch effort to survive in an increasingly foreign body, I had demoted myself again to — well, to a regular member of the group. Nobody reported to me. I was four layers from the top. In effect, I had worked my way to the bottom.

In spite of the group's ability to present great content on our website and to bring in significant revenue, the schism grew between Neoforma's single-minded focus on profitability in the supplies market and my group's focus on the capital equipment market.

There was no doubt in anyone's mind that what we were building in my group would eventually be relevant to what Neoforma was building, but the market dictated that Neoforma would not have the resources to build along more than one road at a time. And our group wasn't on the most expedient road. It was evident that, by every business criterion, Neoforma would have to temporarily shelf the company's capital equipment initiatives. We were necessary to the future, but distracting to the present.

We had been making money, but were at a point that we would require some investment to grow. Neoforma was now ready make the tough decision to postpone my group's development.

I was too. I was tired. Tired of the stress between dependence and independence, between obedience and exploration. I was tired of being depressed. And, most of all, I was tired of holding onto the idea that Neoforma somehow needed me, or perhaps the *hope* that Neoforma somehow needed me.

But we were *not* willing to let go of some of the ideas that had originally inspired us. The capital equipment group had to survive. We had made too much progress to give up. So, in spite of a currently hostile environment for start-up businesses, we worked the crowd to facilitate a way to spin my group out of Neoforma.

I knew it would be helpful for Neoforma if Jeff and I and two key members of the group, Dave and George, left on good terms. And I imagined that it would make some of the people I was leaving behind feel better to know that this early piece of Neoforma history would still survive—and thrive.

So after several months of strangely and increasingly hostile negotiations, Attainia was formed. Our new, small company would set off into a world not too unlike the one that Neoforma had been born into.

Eerily similar to our experience at spinning out from Varian, nobody was comfortable discussing our departure. It was much too awkward. There were no goodbye lunches or closing ceremonies. We were just gone one day—or perhaps we were simply there in a different way from then on. The facilities guy was uncomfortable taking my badge and access key, but I insisted.

Bob and I said goodbye to each other via email.

In spite of the uncomfortable departure, we were excited by the idea that Neoforma was spinning off a new company. Actually, Neoforma had previously spun off at least two companies. With this tradition, Neoforma joined the ranks of many great Silicon Valley companies, including Varian, which has a long history of spinning off technologies and companies, including ones that would contribute to the development of advanced CT scanners, ultrasound equipment and dot matrix printers.

With the right nutrients and caretakers, Attainia would one day grow to its ultimate potential. And who knows what it might seed?

My initial role in the new company, Attainia, was to be limited. I had two other priorities. I had to spend some time with my family and I had to spend some time with myself.

I had to make sense of this bizarre experience and my elusive feelings about it. Every time I closed my eyes, jumbled memories threatened to overwhelm me.

Somehow, I needed to integrate what had happened over the last five years with who I am. I needed to write everything down and organize it somehow, but figuring out how to assemble all of the disparate experiences would take some time.

I had written often, but never anything more than five or ten pages. This was something else completely. It was a new and exciting challenge. It was like starting anew.

February 2001

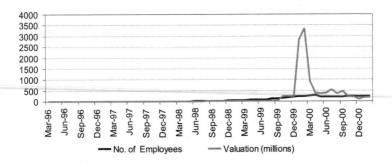

Legend: —— No. of Employees   —— Valuation (millions)

X-axis labels: Mar-96, Jun-96, Sep-96, Dec-96, Mar-97, Jun-97, Sep-97, Dec-97, Mar-98, Jun-98, Sep-98, Dec-98, Mar-99, Jun-99, Sep-99, Dec-99, Mar-00, Jun-00, Sep-00, Dec-00

Y-axis: 0, 500, 1000, 1500, 2000, 2500, 3000, 3500, 4000

Neoforma corporate headquarters in San Jose, California

Film

Neoforma stands as a real company now, entirely separate from me. It provides quarterly financial statements. It hosts annual shareholder meetings.

It even has a picture of its headquarters next to the title, "Company," on its website. It is an imposing, corporate-looking building. The photo captures a sharp corner of the reflective glass and the pre-cast, concrete shell of the building, as it dwarfs a fountain and trees in the foreground. It looks substantial and permanent.

I know many of the people who work there. I know them well because I have known them under stress. I know they are still working behind that tough exterior, conscientiously and passionately. They are continuing to build upon the foundation we built together many years ago.

Jeff and I started Neoforma in a fit of idealistic frenzy. It grew into something much more than we had planned, though much less than we had hoped. It was influenced by forces beyond our control and found its own destiny.

I am proud to say that we did contribute more than we consumed. Several hundred families now derive their sustenance from Neoforma. That, on its own, should be enough.

But there is much more to it than that. Neoforma continues to grow and evolve. It was well worth the early frustrations and sacrifices.

I can't pretend to know the sum of the lessons I have learned, what I might have done differently, what I could do better next time.

The best I can do is capture it all here—to be played backwards and forwards—over and over again.

Afterthoughts

Having just disclaimed all right and ability to draw concise conclusions from my business experience, I will now acquiesce to many early readers of this book who asked me to summarize my advice for managers and entrepreneurs.

Jeff and I did many things right that would have been wrong in another place or time. And we did many things wrong that would have been right in other circumstances. Luck plays a substantial role in the fate of young companies. However, there are some principles that are true beyond place and time. Here is what I would have liked to have had posted above my desk throughout the days at Neoforma:

12 Things to Keep In Mind When Starting Something

1. *Be who you are.* If you aren't true to yourself, your company's culture will suffer. So will you.

2. *Hire for culture first, experience second.* If someone *feels* wrong, they are. However exhausting and distracting hiring is, don't delegate it until after the first hundred employees—and then only very carefully.

3. *Communicate empowerment.* In the maelstrom that is a young company, it is easy for employees to feel helpless or isolated. *All* employees powerfully influence a company's success and direction. Let them know they are valued and their voices are heard. Often and in many ways. Don't waste the potential of *any* employee.

4. *Learn to release, without letting go.* When you delegate (and you must), neither control every detail nor allow the idea to get diluted. Make your plan clear and monitor progress regularly. If you hired well, everything will work out.

5. *Balance is not always found in the middle.* Make and communicate clear decisions. Changing a position is better than not having one.

6. *Do one thing well, then do it better.* Then, while you are still improving the first thing, consider doing one, and only one, related thing well. And so on.

7. *Regularly wear your customers' clothes.* Most entrepreneurs come from the industry they are trying to serve, but when confronted by the challenges of starting or running a business, they quickly lose touch with the customer experience.

8. *The unsatisfied customer is the most important customer.* Therein lies all opportunity.

9. *Never let your competitors drive your business decisions.* Stay focused. If your competitors come up with something good, your customers will let you know.

10. *Never let your investors drive your business decisions.* They are usually smart and can be intimidating, but they aren't as familiar with your business as you are. Their viewpoint is short term, yours should be long term.

11. *Listen to all advice, but trust what you know.* As you confront frequent obstacles, you may begin to question your core beliefs. Don't. Be patient. Ideas that require customers to change behavior often take ten or more years to implement.

12. *Enjoy yourself.* It is very easy, during the inevitable times of monetary starvation and market inertia, to lose sight of how much fun it is to create something new and useful.

Epilogue

In late 2002, Neoforma forwarded me a message from a writer for *Fortune* magazine. She was writing an article, following up with the founders of companies the magazine had written about during 1999 and 2000. She was interested in what had become of an array of momentary business celebrities, including Jeff and me.

Naturally, I thought this was a really interesting subject to explore, so I sent her a message saying that I would be happy to chat with her.

When she interviewed Jeff and me, she asked, "What life lessons have you learned? . . . How much stock were you able to sell before the Crash? . . . What has become of the company you founded?"

I could tell she was seeking some story of drastically altered lifestyle, like the opening of a hot dog stand or an extended stay at a Zen monastery. I said, "I'm writing a book." But I guess a lot of her interviewees were writing books. She didn't ask me much about it.

She seemed a bit disappointed when I told her that Neoforma was still in business, and even more disappointed when I told her that Neoforma was profitable. And she wasn't particularly happy when I pointed out that Jeff and I had been ten or so years older than the twenty-something dotcom darlings of the day, that we had started our business before the Boom, and that we had created the business before we had created the business plan.

"We were just trying to build a good company and offer good services."

I could tell that the picture she was trying to paint — a time of gleeful excess followed by a monumental crash-and-burn — was getting muddied by this conversation.

She asked me to ascribe a meaning to this defining moment in history, which she classified right up there with the Industrial Age and the Depression. I told her that I didn't know, but I was writing a book to help others figure out what it all meant. She thanked me for my time.

Later, when I contacted her to ask when the article would be published, she apologized profusely. She said she had wanted us to be listed as "the only grown-ups we're going to profile." But her editors had cut out our story, telling her that there would be "little reader interest in a real business that doesn't have bells, whistles, or a talking-dog mascot."

Credits

To the past, present and future employees of Neoforma. I have only lightly touched upon the plethora of individuals and families who made Neoforma's creation possible, its growth manageable and its survival assured. Thank you all.

All my love to Anni for always being there, even when I wasn't, Weston for keeping me sharp by questioning everything and Reece for making me laugh when I needed it the most.

Thanks to Jeff Kleck for sharing this wild ride and still managing to end up on speaking terms, Tim Guertin for early support, Jack Russo for making everything possible, Denis Coleman for always being right, Wally Buch for showing that success does not need to dilute one's humanity, Constantin Delivanis for teaching me how to make fire and Bob Zollars for being as big on the inside as he is tall on the outside.

Special thanks to Laynee Gilbert for suffering the very rough first drafts of this work with unblinking eyes and for responding with just the right blend of gracious encouragement, gentle suggestions and unflinching honesty. And to my editor Donna Beech for improving everything without changing anything.

And thanks to Paul Bergholm for making the incomprehensible comprehensible, Greg Brodsky for making the work fun, Peter Glassman for broadening the audience, Candace Hathaway for inflating my ego enough to get me through this, Jerry Kaplan for paving the way, Jamis MacNiven for being Jamis, Kandace Malefyt for coaching me on the ways of the Valley, Chet Szerlag for being the perfect customer, Lisa Sitkin for trying to keep me out of trouble and Graham Van Dixhorn for having the grace to encourage and advise a stranger.

You can contact me regarding this book at wayne@ravel.tv.